WRITING WITH

HITCHCOCK

WRITING WITH
HITCHCOCK

The Collaboration of Alfred Hitchcock
and John Michael Hayes

STEVEN DeROSA

ff FABER AND FABER

New York • London

Faber and Faber, Inc.
An affiliate of Farrar, Straus and Giroux
19 Union Square West, New York 10003

Faber and Faber Ltd
3 Queen Square
London WC1N 3AU

Library of Congress Cataloging-in-Publication Data
DeRosa, Steven.
    Writing with Hitchcock : the collaboration of Alfred Hitchcock and John
Michael Hayes / Steven DeRosa.
        p.   cm.
    Includes bibliographical references and index.
    ISBN 0-571-19990-9 (alk. paper)
    1. Hitchcock, Alfred, 1899—Criticism and interpretation. 2. Hayes, John
Michael, 1919—Criticism and interpretation. I. Title.
PN1998.3.H58 D47 2001
791.43'0233'092—dc21

                                                                                00-045460

Designed by Jonathan D. Lippincott

"Rules and Rigors of a Book-Fed Scenarist" copyright © 1957 by John Michael
Hayes. Originally published in *The New York Times*, August 11, 1957.

For my grandparents
Frances and Louis Gagliano

Contents

Introduction

When asked if he found it easy to sustain his enthusiasm while making a film, Alfred Hitchcock replied, "The most enjoyable part of making a picture is in that little office, with the writer, when we are discussing the story-lines and what we're going to put on the screen. The big difference is that I do not let the writer go off on his own and just write a script that I will interpret. I stay involved with him and get him involved in the direction of the picture. So he becomes more than a writer; he becomes part maker of the picture."

This was an unusual acknowledgment for Alfred Hitchcock to make. For decades, with the help of the press—especially the French critics from the film journal *Cahiers du Cinéma*, who pioneered the *auteur* theory, which held that the director of a film was its true author—Hitchcock perpetuated the myth that he was the sole creator of his films. While he indeed enjoyed a degree of creative autonomy seldom seen in the Hollywood studio system, he was also a producer-director who knew how to get the best work from his collaborators, particularly his writers.

In the 1950s Alfred Hitchcock reshaped and solidified the characteristic trademarks of the Hitchcock style: the use of glamorous stars, sophisticated dialogue, and inventive plots, on an enormous wide screen, in glorious Technicolor. He achieved this by collaborating with John Michael Hayes, an established writer of suspense drama for radio, who had recently graduated from writing B-pictures such as *War Arrow* at Universal to creating star vehicles at MGM such as *Torch Song*.

The Hitchcock-Hayes collaboration produced four motion pictures in two years—*Rear Window, To Catch a Thief, The Trouble with Harry*, and *The Man Who Knew Too Much*—and proved to be one of the most successful director-screenwriter pairings in Hollywood history. Each of these movies has achieved film-classic status, and the professional relationship of these two creative artists was mutually beneficial. Hayes learned a great deal about the art of cinema from Hitchcock, all the while maintaining his individuality as a writer. As for Hitchcock, the collaboration marked the beginning of his most successful period, critically and commercially.

The teaming of Hitchcock and Hayes could not have come at a more ideal time for both men. Hayes was full of energy and eager to be as successful in film as he had been in radio; Hitchcock was at the beginning of an upswing in his career following a string of flops and the failure of his own production company. As things turned out, *Rear Window* was the first in a series of seminal works Hitchcock produced over a decade. Whether he cared to admit it or not, Hitchcock needed good writers. But as his popularity grew in the 1950s—the result of a series of upbeat, exciting motion pictures and his enormously popular television series—he began to believe that he could do it alone, that the "Hitchcock" name was enough to sell his movies to the critics and public alike. For a time, he seemed to be right.

Hitchcock was not solely responsible for this view. The politics of the studio system and the widening acceptance of the *auteur* theory downplayed the significance of the screenwriter's contribution to the art of filmmaking. Frank Capra's most successful films were all scripted by Robert Riskin, yet few people are familiar with Riskin's name. Similarly, Ernst Lubitsch collaborated with Samson Raphaelson on nine films, and John Ford collaborated with Dudley Nichols on eleven. Again, these screenwriters never received the recognition enjoyed by the "*auteurs*" for whom they wrote. But the director who has been most often canonized as an *auteur* is Hitchcock.

"A lot of people embrace the auteur theory," said Hitchcock. "But it's difficult to know what someone means by it. I suppose they mean that the responsibility for the film rests solely on the shoulders of the director. But very often the director is no better than his script." From selection of the basic material, to the hiring (and firing) of every writer, to the final revision of the final shooting script, Hitchcock involved himself in nearly every aspect of developing the screenplays for his films. Although he rarely did any actual "writing," especially on his Hollywood productions, Hitchcock supervised and guided his writers through every draft, insisting on a strict attention to detail and a preference for telling the story through visual rather than verbal means. While this exasperated some writers, others admitted the director inspired them to do their very best work. Hitchcock often emphasized that he took no screen credit for the writing of his films. However, over time the work of many of his writers has been attributed solely to Hitchcock's creative genius, a misconception he rarely went out of his way to correct. Notwithstanding his technical brilliance as a director, Hitchcock relied on his writers a great deal.

Many of Hitchcock's writers believed that their contributions were overlooked because of the industry's general dismissal of the writer's importance and because of the disparaging remarks Hitchcock often made about his writers in interviews. No Hitchcock writer felt this injury more than John Michael Hayes. In François Truffaut's celebrated book-length interview, Hitchcock dismissed Hayes as nothing more than a "radio writer who wrote the dialogue." This comment was made after Truffaut praised *Rear Window* as Hitchcock's "very best screenplay in all respects." Hayes was piqued by Hitchcock's comment, considering the circumstances under which he and Hitchcock parted (which are explained in Chapter 5).

Clearly, theirs was a symbiotic relationship. While Hitchcock needed a writer of Hayes's talent, Hayes also needed Hitchcock. Even though Hayes worked with some of Hollywood's top stars after breaking with Hitchcock—Bette Davis, Clark Gable, Audrey Hepburn, Sophia Loren, and Elizabeth Taylor—all but a handful of the writer's post-Hitchcock films have been forgotten. In spite of a respectable list of credits that includes *Peyton Place*, *The Children's Hour*, and *The Chalk Garden*, Hayes was never able to maintain the level of critical and commercial success that he experienced when writing with Hitchcock. And while Hitchcock's quest for a suitable replacement for Grace Kelly has become part of Hollywood lore, it should also be noted that Hitchcock never found another John Michael Hayes. Following his collaboration with Hayes, Hitchcock never settled on an individual writer with whom he completed more than one consecutive film.

What was Hayes's contribution to this significant partnership? First, richly drawn, sympathetic characters. Prior to working with Hayes, most of Hitchcock's protagonists had been deeply troubled, dark, and complex figures. Hayes also offered Hitchcock an approach to story material that was solid and accessible. In his book *Find the Director*, Thomas M. Leitch correctly points out that a singular theme is at the heart of each of the Hitchcock-Hayes films: the individual becoming one with his community. Whether that community was a Greenwich Village courtyard, a tiny hamlet in Vermont, or a simple family unit, the individual discovers that he can exist happily within what seems to be the confines of social order.

Although Hitchcock touched upon that theme in some of his previous films—for example, *Spellbound* and *Notorious*—it never achieved the kind of accessibility attained by the Hayes-Hitchcock collaboration. Voyeurism, fear of intimacy, fear of death, and the loss of a loved one were never made so palatable as they are in the Hayes scripts. If these films stand out as such, they deserve to be looked upon and studied not only as Hitchcock films—as testaments to his view of the human condition at that time—but also as Hitchcock-Hayes films: documents to their collective view of the human condition.

The films that immediately followed the Hitchcock-Hayes collaboration were a complete reversal: *The Wrong Man*, *Vertigo*, *North by Northwest*, and *Psycho* not only challenged the individual's role within society but put the very identities of these individuals in jeopardy. With the exception of *North by Northwest*, the absence of Hayes from these films resulted in an uncharacteristic lack of humor in Hitchcock's work.

By comparison, at the center of each Hitchcock-Hayes film is an isolated protagonist—someone who, through fear, choice, happenstance, or convention, finds himself in need of redemption. Through each respective narrative, the protagonist is offered a chance to embrace the redemptive qualities of love and become reintegrated into the world he inhabits. Thus, the Hitchcock-Hayes period emerges as the most affirmative in the director's canon.

A journalist once wrote: "John Michael Hayes looks like a Hollywood scriptwriter as played by a Hollywood film star in a Hollywood film about Hollywood. A thoroughly nice guy. He is dark, good-looking and smokes a pipe with a grace and style that would make Crosby look positively clumsy. His dialogue is friendly but forceful. His humor is as dry and snappy as a dead twig under foot. Not unnaturally, John Michael Hayes is a Hollywood scriptwriter."

One of the great clichés about the movies goes: Film is a director's medium. While this is true, film is not exclusively a director's medium. But it is always about movie directors that one hears of the "touch"—the *Lubitsch* touch, the *Wilder* touch, the *Capra* touch, the *Hitchcock* touch. Most movie buffs could cite examples that define the particular touch of each of these star directors. And probably anyone who has seen a movie can cite examples of the Hitchcock touch. But what exactly is the Hayes touch?

First and foremost, the Hayes touch begins with a love of language. Dialogue is Hayes's forte. His scripts were prized for their unique blend of sophisticated repartee and colloquial banter. Few screenwriters would have the audacity to use the word "fripperies" in a script, let alone have a character say, "You've obviously 'fripperied' your lid!" But Hayes also has the ability to find humor in rules of the English language. In *But Not for Me*, when Lilli Palmer asks her ex-husband, played by Clark Gable, if he knows what non sequiturs are, he replies, "Sure. A series of things that don't make

XIV   INTRODUCTION

sense—such as your friends." And in *To Catch a Thief*, Hayes turns a few words about verb forms into a witty double entendre when a jealous Grace Kelly says to Cary Grant and Brigitte Auber that it looked as if they had been "conjugating some irregular verbs."

Hayes's scripts also have what he calls "an emotional roadmap," something that drives the characters to the end of the story. For this reason Hayes always insisted on completing a first draft before turning in the pages to a producer. "One of the hardest things a producer has to do is to wait," said Hayes. "After two or three weeks, he wants to see some pages. But if you give them to him before you're ready, you'll end up in literary litigation for weeks, and lose your perspective before you get going with your story. That's what's wrong with a lot of pictures. They have great openings and no endings."

But the Hayes touch goes beyond his dialogue and carefully constructed storylines. Hayes brought a certain integrity to the job of screenwriter, which had too often been cast in the shadow of famous insults, like when Jack Warner purportedly referred to screenwriters as "schmucks with Underwoods." Hayes was not a schmuck, nor was he particularly fond of Underwoods, and he did not let himself get pushed around in a town that considered writers, if not their words, cheap.

When pressured by the director, producer, and even the head of a studio to change the ending of his script that was already three-quarters of the way through production, Hayes replied to the studio boss's urgent telegram, "BY CHANGING SCENES AS INDICATED THEY MIGHT SOLVE CERTAIN PROBLEMS OF CLARIFICATION BUT RAISE NEW PROBLEMS OF DRAMATIC STRUCTURE, SUSPENSE, SURPRISE. ONE OF THE MAJOR FAULTS OF THE EARLY SCRIPTS WAS THAT THEY LAID OUT EVERYTHING, EXPLAINED FACTS SO THOROUGHLY THEY READ LIKE TRAINING FILMS, NOT DRAMA . . . SO WHAT DO I SUGGEST? I SAY LEAVE IT ALONE." Hayes warned that tampering with the ending at such a late juncture was not merely a matter of a few line changes but could put the entire story out of balance. The ending remained unchanged. Armed with this kind of conviction, Hayes provided structurally sound, often literate screenplays, while remaining true to his principles.

One of the most significant decisions of Hayes's career—and one that is central to this book—was his choosing to stand up to Hitchcock and challenge him in an arbitration over the writing credits for *The Man Who Knew Too Much*. It was an action that Hayes knew would have repercussions. But it was one that he had to take.

The following chapters meticulously detail a fascinating, sometimes stormy relationship between Hitchcock, the world-renowned yet guarded filmmaking genius, and his spirited, congenial collaborator, John Michael Hayes. Their two-year saga boasts a supporting cast that includes James Stewart, Cary Grant, Grace Kelly, Shirley MacLaine, and Doris Day. With emphasis on the development of the screenplays, *Writing with Hitchcock* traces the production of each of the four Hitchcock-Hayes films. What will also emerge for the reader is a portrait of two very different personalities who formed a unique working relationship that began happily but ended in bitter conflict.

Writing with Hitchcock provides the conflicting accounts surrounding the circumstances that brought about the breach between Hitchcock and Hayes. These accounts are supported by primary documents from several departments at the Paramount studio. The book then traces their respective careers subsequent to their disassociation. Finally, there is a comparative analysis of each of the four screenplays. By comparing the screenplay to the final production mounted on the screen, the analyses demonstrate the processes of interpreting script material into shots for the screen, illustrate the contributions of the director and actors, and offer an understanding of the difficult task of transforming conception into realization.

With the centennial of Hitchcock's birth having recently been marked with a score of tributes, conferences, and retrospectives, it is important to acknowledge the contributions of his most significant collaborators. To me, John Michael Hayes is the most deserving of such recognition. Like the comic thrillers of Hitchcock's British period, such as *The 39 Steps* and *The Lady Vanishes*, the Hayes films stand apart as finely crafted works of art. But even more than these early masterworks, Hitchcock's films with Hayes were consistent in their wit, originality, and sheer creative excellence. And the continued appeal of these films has greatly influenced the high regard and affection that the moviegoing public holds for Hitchcock as a filmmaker, an artist, and a cultural icon.

WRITING WITH
HITCHCOCK

Prologue: Pittsburg, California, May 1943

In the spring of 1943, at the height of the Pacific campaign that followed the battle of Midway, the Allied forces were about to initiate a historic military offensive that would be instrumental to an Allied victory against Japan. The strategy was to cut off Japanese supply bases by recapturing a handful of islands, thus effecting a blockade against Emperor Hirohito's navy.

Among the soldiers at Camp Stoneman, under the command of Captain William P. Whelan, in a town called Pittsburg, California, was a twenty-four-year-old private by the name of John Michael Hayes. Like so many who served their country, Private Hayes had left behind a promising career as a radio writer when he was drafted into the Army a year earlier in 1942. The war was an interruption in a life that had been carefully geared toward one goal. As fate would have it, the events of one morning in May 1943 initiated an interesting series of events that brought Hayes even closer to realizing his ambition. Hayes recalled the day he was to ship out for duty in the Pacific:

> I was heading for Kiska and Attu in the Aleutian Islands with a port battalion, to drive out the Japanese, because they had invaded them and had two army bases there. But I was pulled out of the line, just before we shipped out, and brought back to an embarkation camp, to do stage shows for the new theaters they'd built, named after Bataan, Corregidor, and Guadalcanal. They were going to have stage shows and films in them. They were waiting for the theaters to be

finished, but one was completed as far as the film equipment. They had two new Simplex machines, and they needed a projectionist. I didn't know anything about running a movie projector, but they gave me a manual and said, "Until we can draft a couple of projectionists, you're going to run this for us. Read the manual and learn how to operate the machines." I was going to have training films and at night they were going to have movies, but the only movie we had was *Shadow of a Doubt* and I showed it three times a night for a month. I saw *Shadow of a Doubt* ninety times, which is more than I think Hitchcock ever saw it. I knew every nuance in that picture, every line. First I watched it for entertainment, and then I watched it for technique, and then I watched it for background, and I watched it for sound, and I analyzed it and double analyzed it. I could hit the change-over plate on the projector with my back to the screen, because I knew every line of dialogue. So I had this in my bag.

1 / A Perfect Treatment

On the morning of September 9, 1965, Alfred Hitchcock sat in his office at Universal Studios confounded that after a detailed treatment, three complete drafts, and one set of revisions, the screenplay he had been preparing for *Torn Curtain* was not up to par. Hitchcock had spent four months working on the scenario with the novelist Brian Moore, and then engaged the screenwriting team of Keith Waterhouse and Willis Hall to do a hasty rewrite, but still found the script lacking. Peggy Robertson, Hitchcock's personal assistant, knew her employer was in trouble, especially after *Marnie* had flopped a year earlier. Robertson was Hitchcock's most valued associate during his tenure at Universal and had remained part of the director's entourage since serving as script supervisor on *Vertigo* during happier times at Paramount. At Hitchcock's request, Robertson prepared a short list of writers she thought were skilled enough to retool the second-rate script. Hitchcock surely trusted Robertson's judgment, but was adamantly opposed to calling one of the writers she had put on her list, even though a little more than a decade earlier the writer had been responsible for the scripts of some of Hitchcock's major successes. For some reason—pride, anger, principle—Hitchcock refused to call John Michael Hayes. Hitchcock felt he became the Master of Suspense on his own and did not require assistance from someone whom *he* had made a star.

In the spring of 1953 Hitchcock had faced a similar career crisis. His independent production company, Transatlantic Pictures, had failed, and his years at Warner Bros. were a mixed bag of mostly box-office failures. With its track record on the stage in London and on Broadway, Hitchcock hoped that a film of Frederick Knott's *Dial M for Murder* would bring the change of luck he desperately needed. Warner Bros. purchased the rights for Hitchcock, but the studio was in financial trouble. In March the studio halted production on all new projects for ninety days, and the following month they asked their executives to take a salary cut of up to 50 percent.

In a business where you're only as good as your last film, Hitchcock could not afford to let his career come to a standstill. He instructed his agents at MCA Artists to shop around for another studio contract. In his business dealings, Hitchcock was handled personally by the agency's president, Lew Wasserman, in addition to Arthur Park and, later, Herman Citron. In spite of the fact that Hitchcock's performance as his own producer in Hollywood had not yet lived up to his reputation, Wasserman and company shrewdly arranged what became over the next few years a lucrative multipicture contract with the Paramount Pictures Corporation.

Eager to obtain Hitchcock's services, Paramount offered to make a deal if he would develop a script out of a story from a collection called *After Dinner Story* by mystery writer Cornell Woolrich (who wrote under the pseudonym William Irish). Taking Wasserman's advice, Hitchcock chose "Rear Window." Eager to find the perfect writer to dramatize Woolrich's short story, Hitchcock recalled a name he heard often on the radio in connection with comedy, suspense, and detective shows. "Do you know John Michael Hayes?" he asked his agents. The response was that they certainly did—Hayes was also an MCA client.

The Meeting

Through much of his first decade or so in Hollywood, Alfred Hitchcock worked with a number of distinguished writers, including Robert Sherwood, Thornton Wilder, Dorothy Parker, Ben Hecht, and Raymond Chandler. Impressive as this list of collaborators may be, Hitchcock still found himself in the late 1940s and early 1950s with a string of commercial failures. Hitchcock's agents were therefore perplexed by their client's request that they arrange a meeting with John Michael Hayes. By the spring of 1953, the thirty-three-year-old Hayes had been a popular and prolific writer of radio dramas, and although his potential as a screenwriter had been recognized, there was little evidence in his first film credits to indicate he had much to offer Hitchcock. Nevertheless, there was something about Hayes's style that Hitchcock responded to and felt he needed.

Hayes recalled, "Hitchcock had his agents and my agent get together for lunch and they handed me this book which had the short story in it called 'Rear Window.' They told me, 'You're to meet Mr. Hitchcock on Friday night at the Beverly Hills Hotel for dinner. Read the story and be prepared to discuss it with him.'" Hayes virtually memorized the story in order to anticipate what Hitchcock would ask. What color were the eyes of the hero? How many steps up to his door? How many windows across the way? Hayes prepared for a thorough examination.

The dinner was scheduled for seven-thirty in the Polo Lounge of the Beverly Hills Hotel. Hayes dressed as well as he could, memorized his notes and ideas, and drove from the San Fernando Valley, over the Santa Monica Mountains, to Beverly Hills, arriving a few minutes early. By seven-thirty, Hitchcock hadn't arrived. At quarter of eight, he still wasn't there. And by eight o'clock, there was no sign of Hitchcock. The young writer thought he might have gotten the night or, worse, the hotel wrong, which only added to his feelings of anxiety about meeting the famous director. In need of something to calm his nerves, Hayes went into the hotel bar and explained his predicament to the bartender.

Unlike many of his contemporaries in Hollywood, Hayes was a neophyte when it came to liquor and wisely set his limit at two drinks. Unaware of the potency of martinis, which the bartender prescribed as a good drink to calm one's nerves, Hayes knocked back his drink and returned to the lobby as quickly as he could, not wanting to miss Hitchcock. Having skipped lunch that day in anticipation of a big dinner, Hayes quickly felt a warm glow from the liquor as he continued to wait. By eight-thirty, Hitchcock still hadn't arrived, prompting the writer to retreat to the bar for one more drink before returning home.

Having consumed his second martini—his limit—Hayes walked out of the hotel and down the path toward his car, when suddenly a taxi pulled up and out came Alfred Hitchcock, who started up the walk hurriedly. Hayes tried to interrupt him. "Mr. Hitchcock?"

"No. Sorry. No autographs. I have a very important meeting."

"You have it with John Michael Hayes."

Hitchcock stopped and said, "Are you John Hayes?"

"Yes," the writer replied.

"Well, come on. Let's get going," commanded Hitchcock, who never apologized for being late. The two proceeded to the dining room, with the headwaiter fussing over Hitchcock, whose reputation as a big spender and gourmand had been well established even before he arrived in America. As they sat at the booth reserved for the star moviemaker, Hayes must have been impressed, if not intimidated, by the attention he commanded, which made it all the more surprising when the first words out of Hitchcock were "Do you drink?"

Taken aback, Hayes replied, "Well, I've been known on occasion to take a drink."

"Well, what do you drink?"

"I think the last drink I had was a martini."

"Oh, wonderful, my favorite drink," said Hitchcock, adding mischievously, "I like a man who drinks." Hitchcock called the waiter to the table and ordered two double martinis. When the drinks arrived, the two men tipped glasses, and Hayes sipped as cautiously as he could.

Soon after, Hitchcock called for hors d'oeuvres and another double martini for each of them. Hayes had finally gotten the first cocktail down and by now was bleary-eyed, praying he would not get sick. "Mr. Hitchcock, I don't—I think one—" protested Hayes.

"Oh, come on," Hitchcock encouraged, "we've got to relax and get to know each other. As I told you, I like a man who drinks."

Along came the second round of double martinis. Hayes kept imagining he was going to get sick and that Alfred Hitchcock would never speak to him again. And to this point, the director hadn't mentioned *Rear Window* at all. Pouring sweat, trying to keep sober and sound intelligent, Hayes recalled the director asking, "Have you seen any of my movies?"

"Yes, I have, Mr. Hitchcock."

By now they'd finished the hors d'oeuvres and had started a second course of Dover sole with a rare white wine. Hitchcock extolled the virtues of the wine as he poured a big glass for the writer, who tried to sip it politely and act as if he truly appreciated it. Returning to the subject of his pictures, Hitchcock said, "For example?"

Recalling his experience as an Army theater projectionist, Hayes replied, "Well, for example, oh, *Shadow of a Doubt*."

"What did you think of it?" asked Hitchcock.

Hayes began to give an analysis of *Shadow of a Doubt* from frame one to the end of the picture, telling Hitchcock what he thought he had done right and what he thought he had done wrong, where it was strong, where it was weak, and that he didn't particularly like the casting. The young writer continued his assessment of *Shadow of a Doubt* straight through the next course of steak with red wine. Blurred by the combination of martinis and fine wines, Hayes started going through Hitchcock's movies, one by one, indicating some things that he could have done better in *Notorious* and telling the director that he thought the bullet stopped by the Bible in the hero's pocket in *The 39 Steps* was kind of corny. While Hayes talked, Hitchcock said nothing and just continued eating and drinking and munching and crunching and slurping.

At the conclusion of the meal, Hitchcock ordered dessert to be brought with a concoction of brandy and Drambuie. Amazingly, Hayes hadn't gotten sick, but Hitchcock still had said nothing about *Rear Window*—not a single word. Finally, with the dinner finished, Hitchcock said, "Well, I've got to go home." Hayes offered to drive him, but shrewdly Hitchcock decided to take a taxi. After a considerable amount of coffee, Hayes got into his car, put the top down, and drove slowly over the Santa Monica Mountains back home. Upon his arrival, Hayes's wife, Mel, asked, "How did it go?"

"Well, we had one of the great feasts of all time. But I am through, not only with Alfred Hitchcock, but maybe forever in this town. I'd better start thinking of a new profession. Because," Hayes said, "I analyzed his pictures, and I analyzed them like a reviewer, critically." Hayes spent the rest of the weekend waiting to hear how miserably it went. On Monday morning Arthur Park telephoned him and said, "You're in. Hitchcock loved you. You start work tomorrow. Report to Warner Bros., where he's preparing *Dial M for Murder*."

In disbelief Hayes responded, "Are you sure you have the right John Michael Hayes?"

"Why?"

"We never talked about *Rear Window*, or anything."

"You're fine."

The next day Hayes arrived at Warners, and he and Hitchcock discussed *Rear Window* for the first time. Baffled by the experience, Hayes needed a year before he had the temerity to ask Hitchcock about that night. "Well, let me tell you what happened," Hitchcock said. "I went to a cocktail party at Jules Stein's house.* That's why I was late. You know, I was dieting and I had several drinks. I remember meeting you and going in to eat, but I don't remember anything after that. But you talked a lot, and on the assumption that a man who talks a lot has something to say, I hired you." Not one to leave an associate completely at ease, Hitchcock added, "But don't forget, if I didn't like you, two weeks later I could have let you go."

A Partnership Is Formed

Based on their first meeting at the Beverly Hills Hotel, Alfred Hitchcock could not have known how fortunate he was in selecting John Michael Hayes as his screenwriter. Hayes's youth and enthusiasm

---

*Stein was the founder of MCA.

might have reminded Hitchcock of his years at Gaumont-British in the 1930s; perhaps he recognized that they were just the right qualities he needed to get his batteries "well charged," as he later said of this period. Hayes was a sharp dresser who deferred to the director's imperious presence by at first calling him "Mr. Hitchcock," although he was quickly granted permission to call him "Hitch." What's more, Hitchcock could get him cheap.

Hayes met with Hitchcock on the Warner Bros. lot twice before starting work on the treatment for *Rear Window*. At a salary of $750 a week, with no guarantee, Hayes was officially put on the Paramount payroll on June 8, 1953. At this time, Paramount assigned *Rear Window* a story fund number, 84001, to keep an accounting of all costs. (Once the studio approves a project for production, it is assigned a production number.) During their preliminary meetings Hayes discovered that Hitchcock's main concern—as was true of nearly all his films—was with creating a love story.

The Story

First published in the February 1942 issue of *Dime Detective* under the title "It Had to Be Murder," the short story by Cornell Woolrich was anything but a love story. Instead, Woolrich's story is a pure oscillation thriller, its primary objective being manipulation of the reader. The story is told in first-person narration. The protagonist, Hal Jeffries, is confined to a single bedroom with an unscreened bay window. The uncomfortably warm weather and lack of exercise have left him with an inability to sleep, and so, to ward off boredom, he takes to observing the nameless, faceless "rear-window dwellers" around him. After noting the abnormal behavior of one neighbor, a salesman named Thorwald, whose sickly wife has been confined to her bed, Jeffries suspects that the man may have murdered the woman.

Jeffries continues to observe the salesman, soliciting the aid of his black houseman, Sam, and a detective friend, Boyne. However, nobody else is convinced a murder has taken place, and at times even Jeffries doubts his conviction. Soon Jeffries stumbles upon a clue of sorts and comes to believe that the murdered woman is buried under the new cement floor laid in the apartment above the murderer's. Before he can share his theory, the murderer discovers Jeffries spying and tries to shoot him. Jeffries is saved when Boyne and his men arrive, and the salesman is killed while attempting to elude the police. It is not until the end of the story that Woolrich reveals the reason Jeffries is confined to his apartment. The doctor says, "Guess we can take that cast off your leg now. You must be tired of sitting there all day doing nothing."

In his biography of Woolrich, Francis M. Nevins, Jr., suggests that the inspiration for the story can be traced to an event Woolrich himself described in his memoir *Blues of a Lifetime*. On a hot summer evening Woolrich was sitting in his room busy at the typewriter, dressed only in trousers and an undershirt, when he heard the sound of muffled giggling. When he moved to the window, he found two teenage girls staring at him from the apartment building next door.

This experience of being spied on, according to Nevins, made its way into several of the author's earlier works. For example, in "Wake Up with Death," published in 1937, Woolrich's main character wakes up in a hotel room with a hangover, finding the lifeless body of a woman on the floor beside his bed. He then receives a telephone call from someone claiming to have seen him kill the woman from a window opposite his.

In "Silhouette," published in 1939, a middle-aged couple waiting for a bus late one evening believe that they have seen a man strangling a woman behind the window shade of a house on the other side of the street. Woolrich keeps the reader guessing throughout, wondering whether or not a crime was committed. Like "Rear Window," the story is rich in the vivid details of everyday life and— again as in "Rear Window"—the protagonist-witness has no emotional connection to the suspected killer.

Later that year Woolrich's novelette *You'll Never See Me Again* was published. It concerns a newlywed couple who have a quarrel that begins innocently enough but escalates to the point where the bride packs her belongings to move back with her mother and step-father. A few days later the husband calls in the hope of effecting a reconciliation, but is told that his wife never arrived. When the husband frantically tries to find out what became of his wife, a homicide detective is convinced that he killed her.

While the act of being spied on may have influenced Woolrich, it is also likely that he had read a short story by H. G. Wells called "Through a Window," which is remarkably similar to "It Had to Be Murder." Published in 1895, Wells's story concerns a man named Bailey who is confined to a couch in the study of his London flat before a window that overlooks the Thames. With his legs wrapped like a "double-barreled mummy," Bailey watches the comings and goings of the boats and ships outside his window.

Like Woolrich's protagonist, Bailey comes to know the intimate details of those he watches and at times regards the activity out his window as an entertainment to help him pass the time while he recovers from his illness. As does Jeffries, Bailey has regular visitors — a housekeeper named Mrs. Green, who brings him meals, and a friend named Wilderspin, to whom he complains about his idleness and comments on his newfound "eye for details."

The story builds up to a point one morning when Bailey, left alone for the day, notices a figure clad in white fluttering in the distance. Bailey soon identifies the figure as a white-robed Malay sailor who has run amok with a knife and is being pursued by a band of armed men. Bailey sits helplessly watching glimpses of the manhunt outside his window. The sailor continues moving nearer and nearer, until he finally comes through the window and into Bailey's flat. All Bailey can do to defend himself is throw medicine bottles at the madman, who is finally shot and killed at the last moment.

In addition to the similarity of an isolated protagonist immobilized before a window, there are two other telling details that point to the influence of Wells's story on Woolrich. The first of these comes when Bailey sees a boat pass by with a married couple on it arguing. Bailey cannot tell what led to the argument, or how it was concluded; he can only fill in the details with his imagination. It would seem that this single detail intrigued Woolrich so greatly that he would explore the theme in several narratives. The other detail comes when Bailey first sees the white cloth fluttering in the distance. He is unsure if it is a flag or a handkerchief, and finally recognizes the material as the white robes of a Malay sailor. Woolrich employs a similar device when Jeffries watches Thorwald packing his wife's dresses, first believing the dresses on triangular hangers to be pennants.

Consistent throughout Woolrich's several explorations of these details is a sense of self-doubt on the part of the protagonist-narrator; thus the stories become "did he or didn't he" stories, rather than conventional "whodunits." These "oscillation" stories are exercises in tension that Woolrich is able to balance delicately until their suspenseful climax.

"It Had to Be Murder" was given the title "Rear Window" when it was reprinted in a 1944 collection entitled *After Dinner Story*. That autumn Woolrich's publisher submitted *After Dinner Story* to Paramount Pictures, and the following May, Woolrich sold the movie rights to all six stories in the collection for a total of $9,250 to B. G. DeSylva Productions, Inc. Songwriter-producer Buddy DeSylva was then head of production at Paramount, and although the studio released three films based on Woolrich's work over the next five years, none were made from stories in this collection. In 1950 "Rear Window" was sold to Orange Productions, Inc., which was owned by the well-known producer and talent agent Leland Hayward.

The Deal

For a short time in the 1940s Hitchcock had been represented by Leland Hayward, until the latter's agency was bought out by MCA. Hayward first tried to arouse Hitchcock's interest in "Rear Window" in October 1951, when the director was in New York taking part in "Movietime U.S.A.," a nationwide promotional campaign by members of the film industry designed to lure audiences away from their televisions and back into movie theaters. The campaign was one of several attempts made by the movie industry to increase ticket sales since it began in the late 1940s to compete with television for its audience. Hitchcock and his longtime friend and Transatlantic Pictures partner Sidney Bernstein met with Hayward to discuss David Dodge's soon-to-be-published novel *To Catch a Thief*, as well as Cornell Woolrich's story "Rear Window."

While it is unknown how Hitchcock reacted to the story at the time, it is clear he did not immediately pursue the rights (although he did buy the rights to *To Catch a Thief*, which he intended to make at a later date for Transatlantic). It is likely that after reading it in its present form, lacking a leading female character, Hitchcock did not see enough in "Rear Window" to suit his purposes and passed. Hayward then had playwright and theater director Joshua Logan draft a treatment in February 1952. A treatment is a detailed outline of a film's plot, containing character descriptions and occasional suggestions of dialogue. Logan's thirteen-page treatment remained largely faithful to Woolrich's original, but also made several significant changes that bear similarities to the finished film.

The Logan Treatment

Logan's treatment begins with a helicopter view of New York City, moving past tall buildings to get progressively closer to a single city block, with a shot panning the windows of a courtyard and, finally, the window of Jeffries, whom Logan calls Jeff for short. Logan then inserts a shot of Jeff's leg in a cast covered with lipstick marks and women's signatures. Prominently under the foot of the cast (where it cannot be seen by Jeff) is the quote "When you break this cast, you will know the girl who really loves you. Trink." Jeff's love interest, Trink, is Logan's most significant addition to Woolrich's story. Trink is a struggling television actress who travels often for her career. Contrary to Hitchcock's and Hayes's Jeff, Logan's Jeff is eager for Trink to quit acting so they can be married.

In the Logan treatment Jeff is a sportswriter who hates criminals and enjoys playing amateur sleuth whenever the opportunity arises.

He usually gets his friend, a homicide detective named Boyne, to work on cases he's investigated. As in Woolrich's story, Jeff has an African-American servant, Sam. But Logan gives most of Sam's actions from the story to Trink.

Jeff sends Trink to Thorwald's room to "muss it up," then watches as Thorwald discovers Trink in his apartment. From across the courtyard Jeff watches Trink "act" her way out of danger, convincing Thorwald to let her go. Since she "acted her way out," Jeff is convinced Trink is a talented actress. Satisfied that she has proven her ability to Jeff, Trink says she will give up her career and marry him. While reenacting for Jeff the improvisation that got her away from Thorwald, Trink inadvertently allows herself to be seen and recognized by the murderer. As in the story, Thorwald waits until Jeff is alone and comes to kill him, but is himself killed before he can do Jeff any harm. As the doctor removes the cast from Jeff's leg, Jeff finally reads the message shown at the beginning and kisses Trink.

The following spring Hayward sent a copy of Logan's treatment to Lew Wasserman, and within a month's time contracts were being drawn up for Hitchcock to make *Rear Window* at Paramount. In his autobiography Logan recalled his disappointment when Hayward sold the property to Hitchcock, since he had hoped to cut his teeth directing *Rear Window* before directing a film of his own play *Mister Roberts*. Logan's disappointment subsided when Hayward explained that they had doubled their initial investment by selling the story. Hitchcock paid $25,000 for "Rear Window," which included $15,000 for Logan's treatment.

Creating the Characters

Hitchcock and Hayes discussed at the outset the direction their story needed to take. They saw a need to create more neighbors to place in the windows of the surrounding buildings and to build these characters so that each would present a reflection of the relationship between the principals. While Hitchcock busied himself through July and August 1953 with pre-production for the complicated 3-D filming of *Dial M for Murder*, Hayes went all out preparing the treatment for *Rear Window*. Hayes was familiar with Hitchcock's style and had already worked with James Stewart earlier that year on *Thunder Bay* for Universal. Hayes knew the actor would bring a lot to the part. Like most Hitchcock scenarios, the storyline for *Rear Window* would develop from its details, as Hayes explained:

> It started with the fact that we had to give Jefferies [the name is spelled "Jeffries" in Woolrich's story and Logan's outline] a reason to travel around the world, a dangerous occupation, and a reason to get his leg broken. It was more dramatic having it broken in the line of work, and not just slipping on the stairs. Secondly, I wanted to give him an occupation that would give him an occasion to meet a girl like Lisa. Out of that came her profession. He's a foreign correspondent, and his editor said, "Look, we're out of fashion photographers this week. We want you to do a layout on an upcoming model named Lisa Fremont." And he said, "That's not my line of work." They said, "Well, fill in and do the best you can." He did the magazine layout and cover, which you saw, and that's how they met. She was fascinated with him, and of course he was very interested in her as a woman, but not as a wife in the beginning. He figured models are frivolous, and she certainly has never been off the sidewalk and couldn't live in safari clothes. He also kind of felt there wasn't much chance for him—with his earthy style and occupation—with a girl who was wined and dined by wealthy men.
>
> So that's how one thing—to break his leg in an interesting way—led to his occupation, and led to something that would get him together with Lisa. That's how it grew. But there was more you could do with it. He had a telescopic lens we could use later with the picture of the flowers going up and down in the garden. He had flashbulbs to fend off the villain. Out of this grew a whole lot of interesting things.

In addition to James Stewart, who had been attached to the project since the spring, Hitchcock wanted his current leading lady from *Dial M for Murder*, Grace Kelly, for the female lead in *Rear Window*. According to Kelly biographer Robert Lacey, the director was intrigued by the duality of the actress's persona, a cool exterior that belied a reputation for becoming romantically involved with her male co-stars, apparently with little regard for their age or marital status. Lizanne Kelly, who accompanied Grace Kelly in Hollywood during the production of *Dial M for Murder*, stated that the entire male cast and crew hovered around her older sister.

Another Lacey source noted that Hitchcock was particularly astonished to learn that Kelly had had a tryst with the writer of *Dial M for Murder*, Frederick Knott. "She even fucked little Freddie, the writer!" said the director, which is equally revealing of his attitude toward writers as it is of his fascination with Kelly. Hitchcock found Kelly, with her natural beauty, quiet elegance, endless enthusiasm, and appreciation for bawdy humor, a joy to work with and was determined to create for her a part that would show off these qualities. While working on *Dial M for Murder*, Hitchcock asked Hayes to meet with the twenty-four-year-old actress, in order to come up with a character that would best suit her.* As Hayes recalls:

> Hitchcock said of Grace Kelly, "Look at her. She does every-thing well, but there's no fire in her." So I spent a week with Grace Kelly and got to know that she was whimsical and funny and humorous and teasing. She was like the girl next door, but she was very sexy and had all these attributes. I had

*It must have piqued Hitchcock's perverse sense of humor when he sent Hayes and Kelly off alone with each other (to the envy of the men in the *Dial M for Murder* company), rather like the time he left Robert Donat and Madeleine Carroll handcuffed together while shooting *The 39 Steps*. One can imagine Hitchcock wondering whether his leading lady would make a conquest of an-other lowly screenwriter.

to give her a profession, so I gave her my wife's profession—
a high-style fashion model. I combined the best that I saw in
Grace Kelly, the best in my wife, and created the character
of Lisa, and it went very well. And after that, Grace Kelly's
wings spread and we continued the character in *To Catch a
Thief*.

In creating the love story, Hitchcock and Hayes considered
it a more interesting twist to have Lisa pursue Jefferies rather
than the other way around. Recently it has been argued that the
Lisa-Jefferies relationship was modeled on the love affair between
Ingrid Bergman and photojournalist Robert Capa. That Hitchcock
knew of the affair is certain, since it took place in 1945 and 1946,
when *Notorious* was in production. Capa even visited Hitchcock's
set for the purpose of covering the production for *Life* magazine,
which, according to Capa's and Bergman's biographers, was merely
an excuse to be with Bergman in Hollywood and avoid the suspicion of the gossip columnists. In her autobiography Bergman revealed a conversation she had with Capa, in which he confessed
that he was "not the marrying kind," and that if they married and
had a child, he would be unable to pick up at a moment's notice to
cover a news event on the other side of the world. Did Hitchcock
recall Capa's attitude toward marriage when creating *Rear Window*?
    A good case for this reading was made in Steve Cohen's 1990 ar-
ticle "*Rear Window*: The Untold Story," which cites several parallels
between Capa and Jefferies in the film. Capa's association with *Life*
magazine is well known, and although it is never mentioned by
name in the film, there are enough clues that "the magazine" referred to by Jefferies is *Life*. Cohen further argues that Hitchcock
even chose to set *Rear Window* in Greenwich Village because at
one time Capa lived on Ninth Street, pointing out that in the film
the address of the murderer is 125 West Ninth Street. But the location was chosen by the filmmakers due to the simple fact that
the Sixth Police Precinct in Manhattan is located on West Tenth
Street between the same cross streets (Bleecker and Hudson) as

125 Christopher Street (West Ninth in the film). The proximity of the police station to Thorwald's apartment makes their speedy arrival on the scene entirely plausible.

While there are many parallels between Capa and the fictional L. B. Jefferies, Cohen is less convincing in his attempt to make a connection between Ingrid Bergman and Lisa Fremont, who seem quite dissimilar apart from their natural beauty and refinement. Cohen stretches the credibility of his argument when he derives significance from their surnames, whose root meaning in each case is "mountain," suggesting the "berg" in Bergman became the "mont" in Fremont.

John Michael Hayes maintains that he and Hitchcock did not base the love story in *Rear Window* on the Bergman-Capa affair and that the character of Lisa is a composite of Grace Kelly and his wife. While Hitchcock often spoke publicly of his inspiration for scenes and sequences, he rarely did about characterizations. Such matters he usually left to his writers. However, on one occasion, Hitchcock did identify model-turned-actress-turned-beauty-expert Anita Colby as an inspiration for Lisa Fremont.

Anita Colby earned the nickname "The Face" in the mid-1930s, when she was the nation's foremost magazine cover and hat model, and at one time the highest-paid model in America. What contributed to her longevity as a beauty and fashion expert was that "The Face" had a brain, and proved it when she succeeded in becoming a top account executive in the advertising department of *Harper's Bazaar*. Colby's keen business and social sense earned her a unique position in the 1940s as Feminine Director of the Selznick Studio. Many of the leading ladies under contract to David Selznick, including such Hitchcock alumni as Joan Fontaine and Ingrid Bergman, attended what amounted to Colby's one-woman finishing school. No doubt Hitchcock was also aware of the irony that Colby had at one time been linked romantically with James Stewart, and had reportedly turned down a proposal of marriage from the actor.

Whether or not Hitchcock had Capa, Bergman, or Colby in mind during his early story conferences, according to Hayes, there is much from his own life that appears on-screen. In developing the basic conflict in Jeff's relationship with Lisa, Hayes drew upon his own experience with his wife. Hayes explained:

> In the case of Jimmy Stewart in *Rear Window*, when Lisa was in danger, he suddenly realized how much she meant to him, and that if anything happened to her, my God, life was worthless. That came out of my life. Before my wife and I were married, we decided to delay our marriage until I was more successful. We got into an automobile accident, and she was thrown out of the car and onto the highway, amongst broken glass and metal and everything. But in the brief moment when I saw her rolling down the highway before I was knocked unconscious against the windshield, I said, "Oh my God. If anything happens to her, my life won't be worth anything." And I decided I was not going to wait another minute if we ever lived through this thing.
>
> So when I got to this situation in *Rear Window*, we had to bring Jimmy Stewart and Grace Kelly together. Now what scene are you going to play? How is he going to give in? How is he going to say, "Well, you're right," and so forth? This is kind of a dull scene, but we never had to have it. When she was in danger, you looked at his face and knew instantly that he valued her more than anything. So when I came to figure out how we were going to write that scene, I said, "The automobile accident." He saw her and thought maybe it's the last he'd ever see of her, because this man is capable of killing and cutting her up. Mel was capable of having died rolling down the highway, or being terribly injured for life, and so I said, "We don't have to say anything." When I went out and picked up my wife, that was it, we weren't going to be separated again. So when I came to that scene, I drew on my experience for emotion.

Having furnished the emotional conflict—the romance of Jeff and Lisa—Hayes was ready to meld this with Woolrich's story.

The Hayes Treatment

Hayes begins his treatment by setting the mood and visual nature of the story to follow. The back yard of a "Greenwich Village kind of neighborhood, as seen through the picture window of a studio apartment," is sketched in with precise architectural details and succinct descriptions of the inhabitants who occupy the surrounding apartments. Hayes then introduces L. B. Jefferies, who is described as a "tall, lean, energetic thirty-five, his face long and serious-looking at rest, is in other circumstances capable of humor, passion, naïve wonder and the kind of intensity that bespeaks inner convictions of moral strength and basic honesty." In short, a younger James Stewart.

In a few brief passages, through details such as the writing on Jeff's cast, a shattered camera, a series of action-packed news photographs, and a telephone conversation with Jeff's photographic editor (which sets up the basic conflict, Jeff's fear of marriage), Hayes reveals more about Jefferies than Woolrich does in his entire story. At the same time, Hayes introduces a series of neighbors from the surrounding windows—among them a scantily clad ballet dancer, a pair of newlyweds, a husband cheating on his wife with an upstairs neighbor, and a salesman with a sickly wife.

In a departure from Woolrich's story and Logan's treatment, Hayes replaces the houseman, Sam, with Stella McCaffery, an insurance company nurse who visits Jeff daily, checking his temperature and massaging his back to relieve the strain caused by the wheelchair. In the treatment, Hayes describes Stella as

> a blunt and earthy woman, full of the wise and cynical lore of city living. No cant, or hypocrisy, in her dialogue. She says what most of us think, but revise vocally for greater social acceptance. Because of such forthrightness, her comments border on the startling, and are either extremely penetrating, or extremely humorous—and often, both.

Unlike Sam, Stella serves a much greater purpose as a foil for Jeff, chiding him for his "peeping-Tom activities" and shooting down his reasons for avoiding marriage to Lisa. Hayes has observed:

> I like a character like that to act as a Greek chorus, to tell us what might happen and to go to for comic relief. Because you can't have unrestrained suspense all the time. You have to give your audience a chance to laugh and catch their breath and get set for the next scary thing that's going to happen. You can't keep them on a level of fright and suspense through an entire picture. I always liked a character of that nature, who is not really on the sidelines, but sort of a footnote, a commentator on what was going on.
>
> I told Hitch that we'd need a character of this sort to unite the audience with laughter, right from the beginning. He asked me to explain what I meant, and I told him, "When an audience first sits down in a theater, they're all strangers. So when the lights go out and the movie begins, some people are still getting settled in their seats, and the person next to you has your armrest, and somebody in front of you is talking with his wife, and the person behind you is crunching popcorn. So what we have to do is bring this audience together so they feel like they're one." And Hitch thought that over for a moment, then asked, "How would you do that?" And I told him, "With laughter."
>
> So we created the character Stella, and contrasted the suspense with comedy, and this brought the audience together so they reacted as one. Stella also tells us about Lisa, whom we haven't met—"She's only the most perfect woman in the world"—so when we meet her, we know about her. I believe in building your characters carefully. The more you know a character, the more you suffer when suspenseful things happen to them, and so I use that person as a dramatic lubricant between one scene, or one character, and another.

Stella is truly a Hayes character, as she is found over and over again in his work. The first film appearance of a Hayes "Stella" type was the character of Mrs. Stewart in *Torch Song*, for which Marjorie Rambeau received an Academy Award nomination. The Stella type later appeared in *To Catch a Thief* as Mrs. Stevens, *The Trouble with Harry* as Mrs. Wiggs, *Butterfield 8*, *Where Love Has Gone*, and other films Hayes wrote.

Later, Lisa Fremont, a model-turned-fashion-executive, arrives and is described in the treatment as

a lithe, beautiful, honey-haired young woman of perhaps twenty-six years. Her dress and adornment have the exciting perfection of a Vogue Magazine model. Her beauty seems to go deeper than the surface, her eyes alert and her face intelligent. But there is something about her physical movement, the way she walks, turns, sits, that has a professional touch to it. It is as if she is always conscious of the need for dramatizing her appearance. It could be the result of a great insecurity, vanity, or professional training. In Lisa's case, it is the latter.

Hayes sets up an emotional roller coaster for Jeff and Lisa, having Jeff say flat out that "he's given up all thoughts of marriage for a few years." Very quickly, however, the treatment reveals that Jeff is unfair in his assessment of Lisa—she is so much more than just a woman interested in "a new dress, a lobster dinner and the latest scandal." She is very much in love with Jeff, but fearing that kind of commitment, he continually attempts to derail their relationship.

As early as the treatment stage, Hayes sought to create a complex mosaic of variations of the Lisa-Jefferies relationship. As Lisa prepares dinner, Jeff again picks up his binoculars, viewing through them characterizations and situations in the surrounding windows that either parallel or complement those of his own apartment. The Hayes treatment to this point is nearly all character development and has little resemblance to Woolrich's story.

Following this lengthy setup, which occupies the first twenty pages—more than one quarter—of the treatment, Hayes picks up where Woolrich begins. As in the story, Jeff observes the shadowy outline of two figures moving behind the shade of the salesman's window. He then watches as the salesman leaves his apartment and returns three times in the same night. It is this odd behavior that awakens the imagination of Woolrich's protagonist. Hayes, however, adds one significant event. At the moment the salesman leaves his apartment accompanied by a woman, Jeff has fallen asleep.

Unlike Woolrich's Jeff, Hayes's meets with skepticism from both Lisa and Stella when he tries to convince them that something has happened to the salesman's wife. However, Stella becomes intrigued when, along with Jeff, she sees two men in white overalls remove a trunk from the salesman's apartment. By drawing Stella into Jeff's investigation, Hayes manages to entice even the most cynical viewer. Woolrich's Sam had little choice but to act on the whim of his employer, but Stella is an independent agent. If Stella, hard-bitten realist that she is, can be drawn into the mystery, there must be something to it.

As in Woolrich's story, Jeff calls for the assistance of a detective friend, Thomas J. Boyne. Hayes fleshes out the character of the detective, establishing a prior relationship between him and Jeff, when the two were teamed in air reconnaissance during the Second World War as pilot and photographer. The treatment follows the original story line in that the police activities only serve to prove Thorwald's innocence: Boyne reports that his men found nothing incriminating in the salesman's apartment; a ticket agent at the train station identified Thorwald as a man who put his wife on a train bound for upstate; and a postcard was found in Thorwald's mailbox, mailed the previous day, saying, "Arrived O.K. Already feeling a little better. Love, Anna."

The treatment maintains a balance between the Woolrich plot and the conflict between Jeff and Lisa while continuing to develop the storylines of the surrounding apartments. Miss Lonely Hearts, whom Jeff earlier observed in a pantomime scene with an imaginary lover, is drinking and getting ready for a night out; Miss Torso is dating a different man from the one she was with earlier, confirming Lisa's observation that he was not her true love; and the songwriter, who appears in another window, continues composing his tune.

As in the story, Boyne is angry at Jeff for wasting the police department's time and reports that his men located the trunk, found it packed with women's clothes, and watched as it was picked up by Mrs. Thorwald. Boyne's report inspires Jeff to take action. On a piece of notepaper Jeff writes: "What have you done with her?," then watches as Lisa delivers the note. Thorwald's startled reaction convinces Jeff that he is right. This is a key episode from the Woolrich story that remains largely unchanged.

At this point, however, Hayes departs greatly from Woolrich. Lisa returns from delivering the note glowing with excitement—her transformation is taking place—but Jeff is so preoccupied with Thorwald that he fails to notice. Thorwald then leaves his apartment, and Lisa impulsively follows him, in spite of Jeff's protests. As Jeff waits nervously in his apartment, he studies some pictures he took of the garden and notices something odd. He compares one of his slides to the garden as it is now and can clearly see that the zinnias in Thorwald's flower bed have grown shorter.

The shorter zinnias of Hayes's treatment replace the "jump" noticed by Woolrich's Jeff when he saw Thorwald and the building's rental agent walking from the living room to the kitchen in separate apartments. At this point, Woolrich's Jeffries realizes that Mrs. Thorwald is buried in the newly raised cement floor in the kitchen above Thorwald's apartment. Noticing the shortened zinnias, the Jefferies of the film treatment suspects the murder weapon is hidden in the flower bed. It is a simpler visual detail—and one that allowed the filmmakers to exploit Jeff's occupation.

Two hours later Thorwald returns, and Lisa follows, arriving at Jeff's apartment to fill him in. Hayes's treatment reads:

What did he do? Where did he go? Jeff wanted to know. No place that made too much sense to her. He walked to a huge excavation on Martine Street where workers were pouring cement for the foundation of a new insurance company building. He stayed there, watching the work, until the cement was poured and smoothed. Then he went to a nearby bar for a couple of quick drinks. The drinks seemed to relax him, for once he came out of the bar his nervousness was gone and he no longer looked behind himself. Then he stopped in a drugstore for some cigarettes. While waiting for change he noticed some crime magazines on a stand. Then his face went white. He seemed shaken. He picked out one of the magazines, which one she couldn't see, paid for it, and hurried back to his apartment.

As Lisa recounts her adventure, Jeff notices how animated and natural she has become, but he remains preoccupied with the murder. Jeff deduces that Thorwald killed his wife, cut up the body, and then made several trips to the excavation site, where he was able to bury the pieces with the knowledge that they would be cemented over.

The treatment handles the disposal of Mrs. Thorwald's body in a more interesting fashion than the story does. Woolrich's cement floor has become the cement foundation for a new building. However, the scene as written presents the filmmakers with two key dramatic problems. First, the excavation site is never shown, and second, of greater importance, is the violation of a principle true to all Hitchcock's films: if a major character is going to be put in danger, it must occur on-screen. Hayes's invention of a crime magazine that makes Thorwald shudder is a clever nod to the story's origin. But despite its inventiveness, Lisa's adventure of trailing Thorwald did not make it into the subsequent script or film.

The details of Lisa's adventure set the wheels of Jeff's mind in motion, and the crime magazine provides a reason to enter Thorwald's apartment. Jeff suspects the magazine contains a story about a wife-murderer and how he got caught. In Woolrich's story, Jeff merely sends Sam to Thorwald's apartment to "disturb everything just a little bit," in order to bluff the salesman into believing he has obtained something incriminating. But here, Lisa offers to go into Thorwald's apartment to retrieve the magazine. Jeff reluctantly allows her to go, but he first telephones Thorwald, and—pretending to blackmail him—arranges a meeting at the excavation site.

Jeff watches as Lisa goes through the back yard, over the fence, and up the fire escape. After she gets into Thorwald's apartment and finds the magazine, Lisa begins searching the rest of the apartment—to Jeff's horror. As Lisa puts herself in greater danger, Jeff realizes that he truly loves her. The treatment reads:

> "Oh Lisa, darling," Jeff says aloud. "He's already killed one woman. I don't want him to kill you—of all women." And Jeff is shocked to learn how much he loves her. He loves you, Lisa. Get out of there, and get back to him. You've made him understand.

Thorwald returns suddenly and Jeff is helpless. Jeff quickly reaches for the telephone and calls for the police, identifying himself as Thorwald, to report a prowler. At the very moment that Thorwald discovers Lisa and attacks her, the songwriter plays his completed composition. Soon the police burst into Thorwald's apartment and arrest Lisa. As in the story, Jeff is alone when he receives a telephone call from Thorwald, who has discovered his whereabouts.

In the Woolrich story, Jeff prepares for Thorwald's arrival by propping a lifelike bust on his shoulder and crouching down in his chair. When Thorwald enters, he fires his gun and strikes the bust, which crumbles into pieces. Thorwald then leaps out Jeff's window into the courtyard and climbs to the roof of his building as the police arrive. Thorwald fires a shot at Boyne, who promptly returns fire, killing the salesman.

In the film treatment, Jeff fends off Thorwald by using flashbulbs to temporarily blind him. Boyne, Lisa, and the police officers arrive at Thorwald's apartment (where they see the caption for a story in the crime magazine Thorwald bought—"I Was a Wife-Killer") and their attention is captured by the flashes of light across the courtyard. They start toward Jeff's building, where Thorwald is trying to push Jeff out the window. Jeff clings to the ledge as Boyne fires three shots into Thorwald's chest. The police try to reach Jeff, but he cannot hold on any longer and falls from his window into the courtyard, breaking his other leg. Boyne tells Jeff what was found buried in the flower bed—Mrs. Thorwald's head "still nagging." Lisa rushes to Jeff's side:

> Jeff and Lisa come together in love. He tells her what he thought of her when she was in danger. The experience, she said, awakened her also. But the thing that impressed her most was that melody the songwriter was playing in her moment of greatest horror. It was utterly beautiful and she was determined Thorwald wouldn't kill her until the song was finished.

Jeff professes his love to Lisa, saying he cannot wait until they are married. But they will have to wait another six weeks, until his newly broken leg has healed.

The finale of the treatment brings closure to both the murder plot and the dilemma of Jeff and Lisa's relationship. Several ideas developed in the treatment also reach a rewarding conclusion. Lisa reveals that the song inspired her to fight for her life; Jefferies uses the tools of his trade to defend himself; and unlike Woolrich's Jeff, who remains unscathed, Hayes's Jeff has the tables turned when his neighbors watch as Thorwald attacks him and he is thrown out of his own window, from which he had earlier spied on his neighbors.

Hayes turned in his completed treatment to MCA on Friday, September 11, 1953, while Hitchcock was busy directing scenes of *Dial M for Murder*, which had fallen behind schedule. The treatment was then delivered to Marge Wonder at Paramount for retyping. The official studio treatment, dated September 12, 1953, boosted Paramount's belief that they had a winner with *Rear Window*. (The seventy-five-page prose treatment used to be handed out by the Paramount Story Department to new writers as an example of how to write a perfect treatment.) Additionally, James Stewart had enough faith in the film's future success to forgo his salary in exchange for part ownership of the picture. After completing the treatment, Hitchcock and Hayes met again to make adjustments to the basic construction, but the characters, their motivations, and the tone of the film had been set in stone.

Woolrich's story provided the skeleton, but Hayes provided Hitchcock with the characterizations and emotional weight necessary to lift the material from its pulp origins to a level of glamour and wit associated with Hitchcock's best work. The story had been elevated to one about a man's fear of commitment, a theme suggested in Woolrich's story but one that never completely surfaced.

Upon acceptance of the treatment, Hitchcock's agents, Arthur Park and Herman Citron, proceeded to finalize agreements between Leland Hayward's Orange Productions, Paramount Pictures, and Hitchcock's newly formed corporation, Patron, Inc. (combining the names of Park and Citron). While the lawyers drew up the contracts, Hitchcock and Hayes continued to meet at the director's Bel Air home to discuss the screenplay. Hayes recalled, "Hitch was still working on *Dial M for Murder*, in post-production. We did have conferences to keep up with what I was doing, but he gave me my head and let me go ahead and write the screenplay."

"I always insist on sitting with the writer from the very beginning and creating about a 100-page outline of all the details from the first shot to the end," said Hitchcock. "Then I let the writer go away and complete the dialogue and character." Hayes's previous screen efforts, such as *Red Ball Express* and *War Arrow*, afforded him little opportunity to write such strong characterizations. Where he would be criticized for writing "talky" scenes in B-pictures, under the surehanded direction of a Hitchcock, lengthy dialogue scenes seemed to flow with a natural ease. Hayes was at first surprised by the amount of freedom given him by the director to create scenes and inject his own sensibilities into the character of Jefferies.

Hayes infused the treatment with his own experience of having loved ones attempt to dissuade him from pursuing a writing career, which they had considered an unsteady undertaking at best. According to Hayes, the fear of being forced by a loved one to betray one's true nature is everywhere apparent in L. B. Jefferies:

> Jeff is afraid of the fact that if he and Lisa marry, she'll get him to settle down in New York to do portraits, and he'll miss all the excitement of life. She'll make a full-time fashion photographer out of him, and he'd much rather be in Pakistan, traveling in a jeep, taking pictures on the fly. That was exciting for him. He doesn't want to be domesticated.

> He was an action photographer who happened to meet a girl on a shoot, and they formed this warm friendship. The girl liked him. He liked the girl, but realized that, one, she couldn't live his kind of life, and two, he couldn't live her kind of life. Yet he found her very desirable, which makes sense because she was. It's all suggested in the dialogue.

Hitchcock often stated that the better the villain, the better the picture. *Rear Window* did not call for a suave, sophisticated heavy such as those portrayed by Claude Rains or Ray Milland. Hayes, too, agreed that Lars Thorwald was an ordinary human being, not at all the stereotypical villain one might have expected from central casting. According to Hayes:

> When we were casting *Rear Window*, they brought in all sorts of thuggy-looking people for Thorwald, and you knew damn well that they killed their wives. So we got Raymond Burr, aged him, put rimless glasses on him, and tried to disarm him. Yet he was such a good actor, there was an intensity about him that was tremendous, so when he turned and looked directly at the camera, everybody in the theater moved back.

> I've never really written a pure villain. I think when a man becomes a villain, there have to be reasons for it, so I want to explain a little of his villainy. This is just an ordinary

fellow, and one day, he had enough of his wife, he had an affair on the side, and he made a desperate move, which was probably atypical of him, and he thought nobody would notice. Nobody would care in this community, where nobody pays attention to each other, and he accidentally falls victim to a man who has nothing to do but stare out the window. Because of Jeff's photographic ability, he is used to picking up something that isn't right. Thorwald might have gotten away with it if he hadn't fallen victim to a curious man in a different world. That doesn't excuse it. But it's interesting that he was an ordinary villain, because if you'd met him at any other time, you would never suspect him.

The Screenplay

Frequently a writer's "first draft" screenplay is written in "master scenes." This means that the script contains both dialogue and descriptions of action but is not broken down into specific shots. When the writer works with the director, they break down the screenplay's master scenes into individually numbered shots to create a "shooting script." The shooting script then functions not only as the screenplay for the director and performers but also as a shot plan for the production personnel. The shooting script is particularly important for the budgeting and scheduling departments.

A writer and director may develop several drafts of a screenplay before one is distributed to the various production departments at the studio. At Paramount, this initial shooting script was usually called the "yellow" or "first preliminary green" script, and the final shooting script was customarily referred to as the "final white" script. Revisions to the final shooting script were usually printed on blue paper and inserted in the final script, and revisions to the revisions were done in goldenrod.

By the time the agreement between Orange Productions and Patron was signed on October 14, Hayes had completed his first draft script. It was indeed a remarkable job. Hayes had breathed life into the characters, expanding in every way on what had already been an exceptional treatment. From the dialogue emerged a depth of characterization he hadn't achieved before in the medium. He then met with Hitchcock almost daily, turning the screenplay into a Hitchcock shooting script. The writer recalled:

> We sat down in his office and he broke up all the scenes into individual shots, and made sketches of them, and laid out the picture, which he said is now done. "All we have to do is go on the set and make sure they do what we've given them."

The first twenty-one pages of the first draft, or yellow script, are dated October 20, 1953. The remaining pages followed—approximately twelve to twenty at a time—almost every other day through November 30. By the time the yellow script had been completed, it was 167 pages in length and had been broken down into 490 shots.

Few changes in construction were made between Hayes's treatment and the first draft script. Key plot points where Lisa had been absent, such as the first time Mrs. Thorwald's bed is shown to be empty, with the mattress rolled and tied, as well as the moment that Jeff first notices the difference in the height of Thorwald's zinnias, now prominently included her. Hitchcock also dropped the cheating husband from the treatment in favor of a couple with a dog, which would be used to great advantage in confirming Jeff's suspicions about Thorwald. When the dog is found strangled in the courtyard after sniffing around the flower bed, Jeff has good reason to suspect something is buried in the garden.

Hitchcock, who possessed an extensive collection of literature relating to true crime, referred Hayes to two famous British murder trials in order to enhance both the gruesomeness of the murder and the detection of the murderer by using elements from real life. The inspiration for the disposal of Mrs. Thorwald's remains came from the Patrick Mahon case, which was far more grisly than the fate Woolrich had written. Mahon murdered a woman, cut her up, and disposed of her remains by tossing the pieces out the window of a moving train en route from London to Eastbourne. Mahon's dilemma was that he didn't know what to do with the woman's head, which he finally decided to burn in a fireplace.* As he did this, a thunderstorm started, adding to the macabre atmosphere, which reached its climax when the heat of the fire caused the woman's eyes to open. Mahon became so frightened that he ran from the house screaming and was caught. This idea had already been well placed in Hayes's treatment, but Hitchcock had a better idea about what evidence would ultimately trip up Thorwald.

In the treatment, Jeff sends Lisa into Thorwald's apartment to retrieve the incriminating crime magazine. In the script, however, Lisa takes it upon herself to search for Mrs. Thorwald's wedding ring, an idea suggested by the trial of Dr. Hawley Harvey Crippen. In 1910 Dr. Crippen poisoned his wife, cut her up, and buried her remains in his basement. He then pawned several pieces of her jewelry, and also gave some to his mistress, which eventually led to his arrest at sea when he fled England after detectives discovered his wife's remains. Hitchcock was always fond of the Crippen case and enjoyed constructing *Rear Window* so that the chief piece of evidence incriminating Thorwald was the jewelry left behind by his wife, particularly her wedding ring.

To follow the lobster dinner that Lisa had brought to Jeff from the "21" Club, Hayes wrote a poignant scene wherein the pair enter a senseless debate in which Jeff tries to free himself from a commitment to Lisa. Jeff spars verbally with Lisa, trying in every way to put her off, but he is no more convinced of his argument than she is. Lisa exits hurt, but ever more determined to prove herself the stronger and make Jeff "see" what is right before him in his own apartment. Thus, Hitchcock's choice of the song "To See You," heard prior to this scene in the finished film, is in every way significant.

---

*The suggestion of beheading had also been in Joshua Logan's treatment for *Rear Window*. At the opening, Logan's Jeff is surprised when he hears a voice say, "I'm goin' to cut your head off." These are the very first words spoken in Logan's treatment, which turn out to be those of Jeff's houseman, Sam, speaking to a fish that he is preparing for Jeff's lunch.

Hayes loaded the script with crisp, witty dialogue that included some typically Hitchcockian black humor during a meal. As Stella serves Jeff breakfast, she thinks aloud, "Now just where do you suppose he cut her up? Oh—of course! In the bathtub. That's the only place he could wash away the blood." Similar moments occur in *Blackmail, Young and Innocent, Suspicion, Shadow of a Doubt, Rope, To Catch a Thief, The Trouble with Harry, Psycho,* and *Frenzy.*

In the scene prior to the discovery of the murdered dog, the first draft leads toward another disagreement between Jeff and Lisa. It starts with a joke as Lisa says, "I'm going to have a—" Anticipating an announcement of Lisa's maternity, Jeff nearly chokes on his drink. Lisa finishes, "I'm going to have a big day planned for you next Tuesday," revealing her intention to accompany him on his photographic assignment in Formosa, at which point Jeff becomes "quite serious and troubled." This was changed in the final draft to a flirtatious exchange, with Lisa showing off a new nightgown and kimono.

The murder of the dog provided Hayes with an opportunity to indict the occupants of the courtyard for their apparent detachment and refusal to accept social responsibility. The Siffleuse (a professional whistler), as she is known in the script, for her "clarion and melodic" call to her dog, cries out, "Which one of you did it? Which one of you killed my dog? You don't know the meaning of the word 'neighbor.'" It is a delicate moment in the script, which set the moral tone Hitchcock desired, without becoming preachy.

The search for Mrs. Thorwald's jewelry—in particular, her wedding ring, which is referred to by Lisa as a woman's "basic equipment"—truly involves Lisa beyond a mere interest in attracting Jeff. Lisa's feminine intuition pays off in a big way and is a theme carried further by the characters Francie Stevens in *To Catch a Thief* and Jo McKenna in *The Man Who Knew Too Much.* Instead of trailing Thorwald offscreen, as in the treatment, Jeff and the audience observe Lisa enter Thorwald's apartment in search of the wedding ring. The audience expects Thorwald to return before Lisa is able to extricate herself from his apartment. But when will Thorwald come back? Will Lisa find the evidence she is after? This is Hitchcockian suspense at its best.

Layering their script even further, Hitchcock and Hayes added a scene in which Miss Lonely Hearts contemplates suicide. The scene occurs just as Jeff and Stella are supposed to be watching for Thorwald in order to warn Lisa to get out of his apartment. Believing Miss Lonely Hearts is ready to take her life, Jeff immediately telephones the police. Momentarily distracted, Jeff and Stella do not see Thorwald enter his apartment until it is too late. By the time they realize Lisa is in danger, Miss Lonely Hearts's fondness for the Songwriter's sentimental tune prevents her suicide. In the treatment, it is Lisa who is moved by the song, underscoring the drama. With the police already on the wire, Jeff is able to summon them to help Lisa.

Jeff's, Stella's, and the audience's feeling of helplessness is fully exploited by Hitchcock's direction of this sequence, as Thorwald attacks Lisa. The police arrive in time to save her, and she allows herself to be arrested in order to get out of the apartment, but not before signaling to Jeff that she has found Mrs. Thorwald's wedding ring. As François Truffaut pointed out, Lisa's signal to Jeff—her waving of the wedding ring on her left hand—contains a twofold message. The obvious one is that she has come away with the evidence she sought—but the more significant one is that this is her proposal to Jeff! Lisa's signal and "proposal" precipitates the most terrifying moment on the screen, when Thorwald follows her signal and looks directly into the camera. Jeff has just realized that he cannot live without Lisa; with typical Hitchcock irony, the tables are turned on him. The watcher has become the watched, and Jeff's onetime dream of freeing himself from Lisa, even at the prospect of "welcoming trouble," is about to become all too real a nightmare.

Following Lisa's arrest, Jeff telephones Coyne (the name was changed from Boyne in the treatment, and would be changed again to Doyle during production) with the news about the wedding ring. Coyne is now interested and says he will try to get Lisa out of trouble. In the final draft and the film, Jeff hangs up and discovers Thorwald's darkened apartment. A few moments later, Thorwald telephones Jeff, discovering that he is home. This, too, is faithful to the Woolrich story. The first draft, however, contains a moment where Thorwald is seen in long shot, standing in the darkened apartment—"THE CAMERA MOVES IN CLOSER, CLOSER, relentlessly on toward Thorwald's face, until it fills the screen."* Thorwald leaves, and is neither seen nor heard from until he enters Jeff's apartment.

A crane shot moving in toward Thorwald's face reads as a very effective scene, but it is superfluous in actuality, since Thorwald had already looked directly into the camera when he caught Jeff spying during Lisa's arrest. The seed of fear has already been planted. The audience is aware that Thorwald knows Jeff's where-abouts and wonders what he will do. Seeing him look directly into the camera again and watching him leave is less effective than cut-ting to the empty room and hearing no voice on the other end of a telephone call.

Where Hayes's first draft falls short is its ending. Thorwald is shot and killed by Coyne, which is consistent with the story and treatment. There is also an attempt to wrap up the stories of the sur-rounding windows neatly. Stella advises Miss Lonely Hearts, "Just throw away those pills, honey. If this face could trap a man, yours could get there." The newlyweds are observed. "H-a-a-r-r-e-e," calls the bride in a desirous tone, playing on the audience's expectations of a honeymoon couple. "Start without me," calls the young groom, as the camera reveals they have been playing a game of chess. Miss Torso compliments the Songwriter for his lovely tune, and he invites her up to his apartment. Finally, the first draft ends with Coyne, Lisa, and Jeff. Coyne reveals, "You were right. There was something in that garden. And I just got a signal. It's in Thorwald's icebox now." Jeff replies dryly, "That reminds me. Two heads are better than one."

*This unfilmed scene is reminiscent of the famous crane shot in Hitchcock's 1937 Gaumont-British production Young and Innocent, in which the camera sweeps across a crowded ballroom and comes to rest on a close-up of the mur-derer's twitching eyes.

What is unsatisfactory about this ending is the absence of a tag, or coda. The killing of Thorwald is unnecessary. Hitchcock is rarely concerned with the apprehension of the criminals in his films. His concern has always been with resolving the protagonist's dilemma. Thorwald's motivation for murdering his wife is irrelevant, so the mention of insurance money would be eliminated in the final draft. Also, Jeff's glib reference to Mrs. Thorwald's head would be rewritten and given to Stella, for one final wink to the audience.

Pre-production and Censorship

Now that a script was in hand, a production team was quickly assembled. Heading Hitchcock's new Paramount crew as assistant director was Herbert Coleman, who started working at the studio as a driver in 1927. Clarence Oscar Erickson, known to all as Doc, recalled how Coleman was responsible for his joining the production:

> Herbie was there at the very beginning when Hitch came to Paramount. So he was instrumental in getting me on the show as the unit manager. [The unit manager is responsible for coordinating the administrative details of an individual film, such as budgeting and scheduling, in addition to supervising the film's unit or crew.] At that time, Paramount had a number of unit managers on staff, but they were all on assignment. They didn't want to bring in anybody from the outside, and Herbie, who was probably one of the best assistant directors who ever lived, said to the production office, "Look, I don't need anybody, but if you want to give me somebody, why don't you give me Doc." So they assigned me to the show and we became fixtures with Hitch for the next five films.

The roster of production personnel was completed with many who were already familiar faces among Hitchcock's crew—or soon would be—including Robert Burks as director of photography,

Leonard South as camera assistant, George Tomasini as editor, Edith Head as costume designer, Joseph MacMillan Johnson as art director, and John P. Fulton for special effects.

Unquestionably the most famous costume designer in Holly-wood history, Edith Head had a career that spanned nearly fifty years, during which she earned eight Academy Awards. The signifi-cance of her contribution to the look of Hitchcock's films of the 1950s and to those of Grace Kelly cannot be overstated. *Rear Window* was the designer's second collaboration with Hitchcock, and the script called for an extremely stylish wardrobe for its leading lady. "Hitchcock told me it was important that Grace's clothes help to establish some of the conflict in the story," wrote the designer.

> She was to be the typical sophisticated society-girl magazine editor who falls in love with a scruffy photographer, Jimmy Stewart. He's insecure and thinks that she thinks he isn't good enough for her.
>
> Hitch wanted her to look like a piece of Dresden china, something slightly untouchable. So I did that. Her suits were impeccably tailored. Her accessories looked as though they couldn't be worn by anyone else but her. She was perfect. Few actresses could have carried off the look the way Grace did.

In addition to all four Hitchcock-Hayes films, Head's work for the director ultimately included *Notorious*, *Vertigo*, *The Birds*, *Marnie*, *Torn Curtain*, *Topaz*, and *Family Plot*.

The gifted cinematographer Robert Burks began his career in the special-effects department at Warner Bros., where he eventually worked his way up to the position of director of photography. It was while making *Strangers on a Train* in 1950 that Hitchcock began his collaboration with Burks, who, with the exception of *Psycho*, lensed all the director's films from 1950 through *Marnie* in 1964.

While Hitchcock and Hayes continued tightening the script, pre-production and casting commenced. Hitchcock had the walls of his office covered with storyboard sketches for the entire film. This was a practice the director had adopted during his apprenticeship at Famous Players–Lasky in the 1920s, and he subsequently followed it in the preparation of nearly all his later films. The storyboards proved valuable not only to the camera crew and art department as they prepared their contributions to the film but to the editor, George Tomasini, as well, for whom the entire film had been "pre-cut" on paper. Unlike most directors, Hitchcock generally did not shoot "coverage"—the same scene from several angles. Having preconceived the assembly of shots, Hitchcock felt coverage was unnecessary. Pre-cutting was not only cost-effective, but in the days before Hitchcock enjoyed complete creative freedom, it ensured that the producer could not remake the film in the editing room by replacing the director's chosen shots.

It was while working on *Rear Window* that Hitchcock began his long association with George Tomasini, who like Robert Burks worked on all but one of the director's films through *Marnie* in 1964. In Tomasini's case, he was already at work cutting *To Catch a Thief* when *The Trouble with Harry* went into post-production. Were it not for his death from a heart attack at the age of fifty-five, Tomasini probably would have continued working with Hitchcock right up until the director's final film.

Although *Rear Window* would be shot entirely at the studio, Doc Erickson remembers that he was sent to New York to photograph several Greenwich Village courtyards, from which Joseph MacMillan Johnson designed the set. In the film, the courtyard was modeled after Christopher and West Tenth Streets, between Bleecker and Hudson Streets. The immense set—the largest built at Paramount to that date—was constructed on Stage 18. According to a Paramount press release, the set consisted of structures rising up to six stories, which contained thirty-one apartments, fire escapes, an alley, a street, and a skyline. It took six weeks to build.

Hitchcock insisted that *Rear Window* be authentic in every way, dictating in a November 5 memo that actual Greenwich Village ambient sound be recorded so that the soundtrack would be as true to life as possible. Additionally, two days later, Gordon Cole, head of Paramount's property department, made a request of the "21" Club for one wine bucket, two dinner plates, and a half-dozen dinner napkins, to be used in the scene where Lisa brings Jeff supper from the famed Manhattan eatery.*

By mid-November, casting was completed. On loan from Twentieth Century–Fox, the Brooklyn-born Thelma Ritter brought her special comedic talent to the role of Stella, which was almost a reprise of her previous appearances in Mitchell Leisen's *The Mating Season* and George Cukor's *The Model and the Marriage Broker*. As Thomas J. Doyle, Hitchcock cast Wendell Corey, best known for his work in a series of crime melodramas such as *Desert Fury*, *I Walk Alone*, and *Sorry Wrong Number* for producer Hal Wallis. Rounding out the cast in other key roles were Judith Evelyn as Miss Lonely Hearts, Ross Bagdasarian as the Songwriter, Georgine Darcy as Miss Torso, Sara Berner as the Siffleuse, and Irene Winston as Mrs. Thorwald.

The first photography tests for Production #10331, *Rear Window*, were shot on Friday, November 13, 1953. The test involved lighting the neighborhood and courtyard set for both day and night, requiring four male and two female extras, and one car. During these tests Robert Burks supervised the pre-lighting of the complex set. Burks recalled, "I went on the sound stage about ten days prior to the starting date. Using a skeleton crew, we pre-lit every one of the thirty-one apartments for both day and night, as well as lit the exterior of the courtyard for the dual-type illumination required. A remote switch controlled the lights in each apartment. On the stage, we had a switching setup that looked like the console of the

*Fans of the Billy Wilder/Paramount film *Sunset Boulevard* may remember the name Gordon Cole. In Wilder's film, Norma Desmond (Gloria Swanson) believes that Cecil B. DeMille wants to direct her return to the screen when she receives several telephone calls from Paramount's Gordon Cole. Norma later chides DeMille, believing Cole to be one of DeMille's assistants. It turns out that Gordon Cole had seen Norma's car on the lot and wanted to rent it for a Bing Crosby production.

biggest organ ever made!" The pre-lighting allowed for remarkable control during filming and, to the delight of Hitchcock and the Paramount front office, probably reduced shooting time by one half.

With only one week remaining until the starting date, Joseph I. Breen, director of the Production Code Administration (PCA), Hollywood's self-appointed censorship board, responded to the incomplete first draft script in a letter to Luigi Luraschi, head of Paramount's censorship department. Breen enumerated his objections to the sexual elements and other questionable references contained in Hayes's script, paying particular attention to the scenes involving Miss Torso, the honeymoon couple, and any dialogue suggestive of an illicit sexual affair between Jeff and Lisa.

Breen felt that Hayes's description of Miss Torso clad only in black panties was unacceptable. "It is apparent that she is nude above the waist and it is only by the most judicious selection of camera angles that her nudity is concealed," wrote Breen, who added, "We feel that this gives the entire action the flavor of a peep show." Further along in the script, Breen warned against any scenes that would "indicate unacceptable exposure of the girl's breasts," or that would allow the display of "intimate feminine undergarments" when she is seen hanging her laundry to dry. Breen noted that during the scene in which Miss Lonely Hearts brings a young man back to her apartment, the description of the action of the young man whose "hand is doing something with the slide fastener at the back of her dress" was "excessively sex suggestive."

Breen objected to a number of Stella's lines, feeling they were a little too bluntly stated. For example, Breen indicated the line "When General Motors has to go to the bathroom ten times a day, the whole country's ready to let go," should be rewritten to "take it away from the present impression of being toilet humor." The depiction of the newlywed couple was also a cause for concern to Breen, who felt that the occasional vignettes at their window were too suggestive of the "sexual aspects of a honeymoon."

As for Jeff and Lisa, Breen cautioned that too much emphasis had been placed on the fact that Lisa is staying the night in Jeff's apartment. "We think the same story point can be carried if considerably less emphasis were placed on the action and the display of her underwear, pajamas and other paraphernalia . . . and it were indicated that she is going to stay there simply because of the mystery that has risen at this point in the story."

An interoffice memo in the PCA's production file for *Rear Window* indicates that on the first day of principal photography, Alfred Hitchcock and Luigi Luraschi held an on-set conference with PCA officials to alleviate their apprehensions once they had seen "the physical setup under which the action will be photographed." Having seen the extraordinary set, and noting that the action in the surrounding apartments would be photographed from the viewpoint of the protagonist's apartment, many of their concerns had been eliminated. Objections to individual lines of dialogue and the actions of the newlywed couple remained, though. Compromises would be made in the final draft, shooting, and editing. However, in spite of Breen's objections, many of these elements remain, verbatim, in the finished picture.

The Shoot

Principal photography began on Friday, November 27, at nine in the morning. The first shot was the complicated opening camera move. Although planned as a single uninterrupted take, the sequence in the finished film was eventually edited into three shots, the longest of which lasts ninety seconds, beginning with a couple waking on their fire escape. The camera pans left and down to the ballet dancer's apartment, left to the alley and street where children are playing in the sprinkler of a sanitation department vehicle, and over to a woman uncovering a birdcage at a window, all in one shot. Without a cut, the camera retreats into Jeff's apartment and to his broken leg in a cast. The camera then moves over to a table on which there is a broken camera, several action-packed framed photographs, and, finally, to the negative and finished magazine cover showing a glamorous blond model. The camera operator, Bill Schurr, and his assistant, Leonard South, spent half a day executing the scene to Burks's and Hitchcock's satisfaction. The eighth and final take is the one ultimately used in the film.

Hitchcock and his crew proceeded with great speed and efficiency, achieving thirty-four setups (or camera positions) on the second day of production, twenty-one on the third, and eighteen on the fourth. By December 2, the fifth day of production, Hayes had turned in the balance of the final "white script," leaving only the finale to be revised, which he would do near the end of production, while he was on salary for *To Catch a Thief*.

Production continued smoothly through December, with the only major delays caused by the necessity to reshoot many scenes that were filmed with a 10-inch telephoto lens, in favor of retakes done with a 6-inch telephoto lens, which increased the depth-of-field and considerably improved the definition, or sharpness, of images some 40 to 80 feet away from Jeff's apartment. Robert Burks recalled, "We had one shot in the picture that was a key shot in the plot . . . the salesman-murderer is observed by Stewart . . . going through his wife's effects during her absence. He takes her wedding ring out of her purse and looks at it. The first time we attempted the shot, we made it with a 10-inch lens. On the screen, it wasn't clear that the object was a wedding ring. It was obvious that it was a ring, but that was all." Burks tried to correct the problem by adjusting the lights, but Hitchcock still wasn't satisfied. The desired effect was finally achieved when Burks changed lenses and moved the camera onto a boom, out of Jeff's apartment and over the courtyard. According to Burks, "The results were sharp as a tack."

Many of the film's special effects were also achieved "in camera." For example, the instance of Jeff comparing the height of the zinnias in Thorwald's flower bed to their height in the 35mm transparencies he had taken previously was accomplished by rigging the camera with a device designed by special effects expert Irmin Roberts, which used prisms, short-range projection, and quick focus changes. The scene showing James Stewart falling away from the window was achieved by creating a "traveling matte" shot, which combined live action with a prephotographed background. The portion of the shot in which Stewart appears to be falling was photographed on Stage 3 by seating the actor against a black velvet background with a camera overhead. Then, while Stewart acted as if he was falling, the camera in fact moved in an upward direction *away* from him. This image was later superimposed against a stationary shot taken on the actual courtyard set, creating the illusion of Stewart falling into the courtyard.

Rear Window was also Hitchcock's first wide-screen production. The recommended aspect ratio for projection—the width-to-height ratio of the image—was 1.66 to 1, only slightly more rectangular than the Academy ratio of 1.33 to 1. The aspect ratio approximated the shape of the windows surrounding Jefferies's apartment. The overall look and visual effects achieved are memorable, and a testament to Robert Burks's contribution to the art of Alfred Hitchcock.

Although a Paramount press release boasted that *Rear Window*, "in its entirety, was shot on one stage and in one set," this statement is not completely accurate. Following the opening shot of the courtyard and Jeff's apartment, the script called for a brief scene inside the office of Jeff's photographic editor, Ivar Gunnison. Gunnison and his assistant, Jack Bryce, discuss the need to get a photographer to Indochina and agree that the best man for the job is Jefferies. Hitchcock shot the scene but did not use it in the film. While it is no surprise that the scene was not used in the film, since it does nothing to advance the plot, it is odd that Gunnison was played by Frank Cady, since the actor also plays the man on the fire escape (the Siffleuse's husband) in the film. It is possible, then, that Hitchcock never intended to use the scene and merely shot it to alleviate any concerns of the studio that he was making another static "one-set" picture, as he had with *Rope* a few years earlier.

Hayes turned in a new finale on January 5, 1954, which tightened the climactic scenes and included a "tag" that mirrored the film's opening. In a single take, the camera begins on Jeff's window thermometer, showing that the climate has cooled significantly, then proceeds to reveal how the lives of the dwellers in the surrounding apartments have progressed. Miss Lonely Hearts is with the Songwriter, who is playing the recording of his new song for her. Thorwald's empty apartment is being repainted. The Siffleuse is training a new dog. Miss Torso lovingly welcomes home an unassuming Army private. The newlyweds are arguing. Jeff is asleep in his wheelchair with both legs in casts, and finally, the "new" Lisa is revealed, dressed in jeans and a cotton shirt, reading a travel book. When she notices Jeff is asleep, she puts down the book and opens the latest issue of *Harper's Bazaar*.

The shooting of the finale occupied the last week of principal photography. With the exception of a few minor injuries, such as Raymond Burr straining his back lifting Ted Mapes, James Stewart's stunt double, the production came off without a hitch. The final day of shooting, January 13, 1954, was devoted to retaking two scenes in the Songwriter's studio apartment, including Hitchcock's cameo appearance, where he is seen winding a clock. Shots of James Stewart for the promotional trailer took up the remainder of the day. Principal photography closed fifteen days behind schedule (and only slightly over budget), excluding one retake of Miss Lonely Hearts and one added shot of Stella, which were both shot on February 26.

Post-production and Censorship

In addition to submitting scripts and story material prior to filming, it was industry practice for producers to submit a cut of each film to the Production Code Administration before release prints were struck so that the administration could either issue its certificate of approval (or code seal) or make editorial recommendations that, if followed, would result in the film conforming to code restrictions. Although in the early 1950s most major theaters still would not accept a film without a code seal, it was only a matter of time before the PCA would completely lose its stronghold on the industry.

By mid-February a cut of *Rear Window* was submitted to the

PCA and was found unacceptable due to Miss Torso's costume appearing "to be underwear rather than a dancing costume" and two brief scenes in which "she is shown to be nude from the waist up," although she is lying on her stomach. Again, the PCA found the action of the honeymoon couple to be "unacceptably sex suggestive," in addition to the nightgown worn by Grace Kelly, which was found to be "too boldly unconventional." "It was a common practice," Hayes recalled, "that you gave the censors bait, which they focused on, and therefore the things you really wanted to keep didn't appear as harmful. This was done all the time, not just by Hitchcock. So we threw them some bait with Miss Torso, and they got all in a froth about that."

Hitchcock prepared well for the censors, having shot "protection" footage of Miss Torso fully clothed to replace the two scenes he had photographed of her topless. Having taken the bait of Miss Torso, the PCA made no mention of the dialogue which Breen found objectionable in the screenplay back in November 1953. In a telephone conversation, Luigi Luraschi assured PCA official Eugene Dougherty that the offensive shots of Miss Torso would be eliminated completely, and that the emphasis on the honeymoon couple, as well as the footage of Kelly in the negligee, would be reduced considerably. With that, the PCA gave *Rear Window* its certificate of approval on March 30, 1954.

To create the remarkable soundscape for *Rear Window*, Hitchcock prepared a nineteen-page list of dubbing notes on February 18 for George Tomasini and the man whose task it was to score the film, Franz Waxman. Waxman, who had previously composed scores for Hitchcock's *Rebecca*, *Suspicion*, and *The Paradine Case*, faced a unique challenge in scoring *Rear Window*, since each piece of music heard in the film—mostly as popular songs—emanates from the apartments of Jeff's neighbors: "That's Amore," "To See You," "Lover," "Waiting for My True Love to Appear," and "Mona Lisa." The score is also unique in that Hitchcock wanted to use an original song that appears to be in the process of being composed as the story progresses, so that in the final scene the song is heard in its full orchestration, including lyrics, when the Songwriter plays the new recording for one of his neighbors.

Hitchcock's dubbing notes range from the general to the specific, especially in matters regarding the sound effect and ambience tracks. Hitchcock also indicated the point of origin from which each piece of music is heard in the film—whether the music comes from the Songwriter at his piano, Miss Torso's phonograph, an unseen soprano practicing scales, or the jukebox in the café seen through the alley on the other side of the street. Hitchcock's notes reveal his attention to every conceivable detail in order to achieve the mood and effect he desired in each scene.

As a general instruction, Hitchcock noted that when the camera is shooting into Jeff's apartment, the traffic noise and sounds of the neighborhood should be slightly lower in volume than when it is shooting into the neighborhood from Jeff's viewpoint. More specifically, Hitchcock ordered that the voice of Jeff's editor, Gunnison, should be changed to a more authoritative one. "He should sound like Jeff's boss and not his colleague," wrote Hitchcock. He also dictated that when Thorwald enters his wife's bedroom, the music from Miss Torso's apartment should be reduced "so that we can hear the voice of the nagging wife."

At several points Hitchcock suggested the type of music he wanted to use to underscore the action on-screen. For example, during the moment that Jeff's cast causes his leg to itch, Hitchcock indicated, "It might be a good idea if the music coming from Miss Torso's apartment was a little comment on Jeff's scratching his leg, just as a coincidence, of course." For the arrival of the newlyweds, Hitchcock wondered if the scene would be more amusing by including some ironic music coming over a radio. "The wedding march would, of course, be completely out because it would be so obvious and on the nose," wrote Hitchcock. "Perhaps some accidental sentimental tune could come over, but not so obvious as to make the audience feel we have deliberately put this in. This is merely a tentative and nervous suggestion to Mr. Waxman."

Silences were equally if not more important to Hitchcock, for they often allow the audience to enter the mind of a character. "This is only a suggestion to Mr. Waxman, but if we could end the sequence where the knife and sword are shown so that all the music except for background is lost, we would get Jeff's reaction to the knife and sword in dramatic silence." But just as the silences bring us into Jeff's thought process, Hitchcock also uses noise to make the audience identify with Jeff. For the moment when Thorwald is looking at his wife's wedding ring and speaking on the telephone, Jeff tries to hear what Thorwald is saying, but a burst of laughter from the party in the Songwriter's apartment "prevents [Jeff] from hearing even the faintest snatch of the salesman's conversation." Of course as Jeff becomes frustrated when he cannot hear what Thorwald is saying, so does the audience.

Throughout his notes, Hitchcock mentions the footsteps of those coming to and departing from Jeff's apartment: "In view of the fact that we are going to make dramatic use of the footsteps on the stairs at the end of the picture, we ought seriously to consider always hearing departing footsteps when people go out of the room and when people come up the stairs into the room." Hitchcock was very specific about the quality of the footsteps when Thorwald comes to Jeff's apartment: "The footsteps outside the door should clearly indicate the progression of the murderer. In other words, it should start with a faint door closing down below and the progression of the footsteps getting louder and louder." To emphasize Thorwald's footsteps further, Hitchcock dictated that the traffic noise and the sound of Jeff's wheelchair moving around the room should be kept to a minimum. Hitchcock also added, "We should also get the effect of some caution on the part of the murderer as he comes up the stairs."

Finally, Hitchcock noted that the song heard from the phonograph at the end should get louder as the camera reaches Lisa's jeans. However, Hitchcock wondered, "as we fade out on her, the music should go down and end very quietly as the final curtain lowers. In other words, Franz, can we avoid the conventional booming out of the Hollywood score?"

Waxman succeeded in avoiding a conventional Hollywood score, but Hitchcock later complained about the final results. "I was a little disappointed in the lack of structure in the title song," wrote Hitchcock. "I had a motion picture songwriter when I should have chosen a popular songwriter." Harold Rome wrote three sets of lyrics to Waxman's composition, two entitled "Lisa," after Grace Kelly's character, and one called "Love You." In the film, the first version of "Lisa" is used. The reference to forever dreaming in Lisa's arms heard in the song's final lines is appropriate to the image of Jefferies asleep on the screen.

Rear Window previewed at the Academy Theater in Pasadena on April 1, 1954. The audience comment cards were interesting in their diversity. Most of the comments were enthusiastic: "This was one of the most unusual and refreshingly new type of movie[s] I have seen for a long time. After a while I began to feel a little guilty myself looking through that rear window. However, don't change a thing"; "An exceedingly excellent combination of comedy and suspense"; "Good dialogue for a change. Real adult"; "Did not know whether to laugh or be scared half the time."

On the other hand, some viewers seemed to be offended by the occasional risqué dialogue and situations: "Too many suggestive comments"; "Trim the kissing scenes"; "Stewart is getting too old to act with such young girls." And yet one viewer seemed completely lost: "Why did he kill his wife? What was in the [hat] box?" Nonetheless, Hitchcock and the studio were pleased by the reaction of the preview audience.

The Release

Even before the film's release, the effect Hayes had upon Hitchcock was evident. In July 1954 *The Hollywood Reporter* reviewed the film for exhibitors, stating: "*Rear Window* is one of the directorial masterpieces of recent years. To keep it from being cold and technical,

Hitchcock adds to it the warmest love story he's ever packed on the screen. In addition to revealing a new capacity for tenderness, the director shows an unsuspected flair for wisecracking comedy, particularly in the scenes where Miss Ritter and Corey make expert use of the bright dialogue in John Michael Hayes's screenplay."

Rear Window premiered on August 4, 1954, at the Rivoli Theater in New York, and by all accounts Hitchcock had proven himself to be back in top form as a producer-director. As for Hayes, the Writers' Guild acknowledged his achievement by nominating his script for Best Drama of 1954. *Rear Window* also earned Academy Award nominations for best direction, screenplay, color cinematography, and sound recording. Regrettably, it failed to win in any category, but the fact remains that *Rear Window* was a commercial and critical triumph. By today's standards, it is a remarkable achievement that, in a little more than a year (from script development to release), Hitchcock and Hayes managed to transform a twenty-four-page short story not only into the fifth-highest-grossing film of 1954 (at $5.3 million) but into one of the most discussed works of cinematic art ever produced in Hollywood. Whether or not Hitchcock and Hayes would be able to maintain their level of achievement remained to be seen.

2 / A Match Made in Hollywood

Without question *Rear Window* was evidence that the styles, tastes, and, at the time, the temperaments of Alfred Hitchcock and John Michael Hayes meshed. The director could not have known that he was embarking on his most prolific and successful period of film-making—a ten-year run during which he produced and directed ten feature films and twenty television dramas. Similarly, Hayes could not have been aware that he was at the beginning of a thirteen-year association with Paramount Pictures that would result in eleven feature films, including three more with Hitchcock. Had they had the benefit of hindsight, Hitchcock and Hayes might have realized that this was the best of times.

Born one ocean and nearly twenty years apart, Hitchcock and Hayes might never have crossed paths had they not shared a love for telling a good story. Although their adolescent years were not greatly dissimilar—each spent much time alone, was somewhat isolated from two siblings, and had an early interest in the movies—an examination of their childhoods may reveal why the pairing of these two artists resulted in some of the most warmly expressive and enjoyable films ever made and also explain why their partnership could not last.

John Michael Hayes, Jr., was born on May 11, 1919, in Worcester, Massachusetts. The second-largest city in the Bay State and one of New England's chief manufacturing centers, Worcester was also the birthplace of his parents, John Michael, Sr., and Ellen Mable Hayes. Hayes's father worked as a tool and die maker, but his heart belonged on the stage, for he had been a song-and-dance performer on the Keith-Orpheum vaudeville circuit from the age of nine. When he married, the elder Hayes reluctantly gave up his stage career to learn a trade, but he apparently passed along a bit of the greasepaint in his own blood to his middle child and only son, John Michael Jr.

The younger John Michael's paternal grandfather was a mattress maker, who as patriarch entertained the family with Irish folk songs and tales that were passed down from generation to generation in the great oral tradition. It was from his grandfather that young Hayes inherited a gift for storytelling. Hayes had two sisters, Ellen, a year and a half older, and Dorothea, a year and a half younger. The household was closely knit, and the children often helped with the various family businesses as part of their chores.

As a young boy Hayes suffered from a series of ear infections and spent a good deal of time out of school from the second grade through the fifth. With his sisters off to school and little else to do at home for recreation, Hayes found a world of adventure in reading and had quickly gone through all the popular series of books written for adolescents, including *Tom Swift*, the Rover Boys, the Hardy Boys, and the Poppy Ott series. His reading level advanced rapidly, and he soon discovered the works of Dickens, Hawthorne, and many others. This early fascination with reading and folktales led him to wonder how stories were constructed, and he began making up some of his own. Thus, by the age of nine, John Michael Hayes knew that he wanted to be a writer.

In 1929 Hayes moved with his family to Detroit, Michigan, where his father began working for the Ford Motor Company, making dies for pressing automobile bodies. It was while attending junior high school in Highland Park that Hayes first tried his hand at writing, when he took a journalism class and became a staff member on the school newspaper, *The Spectator*. When the Great Depression left nearly 50 percent of the nation's factory workers unemployed, the Hayes family relocated to State Line, New Hampshire, where his maternal grandmother, Ellen Maria Ellis, lived with her new husband, George Farrington. Their home was twelve

miles from the nearest school, forcing Hayes to stay home and re-
sulting in another year and a half away from the classroom. Hayes
continued his own literary education, though, going from farmhouse to farmhouse, borrowing whatever books and magazines he
could get his hands on, including Homer's *Iliad* and *Odyssey*,
Dante's *Inferno*, and G. A. Henty's adventure stories.

Eventually the Hayes family moved back to Worcester, where
John Michael enrolled at the High School of Commerce in order
to take courses in touch-typing and speed-typing. The principal at
the time was Calvin Andrews, whom the students affectionately
called Pop. Andrews was an understanding and benevolent fellow,
as Hayes discovered on at least two occasions. Hayes had become
interested in theater and film, as had a fellow student, Helen
Walker, who was a member of Commerce High's theater group, the
Black Friars. One afternoon the two students cut class to go to the
movies. The film's title, appropriately, was *Crime and Punishment*,
and it was being exhibited at the Elm Street Theater for one week
only in December 1935. Right before the film began, the house-
lights went on and the assistant principal, William J. Casey,
marched down the aisle to where the two students were seated and
escorted them through the lobby and back to Pop Andrews's office.
Hayes and Walker explained that the picture was closing that day
and that this was their last chance to see it, and Andrews chose not
to punish them. However, the principal did say, "I know you are
both interested in the theater and creative things, but you are
school leaders and you have got to set an example."

On another occasion, Hayes and Walker heard that Eugene
O'Neill's turn-of-the-century drama *Ah, Wilderness*, with Lionel
Barrymore, Wallace Beery, and Mickey Rooney, was being filmed
in Grafton, about ten miles from Worcester. Eager to see a real live
movie company in action, the two sneaked out of school and took a
streetcar to Grafton, where they watched the transformation of the
town square to the way it had been some forty years earlier. A bandstand had been built, dirt placed on the roads to cover the pave-
ment, flowers tied onto bushes, and trees put in place. Hayes and

Walker watched as the company constructed the set, and then watched as the scenes were shot. The next day they found that their absence had again been reported, and they were again summoned to Pop Andrews, who was once more understanding. Who knows what might have happened had Andrews been more stern? Helen Walker made it to Hollywood, where she became a leading lady of the 1940s in such films as *Nightmare Alley* and *Call Northside 777*, and Hayes went on to become one of the most popular and sought-after screenwriters of the 1950s and 1960s.

Nearly twenty years before Hayes's birth, on the other side of the Atlantic, Alfred Joseph Hitchcock was born on August 13, 1899, in the London suburb of Leytonstone. The youngest child of William and Emma Hitchcock, Alfred was raised in a very strict atmosphere. His father was a greengrocer and poultry monger, and his mother had two other children to raise, William Jr. and Nellie. The differences in their ages was such that young Alfred spent much time alone, developing an interest in geography and transportation, imagining himself traveling to places far from the family's East End flat.

One of Hitchcock's earliest memories seemed to explain neatly the origin of his fears. "I must have been about four or five years old," said Hitchcock. "My father sent me to the police station with a note. The chief of police read it and locked me in a cell for five or ten minutes, saying, 'This is what we do to naughty boys.' " Hitchcock claimed that his fear of police, imprisonment, and authority figures was forever with him from that moment. Apart from this episode, he rarely referred to his father. Remaining closer to his mother, Hitchcock often recalled the "evening confessions," when he would stand at the foot of his mother's bed and answer her detailed questions about what he had done that day. It was a ritual begun in early adolescence, which continued into early adulthood.

At the age of eleven, Hitchcock was enrolled at St. Ignatius College, where he learned from the Jesuit instructors a sense of discipline and order. He said that the method of corporal punishment at

St. Ignatius was carried out like the sentencing of a criminal. A student who had committed some offense would be sentenced to receive three strikes on his hand with a heavy rubber strap. The student was then left with the decision of when in the day to take his punishment. The fear and dread inherent in having to choose the time to go for one's punishment seems more grueling than the punishment itself, and certainly must have lasted longer than the pain from the blows. Perhaps Hitchcock's understanding of suspense versus shock could be traced to that lesson.

Whether or not these events are entirely true, it is interesting that Hitchcock chose to remember these specific incidents from his childhood. He could have been trying to explain how he devoted his life's work to creating images and stories involving fear and guilt, or they might have been his genuine recollections of his childhood. Whereas John Michael Hayes's memories reflect optimism, understanding, and encouragement from the adult figures in his childhood, Hitchcock's reflect a sense of discipline, suspicion, and cruelty. This is not to suggest that these events were the cause of their individual development as artists, but it is impossible to ignore the fact that their chosen recollections parallel their individual creative visions. There is no question that the tone of Hitchcock's films with Hayes is lighter and more hopeful than in many of his other films. There is a sense of resolution in the Hitchcock-Hayes films absent from *I Confess, Dial M for Murder, The Wrong Man,* and *Vertigo,* the films made just prior to and immediately following their collaboration.

The Apprentice Journalist

By the age of sixteen, Hayes had started writing for Commerce High's yearbook and for a Boy Scout weekly, *The Eagle Trail,* which he had been appointed editor of. About his appointment, the *Worcester Telegram* reported, "The Hayes boy is an exception to the rule which maintains that in modern times no youth knows what vocation he prefers until he is well past voting age." His parents were so proud of his achievement that they drove to Boston and bought a brand-new Royal portable typewriter at a store called Raphael's, for $37, which they were able to pay in installments of one dollar a week.

That summer Hayes became a correspondent for Worcester's *Evening Gazette*, reporting on the local Boy Scout activities, for which he was paid ten cents per column inch. Under the guidance of the city editor, Mo Williams, he did so well that the *Telegram* put him on salary as a cub reporter. Hayes would finish school in the afternoon, go over to the Boy Scout newspaper, and then go to the *Telegram*, where he reported and did regular assignments. Hayes remembered, "I didn't get a lot of sleep, because I was busy. But I became sort of a local celebrity in my neighborhood, which was a poor Irish section of Worcester. On my way to high school in the morning, I'd pick up the *Telegram* and see what stories they had printed. While I was a senior in high school, they did a story about me in *The Christian Science Monitor*, and it was picked up by the Hearst syndicate."

The young writer soon attracted the attention of the Associated Press. Hayes recalled, "I got a letter from the managing editor in New York that said, 'How would you like to work for the Associated Press?' That was just a one-line letter, and I took it to Mo Williams and said, 'I wonder if this is authentic, or is somebody just pulling my leg?' He looked it over and said, 'It looks perfectly authentic to me.' So I wrote back a one-line letter—'I'd very much like to work for the Associated Press.' In return I got a letter back. 'Please report, Washington Star Building, June eleventh, to do a daily story and series called 'A Young Man Looks at His Government.'" Hayes had just turned eighteen.

The Apprentice Filmmaker

Just as Hayes had benefited from someone recognizing his talents early on, so, too, did Alfred Hitchcock. Following the death of his father in late 1914, Hitchcock found employment at the Henley

Telegraph and Cable Company in London, where he earned enough to help support himself and his mother. By 1920 Hitchcock was an art student at the University of London and also put his drafting skills to work in the advertising department at Henley's. Fascinated by the movie industry, Hitchcock enjoyed reading cinematic trade journals, through which he learned that Famous Players–Lasky, which later became Paramount Pictures, was opening production facilities in nearby Islington. Hitchcock put together a portfolio of sketches, scenic designs, and illustrations for silent-movie titles and submitted his work in the hope of securing a position. His ambition paid off, and he was hired as a title designer. Eager to accept new challenges and always a quick learner, Hitchcock soon found himself working closely with the studio's writers, who helped teach him the fundamentals of story construction. He also met an editor and continuity supervisor, Alma Reville, whom he would later marry, and to whose judgment and instinct he would defer on many occasions.

Patricia Hitchcock-O'Connell, the Hitchcocks' only child, recalled how vital her mother's contribution was to her father's career:

> My mother was a continuity girl, but they did everything. They did dialogue, sat in on script conferences, and production. It was quite a job in those days, and she was excellent at it. And then they started working together, and although she took screen credit on very few, she worked with him on every picture. She was the one person who he relied on to tell him the truth.

Before long Hitchcock was given the opportunity to direct a short comedy called *Number Thirteen*, but this was never completed, owing to the studio's financial difficulties, which resulted in a halt of operations. The studio was eventually purchased by Michael Balcon, an independent British producer, who established Gainsborough Pictures and hired Hitchcock as an assistant director in 1922. Hitchcock impressed Balcon with his eagerness and versa-

tility, volunteering to work as art director, screenwriter, and production manager in addition to his duties as assistant director. Here
Hitchcock worked in various roles on a number of productions shot
in England and Europe, most notably at the famous UFA studios in
Berlin. The impressionable English assistant had landed himself in
the heart of the German cinema's "golden silent age," where he was
able to observe the great German director F. W. Murnau while he
was in production on *The Last Laugh*. Hitchcock's experiences in
Germany had a tremendous impact on his future work in terms of
style and visual economy, which set him apart from his contemporaries back home.

In 1925 Michael Balcon gave Hitchcock his first directorial assignment, an Anglo-German production called *The Pleasure Garden*, a backstage melodrama about the lives and loves of a pair of
chorus girls. Filmed in Munich and on location in Italy, *The Pleasure Garden* was quickly followed by *The Mountain Eagle*, a bizarre
tale about a Kentucky schoolmarm who rejects the attentions of the
local magnate and finds refuge in the company of a hermit. Although these first two efforts were well received at trade screenings,
the director always claimed, "*The Lodger* was the first true 'Hitchcock movie.' " Nevertheless, it was Balcon who selected Marie Bel-
loc Lowndes's 1913 mystery novel as Hitchcock's first venture into
the suspense genre. The novel was loosely based on the case of Jack
the Ripper, and Balcon knew that Hitchcock's familiarity with the
middle-class milieu of London's East End, combined with his dramatic visual sense, would make him the ideal choice to direct *The
Lodger*. The film also introduced a theme Hitchcock would explore
over the next fifty years—an innocent man on the run, suspected of
another man's crime.

To his credit, Balcon assigned an experienced scenarist, Eliot
Stannard, to write Hitchcock's first five films for Gainsborough, including the breakthrough thriller *The Lodger*. Stannard was already
a ten-year veteran of the British film industry with more than fifty
scripts to his credit when he began working with the novice director. Ivor Montagu, who helped re-edit *The Lodger* and later worked

as Hitchcock's associate producer in the mid-1930s, described Stannard as a consummate professional, whose method "was to sit down and tap it straight out on the typewriter as he thought of it, without change or erasement." Stannard followed Hitchcock to British International Pictures for three more films—*The Farmer's Wife*, *Champagne*, and *The Manxman*—where his sure-handed writing freed Hitchcock to sharpen the visual skills that earned him the reputation as England's top director.

Confident he had established himself in his new career as a motion picture director, Hitchcock married Alma Reville on December 2, 1926. It was a partnership that would last the rest of his life, though Alma, whose future in the industry seemed almost as promising, took a back seat to her husband when it came to their careers. When he accepted the Lifetime Achievement Award from the American Film Institute in 1979, Hitchcock said,

> I beg permission to mention by name only four people who have given me the most affection, appreciation and encouragement, and constant collaboration. The first of the four is a film editor, the second is a script writer, the third is the mother of my daughter, Pat, and the fourth is as fine a cook as ever performed miracles in a domestic kitchen, and their names are Alma Reville. Had the beautiful Miss Reville not accepted a lifetime contract, without options, as Mrs. Alfred Hitchcock some fifty-three years ago, Mr. Alfred Hitchcock might be in this room tonight—not at this table but as one of the slower waiters on the floor. I share this award, as I have my life, with her.

Following the success of *The Lodger*, Hitchcock moved to the newly formed British International Pictures (BIP), where he directed a string of silent films—mostly studio assignments—with varying degrees of success. While the films allowed for occasional visual inventiveness, the properties did not engage Hitchcock enough for a consistent style to emerge.

An Interest in Radio

John Michael Hayes earned his first byline while writing for the Associated Press in Washington, D.C., in the summer of 1937. It was a temporary but nonetheless welcome assignment. Hayes was on his first prolonged trip away from home, during which he met the renowned radio commentator Lowell Thomas. Thomas became a national celebrity when he was dispatched by Woodrow Wilson to cover World War I. Hayes was immediately impressed by Thomas's work in radio, and he wasted no time in pursuing his newfound interest when he returned to Worcester. Utilizing his years of experience editing and reporting for newspapers, as well as his talent for feature writing, Hayes began writing for small radio stations around northern Massachusetts that did not have writers on staff. Hayes managed to earn enough money that summer to enroll at Massachusetts State College—later the University of Massachusetts—in Amherst for the autumn semester.

While attending college, Hayes kept himself busy with his studies and earned his room and board by helping his professors grade papers and prepare for lectures. An industrious New Englander, he also formed a team of pallbearers with several classmates. Each morning he would read the obituaries in anticipation of getting a job, which in a good week could be as many as four funerals, for which the team received $3 apiece. When the facilities for a new college radio station had been constructed, Hayes immersed himself in that, and his funeral pursuits diminished.

Hayes enjoyed the academic world, and during his senior year was offered a partial scholarship to do graduate work at Duke University. He was also offered a job in the Boston bureau of the Associated Press as well as a position back at the *Telegram*. At the same time, the Crosley Corporation of Cincinnati, Ohio, was sponsoring a nationwide competition that was open to college seniors. The Crosley Corporation made household appliances and automobiles, and also owned three important radio stations, WLW, WSAI, and

WLWO. Crosley wanted to pick a college senior to work as an intern in network and clear channel broadcasting.*

Hayes recalled, "I entered the contest, which went on for months. You had to fill out forms and you had to submit scripts and you had to write a half-hour drama and record it. I did it, and I won the contest." Faced with the choice of graduate study, returning to the newspaper, or an opportunity in radio, Hayes did not take long in deciding on his move to Crosley. The internship required Hayes to do news reporting in addition to writing all kinds of shows—Westerns, comedies, dramas, symphony commentaries, and weather reports. Crosley kept the eager writer working from morning to night for six months. When his internship was over, Hayes was hired by Crosley at a weekly salary of $35, for which he continued to write more than twenty-five shows a week.

England's First Talkie

Although it may have appeared that Hitchcock achieved his status as England's top director overnight with *The Lodger*, he would not find his true voice for at least seven years. The road to Hollywood for Hitchcock was long and arduous, and not without frustrations. In 1928 John Maxwell, Hitchcock's producer at British International, obtained the rights to Charles Bennett's *Blackmail*, a successful play he knew would be perfect for Hitchcock. It was the beginning of one of the most significant associations in the director's career. Before Hitchcock completed shooting the silent film in the spring of 1929, Maxwell informed the director that he could reshoot the last reel to make *Blackmail* a part-talking picture. But Hitchcock went ahead and reshot other key scenes and even invented some new ones, making *Blackmail* England's first all-talking picture.

---

*Clear channel meant that no other station could use the same radio frequency for broadcasting. WLW's clear channel signal, which originated in Ohio, could be picked up by listeners in Massachusetts.

Blackmail, Hitchcock's second crime melodrama, centered on the story of a young woman who kills a man who tries to rape her, and contained themes, such as the transfer of guilt and the conflict between self-interest and public duty, which the director would explore more fully in later masterworks. At once Hitchcock seemed to have mastered the new technology of sound, utilizing the medium in ways that expressed the inner thoughts of a character. For example, Hitchcock conceived a scene in which the young woman, who had stabbed a man the night before, hears only the word "knife" when another character is speaking. The effect demonstrated that Hitchcock could create what he called "pure cinema" even with sound.

Additionally, his leading lady, the Polish actress Anny Ondra, who had previously starred in *The Manxman*, spoke with a heavy accent, totally inappropriate for the London shopkeeper's daughter she was playing. But with the film nearly completed, and with only some scenes remaining to be filmed with dialogue, Hitchcock was even more daring. Rather than recast or rewrite, he had Anny Ondra mouth the dialogue in front of the camera while an English actress, Joan Barry, spoke the lines into an offstage microphone.

Despite Hitchcock's imaginative use of sound in *Blackmail*, it was followed by rather uncinematic film versions of prestigious plays and numerous adaptations of less conventional story material. Although there were flashes of dazzling direction in each, Hitchcock's films of this period—which included *Juno and the Paycock*, *Murder!*, *The Skin Game*, and *Rich and Strange*—lacked a consistent vision. The director remained uninspired by his story material and by his collaborators—but there was hope on the horizon.

In 1934 Hitchcock crossed paths once again with Michael Balcon, who was now in charge of production at Gaumont-British. Balcon was interested in a story that Hitchcock had developed with Charles Bennett while at BIP. The story, "Bulldog Drummond's Baby," centered on a ring of spies that kidnap Drummond's baby in order to ensure his silence when he stumbles on to an assassination plot. Balcon dropped the character of Drummond, acquired the story rights from BIP, and signed Hitchcock and Bennett to a multi-picture contract.

Finding a Style

The writing and production of *The Man Who Knew Too Much*, as it was now called, could not have gone more smoothly, and the film was released in 1934 to enthusiastic audiences, reaffirming Hitchcock's success. Not only had Hitchcock's cinematic vision come into clear focus, but he had also now charted the course that the most successful of his screenwriting collaborations would take. Bennett described a typical workday with Hitchcock:

> In the morning, I used to get up and pick up Hitch in Cromwell Road, where he lived, at ten o'clock exactly. He would be sitting on the curb waiting with Joan Harrison, who was our secretary, and then we would go to the studio where we would discuss the script, and what I was doing with it. Then at about one o'clock, everything would stop, and we'd go to lunch, always at the Mayfair Hotel, and have a wonderful lunch. Then come back and at that point, Hitch would usually go to sleep in the office, and I would do a little work, and possibly doze off too slightly. But eventually, at about five o'clock, we would go back to Hitchcock's flat, where we would have cocktails, and talk more and more and more about the script. And I think more work was done on the script in the evening over cocktails than any other time.

Bennett and Hitchcock would meet each day until they had completed a detailed treatment of about seventy to a hundred pages. Not until this treatment was completed would any of the dialogue be written. In Bennett's case, Hitchcock nearly always brought in other writers specifically for dialogue. What also became evident was that Hitchcock did his best work when he trusted the writer at his side—as he did with Hayes on *Rear Window*.

Over the next three years, Hitchcock and Bennett collaborated on four more films—*The 39 Steps, Secret Agent, Sabotage,* and *Young and Innocent.* Each combined a certain wit, freshness, and originality that became hallmarks of Hitchcock's style. For example, with *The 39 Steps,* it seemed Hitchcock created a genre. The plot involved a double chase, where both the police and enemy agents are after the protagonist Richard Hannay, played with superb nonchalance by Robert Donat. The story remained a model for many of Hitchcock's future films, including *Young and Innocent, Saboteur,* and *North by Northwest.* Hitchcock's key addition, for which there was no basis in John Buchan's novel, was a female character as a love interest. As the icy-cool blonde who eventually warms up to Hannay, Hitchcock cast Madeleine Carroll. The love relationship became the main focus of the story, as it is in so many of Hitchcock's films, leaving the secret plans that the spies were after an insignificant afterthought. Thus the MacGuffin was born. MacGuffin is the term given to the plot device that on the surface motivates the characters but is of little concern to the audience. Although popularized by Hitchcock, the term is credited to Angus MacPhail, chief story editor at Gaumont-British, and was derived from an anecdote, as Hitchcock explained:

It's called a MacGuffin because the story goes that two men are in an English train, and one says across to the other, "Excuse me, sir, what is that strange-looking package above your head?"

The man says, "Oh, that? That's a MacGuffin."

"What's that for?"

"That's for trapping lions in the Scottish Highlands."

So the other man says, "But there are no lions in the Scottish Highlands."

"Then that's no MacGuffin."

It was also during this time that Hitchcock began to refine his technique for turning details from a location into dramatic elements in a plot. The script of *Secret Agent* demonstrated how Hitchcock could construct a story out of such details. Deciding to set the film in St. Moritz, Hitchcock posed the following question:

> "What do they have in Switzerland?" They have milk chocolate, they have the Alps, they have village dances, and they have lakes. All of these national ingredients were woven into the picture. I use this approach whenever possible, and it doesn't merely apply to the background. Local topographical features can be used dramatically as well.

With *Sabotage*, released in 1936, Hitchcock created a film remarkable for its moral ambiguity. As in *Blackmail*, a woman murders a man with a knife and a detective conceals the crime in order to protect her. Unlike *Blackmail*, however, the villain of *Sabotage*, played by the vulnerable, disarming Oscar Homolka, is a somewhat sympathetic character. From this period forward, Hitchcock's villains would essentially fall into two categories—the charming, handsome, romantic villains, such as Cary Grant in *Suspicion*, Claude Rains in *Notorious*, and James Mason in *North by Northwest*, and the clumsy, sympathetic villains, such as Raymond Burr in *Rear Window* and Anthony Perkins in *Psycho*.

Sabotage was followed by one of Hitchcock's most underrated films, *Young and Innocent*. The story of a young man wrongly accused of an actress's murder and a chief constable's daughter who helps prove his innocence, *Young and Innocent* includes a famous virtuoso crane shot that begins with the camera high above the lobby of a hotel, which then moves into a ballroom, sweeping past tables and over a crowded dance floor toward the bandstand, to within two inches of the drummer's eyes, which begin twitching to reveal him as the murderer. This amazing shot was quite an achievement in the days before sophisticated lenses and Steadicams.

Hollywood Bound

With the success in America of *The Man Who Knew Too Much* and *The 39 Steps*, Hitchcock embarked in August 1937 on his first trip to the United States for the purpose of attracting the interest of the Hollywood studios. The warm reception of the British celebrity by the American public intrigued the great independent producer David O. Selznick, who began negotiations to get Hitchcock under contract. By the time Hitchcock returned to England, he knew that he would soon be leaving permanently for America. In the interim, he directed *The Lady Vanishes*, which became the most successful film of his English period.

After a second trip to the United States in March 1938, including his first visit to Hollywood after months of negotiations, Selznick finally managed to sign Hitchcock. All that remained was selecting the right property for Hitchcock's Hollywood debut. Selznick and Hitchcock discussed various projects, focusing particularly on a film based upon the sinking of the *Titanic*, but eventually settled on Daphne du Maurier's recently published novel, *Rebecca*.

Selznick spared no expense on the lavish production, but fought Hitchcock every step of the way on his ruthless methods of adaptation and his technique of shooting a pre-cut picture. Despite the legendary conflicts Hitchcock had with his employer, Selznick was unmatched by any producer for the grandeur and exposure he brought to a production. This was Selznick at his peak, riding high with *Gone With the Wind*, which was being readied for its December 1939 premiere. Having benefited from his highly publicized quest for a leading lady to portray Scarlett O'Hara before finally selecting Vivien Leigh, Selznick conducted a similar search for an actress to play the second Mrs. de Winter. The coveted role finally went to Joan Fontaine. Although years later Hitchcock distanced himself from *Rebecca*, saying, "Well, it's not a Hitchcock picture; it's a novelette, really," the film was voted best picture of 1940 by the Academy of Motion Picture Arts and Sciences and Hitchcock received his first nomination for best director.

Hayes and the Second World War

Shortly after America entered World War II, John Michael Hayes was offered and accepted the position of editor of daytime serials for Procter & Gamble for nearly four times his salary at the Crosley Corporation. Hayes was responsible for reading and editing scripts for the programs sponsored by Procter & Gamble and seeing that the subject matter and dialogue conformed to their moral standards. Although he preferred writing his own scripts, the position provided an opportunity for Hayes to study other radio writers' work. Before he could do anything to change his position, however, in the summer of 1942 Hayes found himself drafted into the Army and headed to the South Pacific.

Hayes had been assigned to limited service, restricted from combat duty due to an amblyopic left eye. When he was pulled out of the line of soldiers headed for the Pacific, Hayes was put into Special Services to entertain the troops. The years spent learning his father's songs and tap-dance routines were not wasted. Hayes performed in plays and musicals at various camps in Missouri and Oregon, and also served as master of ceremonies at the USO in San Francisco. Still, by the time John Michael Hayes was assigned to duty as an Army theater projectionist, Alfred Hitchcock had already made a half-dozen films in the United States.

The Loan-Outs

With the outbreak of war in Europe in 1939, Hitchcock turned to the headlines for his follow-up to *Rebecca*. On loan to producer Walter Wanger and reunited with Charles Bennett, Hitchcock fashioned an entertaining adventure with touches of comedy, romance, and suspense, reminiscent of his British thrillers. However, unlike the British thrillers, which avoided identifying the evil foreign powers, *Foreign Correspondent* afforded Hitchcock the opportunity to play activist. In a stirring piece of propaganda, Hitchcock called on America to defend his native Britain against Nazi aggression. Like *Rebecca*, Hitchcock's second Hollywood effort also garnered an Academy Award nomination for best picture of 1940.

Hitchcock then moved to RKO, where he tried his hand at directing a screwball comedy, *Mr. and Mrs. Smith*, which starred Carole Lombard and Robert Montgomery. Still on loan from Selznick, and irritated at the immense profits that his services gained for his employer, Hitchcock wanted to show that he could direct a modest, director-for-hire vehicle, within budget and schedule. He also needed to show that he was affordable, since his first two Hollywood productions were big-budget extravaganzas. This was followed by *Suspicion*, which in spite of trouble over its ending was a tremendous success and cast Cary Grant in his first of four roles for the director. (See Notes, pp. 304–5, for an examination of the controversial ending.)

Hitchcock then developed an original treatment based on an idea about Fifth Columnists working in America, which Selznick sold to Universal Pictures. To polish the script, titled *Saboteur*, Hitchcock hired Dorothy Parker, who brought a certain wit and spice to a script full of memorable scenes but suffering from poor structure and a weak conflict between the protagonist and villain. (The stilted performances of the film's leads, Robert Cummings and Priscilla Lane, did little to help the film.) "I would say that the script lacks discipline," admitted Hitchcock. "There was a mass of ideas, but they weren't sorted out in proper order; they weren't selected with sufficient care. I feel the whole thing should have been pruned and tightly edited long before the actual shooting. It goes to show that a mass of ideas, however good they are, is not sufficient to create a successful picture."

Still on loan to Universal, Hitchcock selected a story titled "Uncle Charlie" as his next project, which was ultimately called *Shadow of a Doubt*. After the disappointing script of *Saboteur*, Hitchcock was delighted when playwright Thornton Wilder agreed to write the screenplay. Hitchcock admired Wilder's *Our Town*, which painted a portrait of small-town America that the director hoped to reflect on-screen. But the portrait Hitchcock painted in

Shadow of a Doubt revealed a seedy side to the American small town, one that would turn a blind eye on a serial killer and transform an idealistic young girl into a woman who would murder the relative she loves most in order to protect her family. Enriched by performances by Joseph Cotten as the charming but amoral Uncle Charlie and Teresa Wright as his initially worshipful niece, the film revealed the dark side within all of us, exposing through subtle characterization rather than plot our deepest capacity for evil.

  Shadow of a Doubt had been a happy experience for Hitchcock, but before he could seriously entertain any plans for making another film at Universal, Selznick loaned him out again, this time to Darryl Zanuck's Twentieth Century–Fox. Still eager to impress the critics with his quest for great writing, Hitchcock engaged John Steinbeck to write an original story about the survivors of a Nazi U-boat attack called *Lifeboat*, which starred Tallulah Bankhead and Walter Slezak. Although he was growing tired of being bounced from studio to studio, the technical challenges of setting a story in the smallest of places—a lifeboat adrift on the ocean—was appealing to Hitchcock, who earned a second Academy Award nomination for his direction.

Propaganda Films and Plans for Independence

Following his work at Fox, Hitchcock returned to England to contribute to the war effort by directing *Bon Voyage* and *Aventure Malgache* for the Ministry of Information, where his good friend Sidney Bernstein was serving as film advisor. A founding member of the London Film Society, Bernstein was also the owner of England's Granada theater chain. Before Hitchcock departed, however, Selznick decided it was time that he and the director work together again, this time on a story involving psychoanalysis.

  Hitchcock shrewdly persuaded Selznick to allow him to write a treatment while abroad, from which Ben Hecht would write the script upon his return. Hitchcock then hired Angus MacPhail to work on the treatment while he pursued his ulterior motive for the trip to England. Hitchcock and Bernstein began discussions to start their own production company.

Bound for Hollywood

After the war Hayes embarked on a career as a radio writer in Hollywood. "I wrote my first radio plays in longhand," remembered Hayes. "I didn't have a typewriter and had no money to rent one." But Hayes quickly found work writing for a variety of CBS shows such as *The Whistler* and *Twelve Players*. His stay was cut short when he was stricken with a severe case of rheumatoid arthritis. Hayes spent nearly eighteen months at Cushing Hospital in Framingham, Massachusetts, recovering from the condition.

It was a low point in Hayes's life, which he combated by writing a full-length play called *Delaney and Sons*. The drama concerns an Irish family living in a poor, downtrodden section of Massachusetts called "The Island." The patriarch, Dennis Delaney, is a widower and father of six children ranging in age from fifteen to twenty-five. All of Dennis's children still live at home, with the exception of a son named John, who went off to make a life for himself against his father's wishes. Because of a pledge to their dying mother, the Delaney children each give their wages to Dennis so that he may realize his ambition of opening a mattress shop for himself and his family. But we soon see that Dennis is in fact killing his children's spirit by preventing them from pursuing their own lives and dreams. In the end, Dennis comes to realize that by taking his children for granted, he is driving them away.

In *Delaney and Sons* Hayes was able to express some of his innermost feelings. Throughout the time he was in the hospital, Hayes was pressured by his family to abandon what they had considered his precarious dream of maintaining a writing career and instead settle down in Massachusetts, where a friend had assured him a position as a claims adjuster for an insurance firm. Hayes had already seen his father give up the stage and take "honest" work. The prospect of such a move seemed utter doom to him and made him even more determined to resume his writing career. As soon as he was able to walk out of the hospital, Hayes decided he would return to California.

Aware that his family would do all they could to discourage the move, Hayes did not tell anyone of his plans to leave Worcester. On a Sunday evening, while his family was at the movies, the twenty-nine-year-old writer packed his belongings, left a note for his parents, and, with only $15 in his pocket, embarked on a cross-country journey, using two canes, his thumb, and the goodwill of motorists kind enough to offer a ride.

Within a day and a half, Hayes arrived at Zanesville, Ohio, where he spent 75 cents on a telegram informing his parents that he was okay. He continued, nonstop, until he reached Flagstaff, Arizona, where he boarded a bus during a thunderstorm. Hayes finally arrived in Los Angeles with $4.50 remaining and checked into the Mark Twain Hotel for the night, planning to go the following morning to CBS, where he had worked previously. En route to CBS the next day, Hayes passed the NBC radio studios, where there was a line of people waiting to get into one of the popular quiz shows, *Double or Nothing*. Hayes decided to stay and see the show. While he waited on line, one of the show's assistants saw him on canes and let him inside the studio ahead of everyone else. When he got inside, he was asked if he would like to be a contestant. Hayes said yes. The questions they asked were about English literature, and he won $640.

Hayes remembered, "I went down the block to deposit my money in a bank. Next door was CBS. I went in, pressed the elevator button, and ran into Ernie Martin, a friend who had since become a Broadway producer. Ernie looked me up and down and said he needed a writer for a new show with Lucille Ball and he hired me." The show for which Hayes was assigned on the spot was *My Favorite Husband*. Specializing in comedy and suspense, Hayes turned out expert scripts for many diverse series, including *Amos 'n' Andy, The Story of Dr. Kildare, Yours Truly Johnny Dollar, Sweeney and March, Alias Jane Doe, Nightbeat,* and *Richard Diamond, Private Detective.*

It was during this period that Hayes met and courted Mildred Louise Hicks, a high-style fashion model whose professional name was Mel Lawrence and whose beauty rivaled that of the most stunning leading ladies who would later appear in his films; her inner beauty made Hayes consider himself even more fortunate. They were married on August 29, 1950.

E. Jack Neuman wrote for many of the same shows and often collaborated with Hayes, ensuring that they would turn out the work quickly and remain in demand. "The first time we met was at CBS," recalled Neuman.

I was on staff there at one time, and so was John. We just got together right away. This was a year or two after the end of the war and it was very hard to get a place to live, to get clothes, everything, because they were just unavailable. But housing was especially terrifying. One day I was out in the Valley and saw this apartment building being constructed. They were called the Santa Rita Apartments, and I went in and I was able to rent an apartment. I ran into John and Mel; they weren't married at the time. I showed them my new apartment, and John went down and got one for himself. He lived in one wing and I lived in the other. So John and I decided to team up, and we worked out a way to write together which was just sensational. We would meet in the morning at ten o'clock, at my place, or his, and we would plot until noon. Then we would flip a coin to see who took the first act, and who took the second, which was about twelve or fifteen pages each. We would figure out what names we were going to give the characters, and would separate. Then we'd meet at six o'clock. He would read what he had written. I'd read what I'd written. We'd correct each other, turn it over to Mel, who was our in-house secretary, and she'd type the script up. And the next day it was the same thing. But it worked fine because you couldn't tell where one left off and the other began.

Hayes was astonishingly successful writing for several of producer-director William Spier's crime and detective series, particularly *Suspense* and *The Adventures of Sam Spade*. Among the episodes of *Suspense* written by Hayes were "Lady in Distress" starring Ava Gardner, "The Gift of Jumbo Brannigan" starring William Bendix, and "The Wages of Sin" starring Barbara Stanwyck.

While *Suspense* was highly effective as a dramatic thriller series, *The Adventures of Sam Spade* worked as great comedy, almost a satire on the genre. Audiences had become so accustomed to the conventions of the hard-boiled private-eye genre through pulp magazines, radio, and movies that it would have been nearly impossible to have taken them seriously by the late 1940s. Instead, *Sam Spade* exaggerated the plays on words, puns, and metaphors typical of private-eye fiction. In each episode Hayes tried to come up with a larger-than-life client for Spade. The first act was primarily played for comedy, but shifted gears toward real suspense by Act II. In the natural course of events, Spade would solve the caper. Spade was played by Howard Duff, and his loyal secretary, Effie, was played by Lurene Tuttle. The comedic timing of this team was impeccable.

Within three years Hayes was a top man in his field, with over fifteen hundred radio scripts to his credit and a well-earned reputation as "the fastest writer in Hollywood." In a medium that relied on the spoken word, Hayes had become an expert in creating crisp, sophisticated dialogue.

Back with Selznick

In the spring of 1944 Hitchcock arrived in New York to begin work on *Spellbound* with the screenwriter and playwright Ben Hecht. Hecht had already worked with Hitchcock on the final scenes of *Foreign Correspondent* and *Lifeboat*, so he was already familiar with the director's ability to come up with those wonderfully "Hitchcockian" situations that left audiences on the edge of their seats. Despite a somewhat simplistic notion of psychoanalysis and a gen-

eral lack of suspense—the main characters never seem to be in any
real danger until the final moments of the film—*Spellbound*, which
starred Ingrid Bergman as a psychoanalyst and Gregory Peck as her
amnesiac patient, was a huge hit with audiences. It was a masterful
production by Selznick, who proved he could still create a big box-
office attraction, and it earned Hitchcock his third Academy Award
nomination for best direction.

For his next picture, Hitchcock was intrigued by the idea of a
woman being carefully trained and coached with the object of marrying a man as part of a grand confidence trick. It was an idea
briefly alluded to in *Secret Agent*, used with great effect later in
North by Northwest, and given the fullest treatment in *Vertigo*. Capitalizing on the success of *Spellbound*, Selznick reteamed its director, writer, and leading lady, Ingrid Bergman, for a production he
had long hoped to realize: an adaptation of John Taintor Foote's
"The Song of the Dragon." The story was somewhat old-fashioned,
but it provided at least the idea for the character to be a kind of
modern-day Mata Hari, a woman who, despite her tarnished reputation, should be honored for serving her country. Just prior to filming, Selznick sold the entire package to RKO at an enormous profit,
which included a large percentage of the gross, in effect leaving
Hitchcock to be his own producer. Ultimately, the picture that became *Notorious* is perhaps Hitchcock's finest achievement of the
1940s.

"He was an extraordinary screenwriter and a marvelous man,"
said Hitchcock of Hecht. "We would discuss a screenplay for hours
and then he would say, 'Well, Hitchie, write the dialogue you want
and then I'll correct it.' Ben was like a chess player, he could work
on four scripts at the same time." The collaboration could not last,
though, because in addition to being one of the busiest and most expensive screenwriters in Hollywood, Hecht was as notorious a self-
promoter as Hitchcock.

Following *Notorious*, Selznick assigned Hitchcock, as the final
production under their existing agreement, Robert Hichens's *The
Paradine Case*. Selznick allowed for a lavish production—Hitch-

cock's most expensive to date—with a budget of $4 million, which equaled that of *Gone With the Wind*. Starring Gregory Peck and Alida Valli, *The Paradine Case* was, nonetheless, a flawed work, evidence of the director's desire to free himself to be his own producer. Throughout the production Selznick courted Hitchcock, even offering a nonexclusive contract that would allow Hitchcock to make a picture a year for Selznick International and one a year for Hitchcock and Bernstein's own company, Transatlantic Pictures, which formally announced its existence in the spring of 1946.

The Independent Producer

As partners, Hitchcock and Bernstein hoped their new company would make films in England and Hollywood, luring talent from both sides of the Atlantic. They announced that their first production would be an adaptation of Helen Simpson's *Under Capricorn*, a drama set in Australia during the mid-1800s, which would star Ingrid Bergman. (Ultimately, it would be their second production, due to the actress's schedule.) No doubt Selznick felt personally betrayed at the news that two former contract employees, whom he had brought together, were now joining forces without him.

With the necessary financing arranged and a distribution deal with Warner Bros. secured, Hitchcock proceeded with a film adaptation of Patrick Hamilton's 1929 play, *Rope's End*, which was itself loosely based on the Leopold-Loeb case. The story involves two homosexual lovers who, for a thrill, murder an old friend and hide his body in a chest from which they serve dinner to the victim's family and friends. *Rope* provided Hitchcock with several technical challenges. In addition to being his first Technicolor production, the picture was designed to take place in real time. To achieve this, the director conceived a method of telling the story in long takes, of up to nine minutes each in length. The whole production, he hoped, would leave the impression that it was filmed in one continuous shot.* The cast, led by James Stewart, rehearsed for fifteen days as if they were performing a stage play. Despite the anticinematic nature of the film's technique, it was the basic story and characterizations that failed to generate enough conflict or suspense.

By March 1948, Ingrid Bergman was free from other commitments and departed for England with Hitchcock to begin *Under Capricorn*. At last Hitchcock was his own boss, embarking on a large-scale production. Oddly enough, the plot of *Under Capricorn* closely resembled something that might have appealed more to Selznick than to Hitchcock. The story of a weak and haunted heroine dominated by a menacing housekeeper was something right out of *Rebecca*, and the tale of a mistress falling in love with the groom had been a subplot in *The Paradine Case*.

Recently, Arthur Laurents, who penned the screenplay for *Rope*, recalled that Hitchcock had asked him to do the screenplay for *Under Capricorn*. But Laurents did not believe the property would make a successful picture, and when he tried to dissuade the director from undertaking the costume drama, the writer suddenly found himself cut off. To Hitchcock, writers were expendable. Undeterred, he simply engaged another writer and proceeded with *Under Capricorn*. Yet despite the casting coup of obtaining Bergman, the film's lavish Technicolor photography, and several beautifully choreographed long takes, there was not enough in the basic story material to engage audiences, leaving Transatlantic Pictures to face some rough waters ahead.

Becoming a Screenwriter

In 1951, at the age of thirty-one, Hayes caught the attention of Universal-International Pictures and was offered the opportunity to write for the movies. "I went over and auditioned with a story

---

*The reel change would be hidden by moving the camera close enough to an object or a performer's back so that the movement could continue with a new reel, giving the shot a seamless effect. In actuality, there are five perceivable cuts in the eighty-minute film.

for Universal," remembered Hayes. "It was a police story set in Chicago. Three producers sat in on my presentation. One was Aaron Rosenberg."

Hayes was represented at the time by Rosenberg's brother, George. A deal was made quickly, but Hayes surprised the studio executives when he turned down the first two projects they offered because he did not like the basic material. Although a newcomer to pictures, Hayes could afford to be a little choosy, since he was still drawing a higher salary for his radio scripts. The studio eventually got the writer to settle on a World War II action film called *Red Ball Express*, which starred Jeff Chandler and Sidney Poitier.

Hayes, who had conditioned himself to write quickly for newspapers and radio, reported to the writers' building at Universal at eight-thirty each morning and started work. Early one morning, while he was pounding away at his typewriter, the writer from the next office came in, looking sleepy and disheveled from lying on his couch. The writer said, "What in the world are you doing?"

"Well, I'm writing a movie. That's what they do here," Hayes answered.

The writer replied, "But not like that. Your typewriter hasn't stopped going all morning."

"I'm used to deadlines in radio."

"That's not the way you do it in pictures. Suppose you write it in two weeks? You've got to learn to stretch it out over thirteen weeks in order to get a decent salary. They'll get a picture for a thousand dollars."

Working on a weekly salary, Hayes immediately saw the wisdom of his colleague's words, and he slowed down. But by the end of October 1951, Hayes had completed his first feature film screenplay. (Later in his career Hayes would be called upon specifically for his speed and sure-handed writing to script-doctor several troubled productions, including *Butterfield 8*, *Harlow*, and *Judith*. However, by then he commanded quite a bit more to turn out a script in two weeks.)

Hayes's next assignment for Rosenberg at Universal was based on an original story of his own that he had titled *Bonanza* (although it had no connection to the long-running TV Western series). *Bonanza* ultimately became *Thunder Bay*, the story of an engineer who designs an offshore oil rig that can withstand the hurricane-prone waters of the Gulf of Mexico. Starring James Stewart and directed by Anthony Mann, *Thunder Bay* also launched Universal's wide-screen and stereophonic sound systems. To research the original story, Hayes went down to an offshore oil rig during the summer of 1952, where he spent time observing the locale and the people. In spite of the many action sequences, including barroom brawls, offshore oil drilling, Stewart's thwarting of a mob of angry fishermen by wielding lit sticks of dynamite, and a spectacular fistfight on the planks of the oil rig during a brutal hurricane, Hayes's script would be criticized for a tendency toward talkiness—a habit from his years in radio.

Following *Thunder Bay*, Hayes decided to change agents and went to see Harris Kattleman, a representative from the Music Corporation of America's talent agency, MCA Artists. Kattleman introduced Hayes to a busy agent in the writer's department, Ned Brown. Within days Brown had gotten Hayes his first assignment at Metro-Goldwyn-Mayer, a romantic war drama called *I Married West Point*. Hayes spent the fall and early winter months at MGM writing the project, which was intended to star Ann Blyth, but production was canceled when the war in Korea ended. He was then contracted to write *The Rose and the Flame* for Universal in the winter of 1953. Planned as a costumed action-adventure for Tyrone Power, this too did not go before the cameras.

Hayes had better luck with his next MGM assignment, *Torch Song*, which was being mounted as Joan Crawford's return to the studio after eleven years. Producers Henry Berman and Sidney Franklin, Jr., hired Hayes to rewrite Jan Lustig's script, which was based on a story by I.A.R. Wylie called "Why Should I Cry?" *Torch Song* is a backstage musical drama about a self-centered Broadway star, Jenny Stewart, who becomes aware of her self-imposed loneliness when she meets a blind pianist, played by Michael Wilding, who does not fall at her feet but instead sees her true self. *Torch*

Song is one of many projects the studios churned out in the early 1950s, eager to repeat the success of the backstage hit *All About Eve*, which starred Bette Davis. But before Hayes could start on the script, there was confusion over whether or not the studio would allow him to work. Hayes recalled:

> There were two other John Hayeses in town with whom I was confused. One had been an actor in New York. He also wrote for the radio, and later was on the blacklist for having allegedly been a member of the Communist Party. So I was called up in front of a board of MGM executives and asked to explain the Communist activities of John Hayes. I said to them, "I have no connection with this. When this man joined the Communist Party, I was learning to stand up."
>
> Now, one of the producers there at MGM, Charles Schnee, had known me and insisted, "This can't be John Hayes." They soon realized because of our ages that they had the wrong man. So I was told to write a letter to Nicholas Schenck, the head of MGM, and copies were sent to the heads of the other studios so they wouldn't confuse me. Now, while this was going on, MGM kept me two weeks there on salary without using me, in which time I wrote an outline, which I sold to Universal, called *Brady's Bunch*.

Torch Song received notice for its "standout individual scenes and sharp dialogue," particularly in the role of the star's worldly wise, rough-around-the-edges mother, for which Marjorie Rambeau received an Academy Award nomination. This would become a stock character in the Hayes canon, one that allowed him to footnote each film with a little wink to the audience.

After writing the script for *Brady's Bunch*, which had become *War Arrow*, Hayes's next assignment for MGM was a Richard Harding Davis novel called *The Bar Sinister*, which was a turn-of-the-century tale told from the point of view of a bull terrier named Wildfire. MGM was so delighted with Hayes's script that production chief Dore Schary decided it would be a great project in which to showcase all their stars in cameo roles. But the New York office decided it would be a good opportunity to try out some relative unknowns from a young acting group they had under contract, and so production was held up until 1955, when the film, retitled *It's a Dog's Life*, was made with a cast that included Edmund Gwenn, Dean Jagger, and a dog's voice-over narration provided by Vic Morrow.

Hitchcock at Warners

The switch to MCA expanded Hayes's opportunities to work with the "A" studios, more important stars, and, as fate would have it, more distinguished directors. While Hayes was beginning to make a name for himself at Universal and MGM, Hitchcock was recovering from the disappointment of Transatlantic's first two productions, *Rope* and *Under Capricorn*. Hitchcock and Sidney Bernstein agreed to temporarily halt production and search for properties with greater commercial potential. In the meantime, Hitchcock was forced to retreat to the safety of a studio contract, and so he went to work for Warner Bros. Although the contract with Warners allowed Hitchcock to remain his own producer, with control over story selection, casting, and final cut, it was a step backward for a filmmaker who had sought complete independence.

As the first film of his four-picture deal with Warner Bros., Hitchcock made *Stage Fright*, starring Jane Wyman, Marlene Dietrich, and Michael Wilding, in which he continued a trend toward the unconventional by boldly opening the film with a flashback that turns out to be a lie. "It is my hope," he told a *Los Angeles Times* reporter when the film opened in March 1950, "that audiences will be willing to accept a little freshness of treatment now and then. They can't be that conditioned!" But conditioned they were. *Stage Fright* was not the success Hitchcock had hoped for and needed. *The New York Times* said of the picture, "*Stage Fright* is dazzlingly stagy, but it is far from frightening."

After the lukewarm reception of *Stage Fright*, Hitchcock continued his search for a commercial property and came upon an intriguing novel that centered on an exchange of murders. In April 1950 he acquired the rights to Patricia Highsmith's *Strangers on a Train* and immediately began constructing a treatment. By July, Hitchcock had convinced Raymond Chandler, creator of the private eye Philip Marlowe, to write the screenplay. But three months and two drafts later, the two could not see eye to eye, and Hitchcock turned the project over to another writer, Czenzi Ormonde.

One of Hitchcock's greatest popular successes, *Strangers on a Train* is also one of the director's darkest and most complex works. His most thorough exploration of the "double theme" since *Shadow of a Doubt*, the film is a study of the duality of human nature. Above all, *Strangers on a Train* is best remembered for its haunting images and the direction of several dazzling set pieces. The finale, a death struggle on a runaway carousel between Farley Granger and Robert Walker, is one of the most exciting in the Hitchcock canon.

Following the success of *Strangers on a Train*, Hitchcock turned to a more personal project, *I Confess*, based on a 1902 French play called *Nos Deux Consciences (Our Two Consciences)*. The story concerns a priest who hears a murderer's confession but is bound by Holy Orders not to reveal his knowledge, even after the priest himself is indicted for the crime. Starring Montgomery Clift, Anne Baxter, and Karl Malden, *I Confess* was another attempt at a nonconventional thriller, but was not well received by audiences.

The combination of poor story material and uneven casting left Hitchcock with a string of commercial failures he had not experienced since his days at British International Pictures, even though the films often offered brilliant examples of his direction. Hayes has observed, "He relied on suspense and stars to sell his pictures, when basically he should have been concerned with the script more than anything. Hitch's films were frequently unbalanced to the suspense side, to the device side, and not to the characterization or dialogue side." Samuel Taylor, screenwriter of *Vertigo*, *Topaz*, and the unrealized *No Bail for the Judge*, said of Hitchcock:

> He was the master of the situation, the master of the vignette, the master of the small moment. He always knew what he wanted to do with those. He did not have so much of an overall view of the story he was going to tell. That's why he often got into trouble. He never saw it in terms of a completely linear thing, and when he talked to you about a picture, he never told you the story. He told you his favorite scenes. So for him, it was like a mosaic, and when he finally got the entire mosaic put together you saw the story. Now, if he didn't have a good writer, there were going to be pieces missing in that mosaic.

Hitchcock and Hayes

As in England in the 1930s, it was again time for Hitchcock to reinvent himself. Just as Hitchcock's collaboration with Charles Bennett seemed to come at exactly the right moment, so too did his collaboration with John Michael Hayes. According to Hayes, Hitchcock was so pleased with the writer's work on *Rear Window* that he promised him a bonus if the film was successful. But as the weeks and months went by and they began discussing future projects, Hayes got the feeling there was to be no bonus. Additionally, Hayes was hired at the same salary to write *To Catch a Thief*. "My agent said, 'Be quiet,'" remembered Hayes. ' "You work with Hitch and you'll graduate from Alfred Hitchcock University with a degree that will be highly salable.' "

Hayes had good reason to heed Ned Brown's advice. Working for Alfred Hitchcock, with very few exceptions, meant that the picture would be made. With other producers, writers would frequently spend months on a project that never made it to the screen. On the other hand, Brown was a company man, and Hitchcock and Hayes were both MCA clients. Hitchcock certainly brought more money to the agency than Hayes. How could Ned Brown effectively act in his client's best interest while at the same time the interests of a more important client were being represented by the same agency?

3 / You've Never Been to the Riviera?

By the time *Rear Window* had completed production, Alfred Hitchcock and his unit were comfortably set up in their suite of offices at Paramount Pictures. The studio that had long been the home of Ernst Lubitsch, Josef von Sternberg, and Preston Sturges, and had more recently seen the departure of one of its hottest commodities, Billy Wilder, welcomed Hitchcock with open arms and an open pocketbook. Hitchcock was in good company at the studio. Producer Hal Wallis joined Paramount in the late 1940s, creating a series of gritty crime melodramas starring Barbara Stanwyck, Kirk Douglas, Lizabeth Scott, and Burt Lancaster as well as the comedies of Dean Martin and Jerry Lewis. Cecil B. DeMille still made his home at Paramount, as did directors George Stevens and George Seaton, and, for the moment, William Wyler.

Although Alfred Hitchcock worked at a leisurely pace during script preparation—John Michael Hayes had been on salary for twenty-three and a half weeks writing *Rear Window*—the director wasted no time in getting his writer started on another assignment. For on December 3, 1953, the very day after closing on *Rear Window*, Hayes officially started work on his second film for Hitchcock and Paramount, *To Catch a Thief*.

The Novel

David Dodge's eighth novel, *To Catch a Thief*, was published by Random House in 1952. Although it had been submitted in galley form in July 1951 to Paramount Pictures, it was Hitchcock who purchased the movie rights for a reported $15,000 in December of that year. The novel centers on the character of John Robie, a former American acrobat-turned-jewel-thief known as "Le Chat," who in the 1930s preyed upon the Riviera's wealthy visitors until he was captured and imprisoned. Released by the Germans during the occupation, Robie joined the Resistance, becoming a member of the Maquis, and later retired to a quiet life at his Villa des Bijoux.

When a new series of jewel robberies is committed, Commissaire Orial suspects Robie is up to his old tricks and comes to arrest him. After a daring escape, Robie seeks assistance from his former Maquis leader, Henri Bellini, who persuades him to lead an underworld manhunt to apprehend the thief. Robie disguises himself as Jack Burns, a middle-aged New York insurance salesman vacationing in Cannes. There, Robie seeks out prospective victims while Bellini's gang watches for the thief. To complete Robie's disguise, Bellini hires a pretty French girl, Danielle, to accompany him in the casinos.

Robie acquaints himself with Maude Stevens, an American woman with $72,000 worth of insured jewelry and a beautiful daughter, Francie, who wears no jewelry and devotes her time to watching for con artists and gigolos who are constantly after her mother's jewels. Francie is quick to see through Robie's charade and tells him so, volunteering her theory that Le Chat is not an individual but a gang. She then offers to help Robie steal her mother's jewels and threatens to turn him over to the police if he refuses. With his cover blown, Robie decides that he and Danielle should no longer be seen together.

On their last night at the casino, Robie meets an old friend, Paul du Pré, who is struck by Danielle's appearance, as she is a double of his late wife. Paul chooses not to expose Robie and instead asks for an introduction to Danielle. Robie obliges and is left free to deal with Francie, who insists on going to Monte Carlo for the evening. On returning, they learn that Mrs. Stevens's jewels have been stolen. Francie accuses Robie of double-crossing her, having his gang steal the jewels while they were in Monte Carlo.

Robie is forced to tell Francie the truth about himself and enlist her aid, while Mr. Paige, a London insurance agent, begins his investigation of the robbery. A few days later, Commissaire Lepic becomes a hero by shooting and killing a thief in the act of a robbery. The thief turns out to be the Gypsy, one of the ex-Maquis members Bellini set out as watchers. However, Robie is not convinced that the thief Lepic killed is responsible for the recent crime wave.

Robie's one hope is the grand gala to be hosted by Mr. and Mrs. Sanford, whose guests will be wearing some of the most prized jewels on the Riviera. Certain the thief will strike again, Robie gets himself invited to the gala as Francie's guest but is confronted by Paul, who gives him the choice of leaving at once or being turned over to Lepic and Orial. Robie pretends to leave, but instead climbs to the roof and waits for the thief to appear. Before long, a shadowy figure emerges and Robie follows. When the thief misses his footing and clings to a perilous edge, Robie grasps his arm, to discover the catlike thief is Danielle.

Robie brings Danielle to Paul, who is shocked to find that the girl he has fallen in love with is a thief. Like Robie, Danielle has had acrobatic training. Orphaned during the war, she took to stealing in order to survive. Later, she heard of Le Chat, copied his method, and relied on the police looking for a man instead of a woman. Danielle is distraught over her capture, but Robie offers a way out if she will surrender the jewels.

Together with Paul, Danielle sneaks away from the castle, bringing the jewels and instructions to Bellini. Later, Mr. Paige arrives with the recovered jewels in hand, informing Lepic and Orial that he will not betray the thief's identity, so that they may as well give up their search. Paige also informs Lepic and Orial that Robie had been an operative of the insurance company all along. Robie then returns to the hotel to find Francie packing her bags. She tells Robie that she is returning to America and has no desire for him to accompany her. Robie finally realizes he is in love with Francie and, despite her anger, promises to win her.

Although David Dodge claimed that *To Catch a Thief* was based on an actual series of burglaries carried out on the Riviera in 1950 by one Dario Sambucco, the novel was perhaps also inspired by a short story of the same name by Ernest William Hornung. In Hornung's "To Catch a Thief," gentleman thief A. J. Raffles finds himself suspected of a series of jewel robberies committed in his style and sets out to catch his imitator. As in Dodge's novel (and Hitchcock's film), the victims are among the rich and titled—in this case, members of London society. There is mention of one audacious robbery being carried out during a costume ball, and the story concludes with an exciting rooftop climax.

Hitchcock's first mention of plans to film *To Catch a Thief* came in February 1953, when he announced it as a possible production for his Transatlantic Pictures. Although that same year Cary Grant announced his retirement from the screen, Hitchcock confidently told the press in early March that Grant would return to portray the reformed jewel thief.* All he needed to do was convince the actor.

It is easy to see what attracted Hitchcock to Dodge's novel. The double chase, the fetishism, and the exciting climax at a great height were common themes in the Hitchcock canon; the opportunity to shoot a film in one of the world's most glamorous vacation spots only added to the allure. *To Catch a Thief* offered a tremendous change from the claustrophobic atmosphere of the director's Warners pictures, in addition to an immediate escape from his more recent studio-bound projects *Dial M for Murder* and *Rear Window*. Hitchcock was also able to turn a considerable profit, selling the rights to Paramount for $105,000.

Story Conferences

During the first full week of production on *Rear Window* in December 1953, Hitchcock and Hayes had begun conferences for

---

*Cary Grant was also interested in playing the villainous husband in *Dial M for Murder*, but his salary and demands for a percentage of the profits had priced him out of the running.

Story Fund #89030, *To Catch a Thief*. With a polished cast, crew, and script working for him on his current production, Hitchcock was already beaming with a confidence and exuberance he had not felt in a long while. Always thinking in visual terms, Hitchcock began these conferences speaking of the French locales in which they would set their new picture—the Côte d'Azur, Monte Carlo, the Grande Corniche, Promenade des Anglais. In Technicolor and in wide screen, the picture would be spectacular.

"Well, let me do some research," Hayes said.

Astonished, Hitchcock asked in earnest, "You've never been to the Riviera?"

"No," replied Hayes.

"How would you like to go there and walk around and get the feel of it before you write?"

"I'd love to."

Hitchcock picked up the telephone and called head of production Don Hartman. "John Hayes has never been to the Riviera, and I'd like to send him so I don't have to keep explaining to him where things are and what it's like. Just a minute." He paused, turning to Hayes. "You want to take your wife?"

"Yes! I'd love to."

"I'm going to send his wife with him."

Two days later John and Mel Hayes were en route to Cannes to absorb the flavor of the Riviera.

So we went over, and they got a French assistant director as our guide, and we went down and did research. But I said to Hitch, "I don't really need to go. I've written Westerns and murders and other things, and I don't have to do it to know it." Hitch insisted, "It will make it much easier for me and for you to get a feel of the place and not just have to look at picture books." So we spent two weeks there, had a wonderful time, and I thought of the scene in the flower market because of it. It was my wife's birthday (December 10), and as I walked through the flower market, I ordered a whole lot of them, and filled our hotel room with so many flowers, it looked like a florist's shop.

The trip was a welcome vacation (if not something of a bonus), much deserved after the exceptional work Hayes had done on the screenplay for *Rear Window*, which, by the time the writer had returned to Hollywood, was already midway through production. Hayes had begun making notes on the story and characters, this time with Cary Grant and Grace Kelly in mind for the leads.

Dodge never could have foreseen the irony in casting when he wrote his novel. Cary Grant often told the story of his days as a young acrobat named Archie Leach, and of how he was stranded in America when his troupe disbanded. And it is hard not to imagine the future princess of Monaco as Dodge's Francie walks about Monte Carlo speaking of the prince.

Hitchcock did not see a need for preparing as detailed a treatment as had been done for *Rear Window*. Taking the original reader's synopsis, which was only five pages in length, Hitchcock and Hayes made a few changes, eliminated several minor characters, and incorporated, in more detail, several of the novel's key events. The result was a nine-page story outline dated February 23, 1954.

"Plotting was not my greatest talent," said Hayes. "Dialogue, character, and dialogue were. I was presented with the same problem as *Rear Window*. You've got this basic background and all we had to do is just sit down and ask, What if he did this? What if he did that? And gradually our plot grew. David Dodge wrote the book and he was quite surprised that a drama came out of it. But Hitch did it."

Years after the film was released, Dodge wrote: "All that survived in the end were the title, the names of some of the characters and the copyright, which was mine." The key events from Dodge's novel that made it into the outline included the escape from Robie's villa, his seeking Bellini's help, Francie's suspicious questioning of Mr. Burns, the killing of the wrong thief by the police, the final rooftop chase, and Robie alone at the end with Francie.

The changes Hitchcock and Hayes made were simple yet significant. In the novel, Bellini is Robie's best friend and remains so throughout. With Bellini, Hitchcock and Hayes saw an opportunity to create a meaty role for the mastermind behind the new Cat, who exploits his friendship with Robie. The decision to make Bellini a restaurateur came out of Hayes's research trip. Hayes remembered, "I learned that a lot of people in the underground were restaurant workers—cooks, chefs, and waiters. Hitch and I thought we could get them all together as a group in Bellini's restaurant, and this would also give the gang access to the wealthy. They could overhear their conversations, could judge the jewelry they wore, and use the restaurant as a source of great information." And unlike their counterparts in Dodge's novel, the restaurant workers are openly resentful of Robie.

Hitchcock and Hayes happily eliminated the countless coincidences that crowded the source material. The new Cat in Hayes's outline is still the young French girl Danielle, but she no longer works alone. Dodge's Mr. Paige becomes H. H. Hughson and is introduced much earlier as an ally to Robie. Much like Hayes's Stella from *Rear Window*, Mrs. Stevens speaks her mind and has a rough wisdom, which allows Hitchcock to use her as a foil and commentator on what is going on. Dodge's brunette Francie naturally became another in the long line of cool Hitchcock blondes—a successor to Lisa Fremont. Hitchcock and Hayes eliminated a character named the Gypsy, a second copy-cat thief, and substituted Foussard, Danielle's father, who is accidentally killed when he attempts to kill Robie. The police are quick to pin the robberies on Foussard, who, like the Gypsy, hasn't the physical agility to be a cat burglar. Finally, the entire subplot with Paul du Pré was dropped.

Unlike when they worked on *Rear Window*, Hitchcock and Hayes held almost daily story conferences for *To Catch a Thief*. As Hayes recalled:

I would say that Hitch worked more with me on *To Catch a Thief* than he did on *Rear Window* certainly. But still, he realized that I worked better if I was uninterrupted and he didn't interrupt me too much. We never did ten pages and discussed them. We just discussed in general terms story and character, and he let me go on and write until I finished. We did have lunches together and I'd tell him what I was doing, and he was patient enough to wait for it.

Hitchcock discovered early on that Hayes did his best work laying down all the emotion and drama in his first draft. Scenes and dialogue could be fine-tuned later, after the camera directions had been added. Hayes remembered:

Hitch was very penurious. He didn't pay much and never complimented you for anything. If you did it well, that's what you were paid for. On the other hand, if there was something he didn't particularly care for, he didn't slash with a red pencil and throw things around. He would say, "This is interesting, but it's too long. Could we cut it down?" He was very easy to work with.

It was a wonderful experience. I learned a lot from Hitch about gourmet food, cigars, and wine, in addition to learning about screenwriting. Most of my conferences with Hitch were concerned with his reminiscing about how he had solved some cinematic or story problem. It was very enjoyable to sit and have him ramble through thirty years of filmmaking and tell me how he had learned and how he discovered this and that.

Once *Rear Window* was in the can, Hitchcock and Hayes worked on the script for *To Catch a Thief* at a leisurely pace, and the director even found time to teach the writer a basic knowledge of Cockney rhyming slang. Explaining that its origins go as far back as the Elizabethan days, Hitchcock said that rhyming slang began as a jargon used by traders so they could communicate with each other without the customer understanding what they were saying.

But eventually everyone picked it up, and the usage became so sophisticated that in most cases the actual rhyme was left off. For example, rhyming slang for stairs is "apples and pears," but in conversation, one would say, "going up the apples" to communicate going up the stairs. One such example given by Hitchcock went: "I had an actress once say to me in London, 'Half a cock, while I lemon my Germans, would you?' She wanted to go to the toilet, which in polite English is 'I'm going to wash my hands.' Half a cock linnet, that's *minute*, while I lemon squash, which is *wash*, my *hands*, which are German bands. In those days, in Victorian times they had these little German bands on the street corners."

"Hitch could be very generous outside of the office," remembered Hayes. "And he enjoyed playing host."

> He supposedly hated eggs, and yet he was absolutely crazy about soufflés and quiche Lorraine, which he insisted we put in the screenplay after we had it one afternoon for lunch. Those were some of the most enjoyable times at his home, in his kitchen, with Alma, who in my opinion really deserves a lot of credit.

The basic story, again, would be a romance. The title, derived from the axiom "Set a thief to catch a thief," is here given a second meaning. Although Robie will have to catch his own imitator, his quest—the pretext for the story (or its MacGuffin)—is given less emphasis than the means by which Francie sets out to catch Robie. The jewel robberies, the threat of imprisonment to Robie, and ultimately the threats on his life are all treated in a lighthearted manner. The romantic plot between Robie and Francie in *To Catch a Thief* is similar in its design to *Rear Window*'s. In both films, the female is the pursuer and the male protagonist avoids intimacy. John Robie, like L. B. Jefferies, enjoys his independence. Jefferies eluded intimacy by traveling the globe, never remaining in one spot long enough to be caught; Robie, on the other hand, has retreated to the isolation of his cultured haven. Jefferies had to have his leg broken

in order for Lisa to win him; Robie is forced out of isolation by his
need to catch the new Cat, thus allowing Francie to catch him in
turn.

The stories' fetishism is also reversed. Whereas Jefferies becomes interested in Lisa as her involvement in the investigation of
Thorwald grows, Francie becomes more interested in Robie when
she suspects he is a famous jewel thief. In this context, *To Catch a
Thief* looks forward to its more serious counterpart, *Marnie*, produced and released nearly a decade later. In that film, a wealthy
businessman becomes sexually obsessed with a woman he knows to
be a compulsive thief. It is perhaps more than a coincidence that
Hitchcock wanted to reverse the roles by casting Grace Kelly, then
the princess of Monaco, as the female thief and object of sexual
blackmail. (Princess Grace's return to the screen was not to be, and
Hitchcock cast Tippi Hedren in the lead role of *Marnie*.)

The Screenplay

With the romantic angle fully developed, the director conceived
several of those dazzling Hitchcockian set pieces for Hayes to weave
into the story—among them a car chase along the Grande Corniche, the wrecking of a huge carnival float, and a lavish costume
ball—and in a short time Hayes completed his first draft. Together
with Hitchcock, Hayes broke down the 212-page script into 651
shots. The first draft, dated March 23, 1954, retains the structure of
the outline.

Hayes opens his first draft of *To Catch a Thief* with great visual
economy. A series of scenes of jewel robberies is intercut with those
of a black cat prowling on rooftops at night, followed by scenes of
plainclothes detectives en route to question a suspect—the protagonist, John Robie, the Cat. Robie is first seen quietly tending the garden at his villa high in the mountains overlooking the Riviera, but
then, before the police can take him into custody, he escapes in one
of their own cars and wrecks it. As the police watch the first car ca-
reening down the side of a mountain, Robie somehow manages to

steal the second police car from under their very noses, with which he drives into town before abandoning it at a used-car lot.

Arriving at the restaurant of his former Resistance leader, Augustus Bellini, Robie concludes that he will have to catch the thief himself. At this early stage of the script's development, Bellini is somewhat sketched in, more comically drawn than mysterious, retaining his constant chuckling from the novel and often pinching the bottom of his cashier, Antoinette. Atypically for a Hitchcock script, we are given little, if any, clue that Bellini might be the mastermind behind the robberies, other than a mild attempt on Bellini's part to dissuade Robie from pursuing the thief. Hitchcock and Hayes tread the line very closely, seemingly unsure of how much they want to reveal about Bellini.

Following his conversation with Bellini, Robie again eludes the police, this time by sea. Danielle, the pretty French girl from Dodge's novel, has become the daughter of Foussard, the wine waiter at Bellini's restaurant. Danielle pilots Robie via motorboat to the beach club at Cannes. En route, Danielle betrays her admiration for Robie, as well as her opinion that he is guilty. At the beach club, it appears that Robie is being closely watched by a suspicious concession attendant named Claude.

Through Bellini, Robie meets H. H. Hughson, an insurance agent for Lloyd's of London. Hughson's interest is in the recovery of his client's jewels; Robie's, in obtaining information in order to outwit the new Cat. Hayes set their meeting at the colorful flower market in Nice, and Hitchcock concocted a wild chase through a carnival procession to conclude the sequence.

Hitchcock and Hayes laid out the chase to include a carnival float with a gigantic figure of "Father Neptune, King of the Seas, and his court of fishermen and mermaids." Trying to elude the police, Robie leaps onto the float and hides himself inside the enormous head of King Neptune, causing a great disturbance among the operators of the float, and hell breaks loose before he is captured.

In a March 16 memo to Hugh Brown of Paramount's Budget

Department, Hitchcock requested information on any Nice carnivals that might be held after May 15, stating, "I would like to stage a section of the film where Cary Grant can be chased by the police from the flower market into the carnival procession and onto one of the big floats . . . that carries an oversized figure with a huge head." He continued, "We would want to wreck the float if possible in the actual street, but it is not my intention to shoot this phase of the float during the actual carnival. My plan would be to get the long shots from the actual carnival and restage this particular section another day."

Apprehended, and released soon after, Robie explains to Hughson while serving lunch at his villa that he has been given ten days to offer a defense against the charges. In so doing, Hitchcock sets the clock ticking. Hayes also has Robie point out to his stodgy British guest that we are all thieves in some way. The scene also allowed for Hitchcock's recurring motif of using black humor during a meal. Speaking of Robie's days in the Resistance, Hughson asks, "Did you kill many people?" Robie replies blandly, "Seventy-two." Later, as Hughson admires Germaine's quiche Lorraine, Robie says, "Germaine has very sensitive hands . . . She shot a German general once . . . at eighty yards." In the film Hitchcock changed this line to "She strangled a German general once. Without a sound." Hitchcock had a particular fondness for strangulation, as evidenced by *Shadow of a Doubt*, *Strangers on a Train*, *Rope*, and other films.

Later, in the casino, Robie makes the acquaintance of Francie and Mrs. Stevens while assuming the guise of Oregon lumber magnate Conrad Burns. "Right now building is booming," he replies when Mrs. Stevens asks about his income. Francie is practically silent throughout the scene, which makes it all the more surprising when she boldly kisses Robie on the mouth after he accompanies the ladies to their suite. Hitchcock was fascinated with the dichotomy of what he called sophisticated drawing-room types who become whores once they're in the bedroom. "An English girl," explained Hitchcock, "looking like a schoolteacher, is apt to get into a cab with you and, to your surprise, she'll probably pull a man's pants open." Hereafter, Francie continues courting Robie, inviting him for breakfast, a morning swim at the beach, and a picnic lunch.

At this stage, the focus of the screenplay turns toward the pursuit of Robie by Francie, and only occasionally do the filmmakers remind us of the potential menaces to Robie's life and/or freedom. But even these threats are handled in the first draft in a rather light tone. Robie first receives a threatening note from the thief: "DEAR MR. BURNS, IF YOU INTEND TO REMAIN IN CANNES ANY LONGER, IT WOULD BE ADVISABLE FOR YOU TO INSURE YOUR LIFE WITH MR. HUGHSON OF LLOYDS." And later he is tailed by two detectives who seem more interested in looking at snapshots of beautiful women and playing soccer with a small stone. The detectives' ineptitude reaches its climax when they crash their car in order to avoid a chicken crossing the road. Although treated comically, the stakes have been raised, as Robie's life is threatened from one side and his liberty from the other. This is the classic Hitchcock situation of the double chase.

While at the beach, Robie is signaled by Danielle, whom he swims out to meet at the hotel's float. Danielle again tries to get Robie to leave, warning that his former Maquis comrades might kill him. Later, Francie offers to take Robie for a drive, to be followed by a picnic lunch. Before departing, however, Robie joins Hughson and Commissaire Lepic for a brief scene on the hotel terrace. Lepic is suspicious of Hughson's association with Robie, as the latest robbery resulted in nine new insurance policies being sold by Hughson. "You don't think that I steal so Hughson could sell policies, do you?" asks Robie. Francie pulls up in her convertible, and they're off. While Hitchcock keeps Robie and Francie on the go, allowing more local color to be displayed on the screen, Hayes borrows some dialogue from two scenes in the novel and adds his own sophisticated level of pun and sexual double entendre.

In the quartet of Hitchcock-Grant films, there is always a wild automobile ride which offers either the risk of plunging over a precipice or an instance of drunkenness, and in *North by North-*

west, both. Hitchcock enjoyed playing against Grant's persona in this way, and in *To Catch a Thief,* he disarms the suave, cool ex–cat burglar by showing his apprehension as Francie races along the treacherous winding roads. Through a single close-up of Robie's hands tightly gripping his knees, Hitchcock reveals the character's fear. Francie stays ahead of the police and finally unmasks Robie. Continuing the theme of feminine intuition from their previous film, Hitchcock and Hayes have Francie boast about her cleverness and playfully blackmail Robie into coming to her suite for cocktails and dinner that evening.

For the evening seduction scene, which is the midpoint of the film, Hayes was given free rein to ignite the script with dialogue that would surely have the censors in an uproar. Hitchcock also had it in mind to ignite the screen, as it were, envisioning the climax of the love scene as a flurry of colorful, exploding fireworks. The director who had always regarded "avoiding the cliché" as one of his hall-marks here embraced the cliché wholeheartedly.

As in the novel, Mrs. Stevens's jewelry is stolen, but here Fran-cie's call to the police sends Robie into hiding. In the first draft, Robie meets with Hughson on a small rowboat while disguised as a fisherman. Midway through the first draft, Hitchcock and Hayes de-cided to make the threatening notes Robie receives into coded weather reports. Over wine and sandwiches, Robie explains to Hughson that he is now certain that Bellini is behind the robberies, since in the Resistance days they used similar "weather reports" as a means of underground communication. Although the idea for us-ing coded weather reports for the threatening notes came before the first draft was completed, they were not initially written that way. The notes would be changed in the next rewrite. The latest note is intended to bait Robie to fall into a trap. But Robie intends to re-verse the trap, having the police arrive in time to catch the new Cat. Along with the early scene between Robie and Bellini, this scene would endure the most rewriting.

That night an attempt is made on Robie's life, which results in the death of Foussard, Danielle's father. Lepic quickly reports to the newspapers that Foussard was the Cat. But Robie tells Lepic and

Hughson that Foussard had a wooden leg and couldn't possibly have committed the robberies. Later, Francie apologizes and confesses her love to Robie, who asks that she get him an invitation to the Sanford gala, where he is certain the Cat will strike.

For the finale, Hitchcock conceived a grand costume ball sequence, an opportunity Dodge missed, as the climactic moments of the novel take place the night before the gala. Paramount's Paris office supplied the research department with information on French customs and traditions, including Le Bal de Biarritz, a grand gala held annually at the end of the summer season. The research file contains photographs from the event that show guests wearing eighteenth-century costumes, women bedecked with jewels, partygoers passed out in a drunken stupor, and couples reclining on a lawn, kissing. It was a vulgarized depiction of the filthy rich, which Hitchcock relished showing.

In Hayes's finale, Robie and Hughson wear identical costumes and switch places, in a situation reminiscent of Hayes's own radio play for *The Adventures of Sam Spade*, "The Flopsy, Mopsy, and Cottontail Caper." Hughson plays decoy to Lepic and his detectives, dancing all evening with Francie, while Robie sneaks away, unobserved, to the roof of the Sanford villa, where he remains until the thief appears. As in the novel, the thief turns out to be Danielle. When Danielle slips and clings to the edge of the roof, Robie saves her, but not before forcing a confession to the police below. The first draft ends abruptly, with a single shot of Robie's villa at night, darkened, except for an illuminated window of the upstairs bedroom and a black cat curled contentedly on a patio chair as a succession of fireworks explode in the sky.

With the first draft completed, Hitchcock sent Hayes to work with a translator, since it was required to submit scripts in both French and English to the National Center of the Cinema and the French trade unions in order to obtain permission to film in France, as well as to acquire the necessary work permits for the American crew. "Hitchcock had me translate the script into French," Hayes remembered, "but more than that, we translated it back into English, so that the French actors would speak English with French idiom. I worked long and hard with a translator to get the script ready on time. I can't imagine many producers doing that. But Hitch did."

Pre-production

To Catch a Thief was to be the first of a three-picture deal between Hitchcock and Paramount wherein the studio would retain ownership of the film. Under this agreement, the director was to receive a salary of $150,000 per picture, plus 10 percent of the profits after twice the production cost was earned back.* For his services Cary Grant was to receive 10 percent of the gross. By the end of March 1954, the contracts had been finalized and Hitchcock's production team—most had worked on *Rear Window*—began the scheduling, budgeting, and designing necessary to mount a major Hollywood production abroad.

Although billed in the screen credits of *To Catch a Thief* as second-unit director, Herbert Coleman had become Hitchcock's right arm, supervising many of the production details before departing to scout locations, secure permissions, and oversee the considerable second-unit photography that had to be filmed to the director's precise specifications. Doc Erickson accompanied Coleman to France as unit production manager and found himself an increasingly important member of the company, having been allocated many tasks unrelated to his budgeting and scheduling duties.

By mid-April, with a budget rapidly approaching $3 million, Hitchcock was forced to make cuts in the script. He completely eliminated the Nice carnival chase, which had been estimated at $48,000. The sequence called for one carnival troupe, including one float, one stunt double for Robie, four bit players as detectives,

---

*In the case of *To Catch a Thief*, there was an exception to this agreement, in that Hitchcock's percentage would be determined after Cary Grant's percentage had been deducted from the total gross receipts. *To Catch a Thief* was also the only picture produced under this arrangement. The ownership of the remaining Hitchcock-Paramount productions reverted to the director eight years after their initial release.

six additional players dressed as policemen, fifty adults and children as extras, and six women dressed as mermaids. Hitchcock also reduced the number of shooting days for the expensive location production, planning instead to re-create many scenes back on the sound stages at Paramount with rear projection.

In the key supporting roles of Mrs. Stevens and Hughson, Hitchcock cast Jessie Royce Landis and John Williams. Landis primarily worked on the stage, but over the years turned in a series of key character performances on the big screen as well. In fact, Landis played Grace Kelly's mother a second time, in MGM's *The Swan*, and also made a brief but memorable appearance as Cary Grant's mother in Hitchcock's *North by Northwest* (even though they were almost the same age). John Williams had previously appeared in the director's *The Paradine Case* and *Dial M for Murder*, but he most recently had played Audrey Hepburn's father in Billy Wilder's *Sabrina*. As Bellini, changed to Bertani in the final script, Hitchcock cast the venerable French actor Charles Vanel, and as Danielle, the young acrobatic thief, the director chose Brigitte Auber, whose performance in Julien Duvivier's *Under the Paris Sky* he had admired. The remaining actors would be hired in France.

Now on his fifth picture with Hitchcock, director of photography Robert Burks faced the challenge of lensing *To Catch a Thief* in Paramount's new wide-screen format, VistaVision. The process, developed by the studio, created a larger negative frame by running the 35mm film horizontally through the camera rather than vertically. The image was eight sprockets wide—twice that of the conventional method—which resulted in a larger and sharper negative. Unlike CinemaScope, VistaVision, which came out a year later, was not an anamorphic process, so that there was less distortion as well as a greater depth of field.* The process was expensive, however, in that twice as much film needed to be exposed.

---

*CinemaScope employs a special anamorphic camera lens that squeezes the wide image onto the film, and a lens that unsqueezes the image when it is projected onto a wide screen.

While the crew prepared for the journey, Hayes managed the revising and editing of the script, which kept him busy through May 3, a day before Hitchcock departed for New York. The revised first draft was immediately submitted to the Production Code Administration, whereupon Joe Breen responded in a May 6 memo to Luigi Luraschi by calling attention to the script's "unacceptable elements."

Breen objected to Bellini's constant pinching of Antoinette's posterior and cautioned the studio on "handling the scenes around the beaches," where he made an explicit ruling that any scenes showing bikinis or French-type bathing suits could not be approved. Breen also found in the dialogue "an unacceptable attempt to justify Robie's past career as a thief" and asked that "this material be rewritten, in such a manner as to eliminate the excusing of Robie's criminal acts, and the impression that thievery is a widely accepted practice in all walks of life."

Breen also expressed concern over the "chip gag," in which Robie drops a casino chip down the front of a woman's dress as a means to strike up a conversation with Francie and Mrs. Stevens. "The French woman's cleavage should not be emphasized," wrote Breen, and, further, "Robie should not be waiting with 'poised fingers,' as though he were about to retrieve the chip from her dress."

The scenes between Robie and Francie were loaded with sexual innuendo. Breen cautioned against such lines as "One with everything—diamonds, excitement, *me*"; "At least I didn't offer him my treasures in a semi-darkened room"; and "Miss Stevens, you have confused an ancient medium of exchange for mutual understanding."

Breen found the fireworks-seduction scene "completely unacceptable," adding that "in a story of this type it would be impossible to get the proper moral values as required by the code in treating the subject of illicit sex." In closing, Breen noted that "the tag of this story seems to be a reprise on the foregoing illicit affair and as such is unacceptable."

The Rewrites

By the time the PCA responded to the first draft, Hitchcock had already departed from Hollywood for New York to promote *Dial M for Murder* and *Rear Window*, which were due for release in late May and August, respectively, and to announce that he would follow *To Catch a Thief* with an adaptation of an English novel by Jack Trevor Story called *The Trouble with Harry*. Hitchcock also thought it worth mentioning that Hayes had done "a remarkably fine job on the screenplay of *Thief*, despite the fact that when you're forced to cut such a script you're left with an awful feeling of guilt." Hitchcock rarely complimented a collaborator in so public a manner.

Soon Hitchcock left for England to promote the British release of *Dial M for Murder*, and the cast and crew for *To Catch a Thief* departed for France. Before journeying to Cannes, the company enjoyed a tour of Paris, where Hayes discovered his fear of heights when a member of their group approached him from behind while he was on top of the Arc de Triomphe, and playfully nudged him toward the edge. By the third week of May, the cast and key production personnel were registered at the famed Carlton Hotel in Cannes, where Hayes continued writing. On Hitchcock's arrival, the two began marathon rewrite sessions, as an excerpt from a May 25 letter from Doc Erickson to Hugh Brown suggests:

> The condition of the script is not good. Hitch went to work with John Hayes immediately upon his arrival yesterday noon and will be working with him all day today, but he feels there is considerable polishing to be done yet. Physically there are no changes in the story and therefore we are planning our work here based on the green script, but you know how difficult it is to plan efficiently when you know there is a re-write coming. I doubt very seriously that we will have any sort of new script before the end of the week.

Naturally, with Hitch working on the script every day, we will have very little opportunity to show him any of the location sites for the pre-production shooting.

In a week's time, the director and writer polished their script, eliminating or altering aspects that the PCA found objectionable and concentrating on the obvious weakness in the characterization of Bertani. They also changed the opening sequence so that instead of stealing one of the police cars, Robie escapes from his villa riding a bus. This is accomplished by luring the police from the villa when Robie's housekeeper speeds away in his car, and it anticipates the final moments of the film, when Hughson acts as a decoy for Robie.

In the new script, Hayes developed Bertani into a much more complex character. Bellini's comic pinching of Antoinette's bottom was thrown out, in favor of Bertani's carefully chosen wardrobe and evident strength as a leader of men. More than once Bertani checks his appearance in a mirror—a frequent Hitchcock clue to a character's duplicitous nature. The dialogue also reveals that Bertani may have attained his restaurant through questionable means. "It was a present from an elderly and unfortunate woman for whom I have done a favor in the *past*," exclaims Bertani. "I heard it was a loan. But after she died, they never could find the note you signed," replies Robie. In this draft, the filmmakers' intentions are much more apparent in that Bertani is eager for Robie to go into hiding and do nothing to trap the copy-cat thief.

Minor changes included Mrs. Stevens being named Jesse, after the actress portraying her (although Landis spelled her name Jessie). The threatening notes to Robie were now written into the script in the form of weather reports. Francie was now included in the scene between Robie and Danielle on the hotel's float. It is the only scene where Francie and Danielle share the screen together, allowing an opportunity for Hayes to explore a rivalry between the two. The scene among Hughson, Lepic, and Robie on the Carlton Hotel terrace was eliminated, moving the film directly from the beach sequence to Francie's invitation to take Robie for a drive and a picnic lunch.

Another scene that had been completely rewritten was the one between Robie and Hughson after the Stevenses' burglary. In the later version, Robie and Hughson are sitting at the end of a pier, fishing (changed from sitting in the rowboat of the first draft). Robie tells Hughson that he is certain he knows the identity of the person behind the new Cat, but he withholds the details. The wealthy Brazilian couple, the Souzas, are renamed Silva, allowing for a play on words in the new threatening weather report. "LIGHTNING WILL DEFINITELY STRIKE. THE WEATHER MAN SAYS DON'T TOUCH ANYTHING SILVER" reads a portion of the note. The word "silver" is meant to bait Robie for a trap at the Silvas' villa.

The finale unfolds as it does in the first draft, but with an added scene in the main entrance hall of the Sanford villa. As Lepic takes Danielle away, he tells Bertani to be at the police station at ten the following morning. During this scene, Bertani twice requests that he be allowed to report at noon. Hitchcock got the idea during a research visit to a New York City police precinct, when he overheard a police officer in conversation with a wanted man. The suspect requested that he be allowed to give himself up on the following Monday so that he could keep a date that weekend. The officer, according to Hitchcock, agreed. The scene was filmed, but later omitted. "It would have made an amusing payoff," Hitchcock said, "but it would also have deflected the story, and at this stage the spectator would want to know what happens to the principal characters. Besides, it might have seemed incredible. Very often the truest things appear too far-fetched."

In the new tag, Francie and Mrs. Stevens are standing in front of the Carlton Hotel as two bellboys put their luggage in the trunk of a chauffeur-driven limousine. Robie and Francie say their goodbyes and the women leave. Hughson looks on, bewildered, and has the following exchange with Robie:

                    HUGHSON
I say—Robie—you're not simply going
to let her drive away from you—are
you?

                     ROBIE
Yup.

                    HUGHSON
But—but that girl's a prize.

                     ROBIE
We're meeting again—in exactly six
months. Right here, as a matter of
fact—up on the fourth floor.

                    HUGHSON
You don't seem to know much about
romance, old fellow. I'll bet ten
pounds sterling somebody else will
marry that girl before she comes
back.

                     ROBIE
Not a chance.
   (Looks directly at Hughson)
You see, last night I learned that
she didn't go on a trip to <u>get</u> a
husband—but to <u>lose</u> one. Her
divorce won't be final for six months.
Care for a drink?

Hughson's expression says he might as well
have a drink and the two of them turn and
stroll leisurely toward the Carlton
Terrace, the CAMERA PANNING THEM AWAY.

While this was certainly a more fitting tag than that of the first draft, the search for a satisfactory ending would continue.

On the Riviera

Principal photography for Production #11511, *To Catch a Thief*, began on Monday, May 31, in Saint Jeannet, France, the location for Robie's villa, with only fifty-four pages of the revised final script completed. The first day's shooting was limited to three scenes involving the police car and the bus that Robie uses for his escape, as intermittent rain showers delayed production. It is ironic that Hitchcock and Hayes should have the threatening notes composed as dubious weather reports, for in November 1953 a report issued to Paramount Pictures by the National Weather Institute forecast for the French Riviera twenty-four "good shooting days" and only three days of rain during the month of June 1954. The forecast could not have been more wrong, and after only two weeks, the production was three days behind schedule.

The rain delays allowed John Michael Hayes and Cary Grant time to walk around Cannes. Enjoying a tranquil moment, the actor explained to the writer, "John, this isn't like America. In Europe, they don't worship stars. We'll just go down rue Commandante André, there's a store down there I know." The actor wanted to buy a shirt. "By the time we got to the store," Hayes recalled, "the word got out, and a crowd gathered that blocked the street and almost broke the window. We had to escape out the back door with a car we called for, with Cary ducking down." However, Grant still managed to get the shirt he wanted, which was the striped shirt he wore in the opening sequences.

Notwithstanding the unusually rainy weather and a frantic rush to complete the shooting script, Hitchcock remained cheerfully calm, as Doc Erickson recalled:

> We managed to arrange our work so that we could have dinner, and dinner was always delightful with Hitch. It was always Herbie and I, and Alma, of course, and there would be

maybe one or two other select people, from the crew or cast that Hitch might invite. And we had wonderful times—the drinks, the wine, and the fish course, more wine, and the main course, more wine and dessert, the after-dinner drink, and then you'd fall into bed.

Fashion designer Oleg Cassini, who was ardently pursuing Grace Kelly at the time, having asked her to marry him, joined the company in Cannes and also remembered Hitchcock's passion for fine dining:

We would often have dinner together—the Grants, the Hitchcocks, Grace, and I—a grand occasion always, very carefully orchestrated by the director himself. He had one of the most curious eating habits; his diet consisted of one spectacular meal each day. He would fast until evening, drinking only water during the filming. Then he would take a bath and we would gather for dinner at the restaurant of his choice, for the precise meal of his choice. We always ate in restaurants rated three stars or better. Still, Hitchcock would review everything in advance: the wines, the soup, the fish, the meat, the sorbet between courses, the dessert, the fruit and cheese. He would preside over it all, like an emperor, savoring each morsel. I've never seen anyone enjoy a meal more. He would grow expansive then; we would discuss philosophy. He was, of course, a complete autocrat. He believed anyone on a film (except him) could be replaced. I argued the opposite, the importance of individuals, especially the unique "chemistry" generated by stars like Cary Grant and Grace Kelly. They could not be replaced. Hitchcock believed, though, that he could make anyone a star. He was wrong, and would spend the rest of his career proving it, as he searched—unsuccessfully, of course—for an actress who could replace Grace Kelly.

While the director entertained his cast and crew at dinner, openly discussing future projects, Doc Erickson remained in close contact with the studio's ever-watchful budget department. "So far we are in the best of health and the general morale of the troupe is excellent," wrote Erickson to Frank Caffey in a letter dated June 1.

The three musketeers—Coleman, McCauley, and Erickson—will be up to their ears breaking down the new script and getting together on a schedule.

On June 6 he added:

We have discussed with Hitch the length of the script and the length of the shooting schedule. He feels that the script cannot be cut, and therefore, we have to lengthen the schedule accordingly.

By June 10, Hayes had turned in the remainder of the shooting script. Although Hayes remained in Cannes for the duration of location photography, and continued revising the script during production, Hitchcock had the studio take the writer off salary for To Catch a Thief effective June 12 and begin paying his salary for The Trouble with Harry on June 14. The latter picture had been tentatively scheduled to commence production in October, so Hitchcock gave Hayes the novel to begin his adaptation. Hitchcock's contract with Paramount regarding the "story cost" of To Catch a Thief suggests the director may have had an ulterior motive for the quick switch in payroll allocations. The contract dictated that the "total story cost including rights and writer will in no event exceed or be less than $125,000." As the story rights cost $105,000, if Hayes's salary, living and travel expenses totaled less than $20,000, the difference would be paid to Hitchcock by Paramount. Any costs in excess of $20,000 would be reimbursed to Paramount by Hitchcock. By this time, Hayes's salary had already reached $20,625 and expenses for his December research trip had totaled $3,993. By putting Hayes on salary for *The Trouble with Harry*, Hitchcock got the studio to pick up the tab for the writer's revisions on *To Catch a Thief*, which continued throughout August, while also getting Hayes to begin scripting the new picture.

As the weather improved, production moved along more swiftly. To hasten the shooting, Hitchcock decided to abandon filming the Carlton Hotel lobby sequences on location in favor of shooting them later at the studio, where Joseph MacMillan Johnson was already supervising the design and construction of sets to match the locations. The director also added another costume change for his leading lady, having Erickson send a telegram to the designer, Edith Head: "NEW CHANGE FOR KELLY REQUIRED—SCENES 306 THROUGH 312 BEING REWRITTEN—FRANCIE INDICATES WILL DRESS AND MEET ROBIE IN LOBBY—DO NOT WISH TO DISCLOSE SPORT OUTFIT UNTIL LOBBY SCENES." In all, Edith Head provided the actress with eleven costume changes in *To Catch a Thief*. Years later, she recalled the film as a personal favorite among her assignments:

> When people ask me who my favorite actress is, who my favorite actor is, and what my favorite film is, I tell them to watch *To Catch a Thief* and they'll get all the answers. The film was a costume designer's dream. It had all the ingredients for being fun, a challenge, and a great product. The director was Hitchcock. The stars, Cary Grant and Grace Kelly. The location, the Côte d'Azur in the south of France. Grace played the part of possibly the richest woman in America, with the most fabulous clothes and the most fabulous jewels. Her mother, played by Jessie Royce Landis, was equally elegant.
>
> The story revolved around a world of people with great taste and plenty of money. Even the extras were meticulously dressed. At the end of the picture we had a fancy masquerade ball, presumably at the court of one of the great kings of France, so every woman was running around dressed like Marie Antoinette. That was the most expensive

setup I've ever done. Grace wore a dress of delicate gold mesh, a golden wig, and a golden mask. Hitchcock told me that he wanted her to look like a princess. She did.

Happily out of semiretirement, Cary Grant was accompanied by his third wife, Betsy Drake, and truly enjoyed the process of picture-making. Having collaborated twice before, the actor and director were comfortable working together, and Hitchcock trusted Grant completely in matters of performance. "Cary is marvelous, you see," said Hitchcock. "One doesn't direct Cary Grant. One simply puts him in front of the camera."

That level of trust was so great that Hitchcock even let Grant choose his own wardrobe for the movie. "Edith dressed the women but she didn't design my costumes," recalled Grant. "I planned and provided everything myself. In fact, I bought everything in Cannes, just before we began shooting. She didn't go with me when I purchased the clothes, nor did she approve anything. I was the only one who approved my clothes. Hitch trusted me implicitly to select my own wardrobe. If he wanted me to wear something very specific he would tell me, but generally I wore simple, tasteful clothes—the same kinds of clothes I wear off screen."

When it concerned the script, however, Hitchcock was more judicious with the allowances he gave his star performers. John Michael Hayes recalls that Cary Grant often arrived on the set in the morning with pages of script that he had gone over the night before, saying, "Hitch, I have an idea."

"Do you," the director would say. "Talk to John."

Hayes was then given the task of stalling Grant until it was too late to work in his suggestions. "Well, that's very interesting. Let me think about it," the writer would say. Eventually the crew was ready with the next setup, and it was time to shoot the scene.

Later Grant would insist on running through a scene both ways to get Hitchcock's approval. Hayes remembered the actor being unnaturally awkward when doing the scene as written, then doing his own version to perfection, saying, "What do you think? Which one is best?"

"We had to come up with a gimmick to forestall this," said Hayes, "because Hitch planned every script very carefully, down to camera angles, way in advance and didn't like to improvise too much on the set . . . so the next time Cary did that, we had everybody on the set primed. When he did the scene as written, everyone, from the grips to the lighting boys, broke out into applause."

"I guess it's all right the way it is," said Grant, who eventually caught on and enjoyed the joke.

In her third and, as it happened, final film for Hitchcock, Grace Kelly was at the pinnacle of her career and never looked more lovely. On one of their days off, Hayes accompanied Kelly and Grant's wife Betsy Drake on a tour of Monaco, and the writer taught Kelly how to play roulette. She won some money, after which the trio went to lunch and continued their sightseeing, ending up outside the Grimaldi museum. Kelly was delighted by what she could see of the gardens, the gates to which were locked. Hayes remembered, "Grace said, 'I wonder if we could find some way to get in.' So I said, 'Well, I'll see if somebody can get to the Prince, or his public relations man, and get you a tour of the garden while you're here.' But we finished the location photography before a tour could be arranged."

The following year, when Grace Kelly returned to the Riviera, she was a sensation at the Cannes Film Festival. This time she did meet Prince Rainier, who gave her a personal tour of his gardens. Within a year's time, she had retired from the screen to become Princess Grace of Monaco. Years afterward, Hayes remembered, "Later, when she invited my wife and myself to the palace, Grace said, 'Now I can show *you* the garden.' "

Back at the Studio

The principals and first unit wrapped location production on June 25, allowing ample time for everyone's safe return to Hollywood for the studio shooting, which was to commence on July 6 with the scene of Kelly kissing Grant in the Carlton Hotel corridor and the fireworks/seduction sequence in her suite. Before the holiday weekend, Hayes turned over his script pages to the studio typing pool, which turned out the retyped shooting script by July 2, so the censorship department could submit the new script to the PCA for approval.

While Hitchcock proceeded in the studio, Herbert Coleman continued supervising the second unit in Cannes, which was photographing the chase sequences and aerials, then sending the completed footage to Hollywood for the director's approval. One example of Hitchcock's meticulousness is expressed in a July 8 cable to Coleman, after having seen the rushes:

Dear Herbie,

Saw shot where car avoids oncoming bus afraid it does not come off for the following reasons. Because we, the camera, are rounding a bend, the bus comes upon us so suddenly it has gone past before we realize the danger . . .

I think there are two corrections that could be made . . . first, that we should be proceeding along a straight bit of road with bend at end so we are aware of bend long before we come to it . . .

When we reach bend we should then be shocked to find bus appearing around bend and coming straight at us because sharpness of bend should almost send bus over to wrong side of road but we ourselves should never actually make turn at bend . . .

Other point is that in present shot only half the bus appears on the screen. This I realize arises out of fact that you are veering out of its way . . . This latter fault could be corrected by keeping camera panned well over to left so that as camera car swerves the camera pans over at same time from left to right . . .

I also feel that scene three seventy five slate 732X1 now looks as though it is a viewpoint from Sunbeam although I know it is intended as an establishing shot. Could this not be

redone so that camera is shooting back on a three quarter angle slightly ahead of police car . . .

HITCH

By July 9, Joe Breen had reviewed the new script, and in a letter
to Luigi Luraschi he again cautioned against Robie's "poised fingers" in the scene with the casino chip. Breen also warned that the
suggestion of the detectives looking at French postcards was unacceptable and asked that Robie's line "Two weeks with a good man at
Niagara Falls" be rewritten. Although there had been no specific
mention in his review of the first draft, Breen now felt that "the symbolism of the fireworks is pointed and we ask that it be eliminated."

Production continued with the Carlton Hotel raft sequence being re-created in Paramount's "A" tank on Set #12. On Tuesday,
July 13, Cary Grant, Grace Kelly, and Brigitte Auber first took their
places in the pool to film the critical scene, which is fraught with
jealousy, sexual tension, and humor. Auber expertly conveyed each
of these feelings in her portrayal of Danielle. Of the French actress,
Hayes recalled:

She had a casual way of wearing a blouse, which exposed
her bosom frequently. And Hitch, of course, was delighted
with her. She brought a lot of humor and vivacity to the part.
Grace was more reserved and Brigitte was more playful,
more childlike. And, of course, that was disarming. You
couldn't think of her as the jewel thief. She was just a lovely,
effervescent young girl, in love with this older man, who
kept saying, "Leave me alone. Go back to your dolls." And
she was trying to show that she was more of a woman than
Grace Kelly. And being more of a woman meant being built
better, so when Grace said something to the effect that she
was just a child, she says, "Shall we stand in shallower water
and debate that?" Which is a line that tickled me.

Hayes continued rewriting, less to oblige the censors than to accommodate Charles Vanel, whom Hitchcock had apparently cast

without knowing that the actor did not speak English. The writer remembered:

> They tried to teach him phonetically, and that inhibited all the scenes we wanted to do with him, because he hardly moved and talked in simple sentences. We couldn't get the subtlety in his part that we wanted, that he could very well have been masterminding this thing. Hitch hired him because he saw him in *The Wages of Fear* and never bothered to check whether he could speak English at all. They had his lines on a blackboard, and he tried to look offstage and read the lines. It was too bad, because he was an accomplished actor, with all the subtleties of gesture and intonation, and of course we got none of that.

By the first week of August, Hayes had rewritten much of Vanel's dialogue, shortening speeches and, in the process, sacrificing characterization. To balance the scenes with Bertani that had been rewritten, Hayes had to change the scene between Robie and Hughson on the fishing pier. The final changes of the latter scene, dated August 27, made no mention of Robie suspecting Bertani and eliminated the second threatening "weather report." The overall effect of this compromise was to lessen the tension in a script already light in its thriller aspects.

After working closely with the dialogue coach, Elsie Foulstone, Charles Vanel was ready for the cameras. The scenes inside Bertani's office and kitchen were shot on a closed set from Wednesday, August 4, through Saturday, August 7. Ultimately, though, Vanel's English dialogue was entirely redubbed by the French actor Jean Duval.

The company began shooting the finale the following week, using all of Stages 14, 15, and 16 to re-create Cannes's famed Goldman Villa. On this set, Cary Grant and Brigitte Auber both used their acrobatic training to scamper about on rooftops some eighty feet above the stage floor. While preparing to film the rooftop climax, Auber noticed that mattresses had been spread out in what

seemed a feeble attempt to prevent serious injury. The French actress then saw four Catholic priests enter the stage, though she
didn't know they were merely visiting the studio. "*Mon Dieu*," ex-
claimed Auber. "You Americans think of everything."

In spite of delays that ultimately put *To Catch a Thief* twenty-
two days behind schedule, Hitchcock maintained a light mood on
the set during the filming of the final scenes, which included the
costume ball. "Hitchcock had Edith Head create this elaborate gold
gown for the sequence," recalled Grace Kelly, "and it was impossible to get into, it took forever. While I was being stuffed and sewed
into the dress, the assistant director [Daniel McCauley] was outside
banging on my door shouting 'Mr. Hitchcock is waiting, Mr. Hitchcock is waiting.' Finally I got to the set, and instead of scolding me,
he just looked at me and said in that inimitable way of his, 'Grace,
there's hills in them thar gold.' "

On Friday, August 13, the company paused for champagne and
cake to celebrate the director's birthday. Oleg Cassini recalled that
the celebration began when Hitchcock's secretary announced,
"Could I have your attention for a moment? Would you all come
into the other room, please, and have a piece of Mr. Hitchcake's
cock?" Whether her slip was intentional or not, it was the kind of
play on words that amused the director. The evening before, *Rear
Window* had had its Los Angeles premiere at the Paramount Hollywood Theater and, by all accounts, was a certified hit, which only
heightened the tone of the birthday festivities.

Late in the filming, Hitchcock had gotten wind of Hayes's fear
of heights and decided to cast the writer as the butt of one of his
practical jokes. During a break in shooting the finale, Hayes remembered being summoned over the bullhorn: "John Michael
Hayes, please report to Mr. Hitchcock on Stage 16."

Now, Hitch allowed a certain amount of visitors to come in,
and they're mumbling, "It's Hitchcock's writer. It's probably
something very important." I go over and he heaves himself
out of the chair, and says, "Come with me." It was the party

scene at the end, and they had built wooden steps and scaffolding all around the sound stage, so they could photograph from the rooftop down. He goes laboriously up these stairs and scaffolding, up over the top of the roof, looking down into the courtyard. We're up pretty high, and all you've got is a wooden railing, along with a stud every few feet, and Hitch says, "I'll tell you why I brought you up here." I said, "Why?" "I wanted to see if heights frighten you as much as they do me." I said, "They certainly do, Hitch." "You know, everybody runs up and down these things so easily," he said, "and I'm terrified. I'm glad to find out I'm not the only one." This was, in effect, his conversation, and he stopped the whole picture for it. And he said, "You know, they probably think we're making some important decision up here, little do they know we already made it in the office three months ago. Let's go down." He did have his pixie side.

Indeed, Hitchcock seemed to be at his most jovial during this period, taking time to entertain reporters and, in another rare instance, to note the contributions of his writer and crew. "Proper casting, not only of performers," the director continued, "but of writers, and a close relationship between the artistic and technical people involved in a production, are all vitally important to the success of a good suspense film."

For his traditional cameo appearance, Hitchcock chose to be seated on the bus with which Robie makes his escape early in the picture. *Variety* reported: "Originally, Hitchcock was to be photographed full-face by Robert Burks, in charge of cameras. Just before the shot was made, however, Hitchcock instructed Burks to shoot only half his face, thus slicing his part in two."

As the end of production drew near, the final tag remained a scene of debate among the director, writer, and the two stars. "We had a fight only once," Hayes remembered, "and that was over the ending of *To Catch a Thief*, and it got to be quite bitter."

I must have written a dozen endings for that picture. I had a scene that I liked. Cary Grant would like one. Grace Kelly would like one. And Hitch wouldn't like it. And then Cary Grant and Hitch would like one, and Grace Kelly wouldn't like it. But Hitch got angry because I showed the scene to Grace and Cary, to get their opinion of the one I liked, and that was his function, not mine, and he was right. Although I did it innocently, not with any sinister intent. I wanted to make the best picture I could. The ending that I liked was with the little Sunbeam, Francie's car, with which she took him for a ride over the Corniche and scared the hell out of him. I wanted the last love scene to be played in that car, on the edge of the road, overlooking Monte Carlo. There's a cliff and this town way down there. I wanted them to be hugging and kissing, and the car starts to roll forward, and they don't notice, they're so absorbed in each other. It keeps rolling toward the edge of the cliff, and finally Francie says, "John?" He says, "Yes." She says, "Will you do me a favor?" "What?" he asks. "Would you put your foot on the brake, please?" He puts his foot on the brake and the bumper is just hanging over the edge, and I wanted to end there. But I couldn't convince Hitch to do it.

The new ending turned in on August 30 mirrors the opening sequences, as Robie's car is chased by a black sedan up the mountain roads toward his villa. He enters the patio and finds that he has been followed by Francie, still in her ball gown and eager for Robie to give her due credit for helping him catch the new Cat. Robie does just that, admitting, "I guess I'm not the lone wolf I thought I was, Francie." But when she turns to leave, he pulls her toward him and kisses her passionately. She smiles, having broken through his isolation, and says, "So this is where you live? I think I'm going to like it." In shooting the scene, Francie's closing line was changed to "So this is where you live? Oh, Mother will love it up here!"

"I didn't want to wind up with a completely happy ending,"

Hitchcock told Truffaut, "it turns out that the mother-in-law will come and live with them, so the final note is pretty grim."

Principal photography was completed on Saturday, September 4, and editor George Tomasini immediately began putting together an assembly of the picture while the director and crew turned their attention to *The Trouble with Harry*, which was scheduled to begin production on location in less than three weeks. Before then, however, Cary Grant made himself available for retakes for some of the convertible scenes on September 14 and 15.

Post-production

Although Hitchcock generally worked without interference from the front office at Paramount, production chief Don Hartman had some suggestions when he saw a cut of *To Catch a Thief* in October 1954. Hartman asked that the opening scenes between Lepic and Robie be redubbed into English. He also thought that the level of Bertani's offscreen lines needed to be raised, and that his speech "Foussard's daughter will take you by boat" needed to be redubbed. Regarding the Carlton Hotel lobby scene, he indicated: "Re-write and re-shoot the insert of the threatening note." For the scene at the Silvas' villa, he asked that "a close shot of the man wielding the monkey wrench" be shot, using a "good photographic double for [the character] 'Claude.' "

The new threatening note to Robie now completely eliminated any reference to the dubious weather reports, reading: "Robie, you've already used 8 of your 9 lives. Don't gamble your last one." In addition, some minor dialogue changes were made in Robie's opening scene with Bertani. Grant received $6,250 for two days of retakes with a double for Bertani. A studio memorandum suggests playwright Alec Coppel was responsible for the new threatening note and dialogue since Hayes was busy getting his script for *The Bar Sinister* ready to go into production at MGM. Coppel received $1,250 for a week's work from November 12 through November 18.

Hitchcock also decided to change the main title background

shot. The original had been a shot of an open jewel case filled with an expensive array of women's jewelry, glistening in a moonlit hotel room in Nice. The shot concluded with a pair of black-gloved hands entering the frame and silently removing the case's contents. The new background shot was an exterior of a New York travel agency window. At the end of the title sequence the camera dollies in to a travel advertisement with the caption "If you love life, you'll love France." The retakes and new main title were shot on December 1 and 2.

For their anniversary, Alfred and Alma Hitchcock returned to Europe, spending Christmas in St. Moritz. Post-production continued in January 1955, with the Hitchcocks stopping in Paris, where additional dubbing of the French actors' voices was being completed. John Williams also spent a day dubbing lines in New York on January 18. Well rested after his holiday, Hitchcock returned to Paramount, where composer Lyn Murray was busy writing the score. Murray had been recommended to Hitchcock by producer William Perlberg after he scored *The Bridges at Toko-Ri*. Before leaving for Europe in December, Hitchcock gave Murray three pages of single-spaced notes indicating precise directions for music and sound, and the effect each of these elements should achieve. Murray recorded the score in early February. The finished score is bright and whimsical, with just the necessary hint of menace in key places to thrill the audience.

On February 24 Geoffrey Shurlock, who had succeeded Joe Breen as director of the PCA, issued the administration's certificate of approval for *To Catch a Thief*, "with the understanding that in all prints . . . the love scene between Cary Grant and Grace Kelly, in Miss Kelly's hotel room . . . will be terminated by a dissolve before the couple lean back toward the corner of the sofa." Hitchcock did not alter a frame of the sequence, which had been scored with a tenor saxophone played in a "very sensuous manner." Instead, Hitchcock had Murray tone down the music, putting more emphasis on comedy and less on sex, which appeased the censors. By the time the film had been submitted to obtain a code seal, the PCA's power had begun to diminish, and many points Joe Breen had cautioned against in the screenplays were left intact in the completed film.

The Hollywood Reporter's reaction to the preview screening in July commended the director for the variety of his output, but complained "when one experiments constantly, one is bound to have some mistakes and failures and in the opening third of this film in my opinion, [Hitchcock] makes more boo-boos than he has made in his entire career." The film was also criticized for being poorly dubbed. Both criticisms were attributable to Hitchcock's decision to keep Charles Vanel in the role of Bertani.

The Release

To Catch a Thief premiered at the Paramount Theater in New York on August 4, 1955. The film delighted audiences, but reviews were mixed. Bosley Crowther of The New York Times said, "In his accustomed manner, Mr. Hitchcock had gone at this job with an omnivorous eye for catchy details and a dandy John Michael Hayes script . . . To Catch a Thief does nothing but give out a good, exciting time. If you'll settle for that at a movie, you should give it your custom right now." Other reviews were less enthusiastic. Nevertheless, To Catch a Thief was a box-office smash and earned Hayes recognition from the Writers' Guild, which nominated his script for best comedy. The film also received Academy Award nominations for color cinematography, art direction, and costume design. For his cinematography, Robert Burks won the Academy Award.

By the end of production on To Catch a Thief, Hitchcock had completed three films in less than eighteen months and was well into pre-production on a fourth. His commercial slump had ended with Dial M for Murder and Rear Window. It seemed the lighter approach toward his material, as well as the fresh characterizations of Hayes, struck a chord with audiences and affected the director in turn. He would continue in this commercial vein but would slowly introduce darker, more personal themes into the foreground of his films.

Embarking on his third Hitchcock film, and contracted to Paramount for another two, Hayes graduated to the "A" list of writers. After *To Catch a Thief*, Hayes was no longer working on a week-to-week basis but now had guaranteed status. The success was garnering Hayes much attention within the industry, and his services were sought by some of Hollywood's most successful producers. Attention within the industry was fine; Hitchcock could maintain that his mentorship, and the association with his name, had boosted Hayes's credentials. But when Hayes began getting attention from the press, thus taking away some of the spotlight that usually shone on Hitchcock alone, the writer's days were numbered.

4 / An Expensive Self-Indulgence

In the short time he had worked closely with Alfred Hitchcock, John Michael Hayes had moved several rungs up the screenwriting ladder. Although the relationship was one of two professionals who mutually respected each other, Hayes admits that at times the dynamic was that of mentor and protégé: the older, experienced master and his young charge. Other writers who worked with Hitchcock had the same feeling. Ernest Lehman, who wrote *North by Northwest* as well as the director's last film, *Family Plot*, likened his early relationship with Hitchcock to "sitting at the feet of the master." Hitchcock preferred it this way, which is why he seldom worked with anyone who was on a par with him in stature or reputation.* Nevertheless, Hitchcock taught Hayes how to think cinematically and economically. The writer recalled:

When we were in the office working on the script, Hitch visualized being on the stage and faced with the problem of blocking every scene. He thought about every shot in advance, so he wouldn't have to sit on the stage and waste everybody's time thinking about what to do. When we fin-

*This is also the reason why Hitchcock's films were frequently adapted from lesser-known novels and plays. Hitchcock learned a valuable lesson from his first Hollywood production, *Rebecca*, which was billed as "David O. Selznick's production of Daphne du Maurier's celebrated novel . . . directed by Alfred Hitchcock." Thenceforth, whatever the source material, Hitchcock would make it his own. After all, it was "Alfred Hitchcock's *Rear Window*," not "Alfred Hitchcock's film of Cornell Woolrich's classic suspense story . . ."

ished a setup and he said, "Cut—print! Let's move on," everybody sprung into action. The grips, the set decorator, and everyone knew what the next shot was going to be. He would turn his back and light a cigar, and we'd talk about politics or baseball, and he knew what they were setting up from the next scene in the script and the sketch. He didn't shoot coverage the way other directors did. Some directors who are going to use nine thousand feet in a film, shoot a *hundred* and nine thousand feet of film. Hitch would shoot, say, fifteen or sixteen thousand feet, and you could put all the leftover film in a small box. He was a delight on the set.

But Hayes also remembered on occasion that Hitchcock could display a possessive streak, as though after he granted someone the privilege of working with him, Hitchcock expected that person to set aside all personal desires and be available to respond to every whim and fancy.

Hitch would frequently invite me to his house for dinner, and I did go up to his house in Santa Cruz, but he never invited my wife. And it was always dinner with movie talk. Hitch did not want the table conversation to veer from Hitchcock and his movies. Work was all-absorbing in his life. There wasn't much else besides food, drink, and work. I always felt that he didn't have parties because unless he was the center of attention, he didn't like it. In fact, I started turning down invitations to go to dinner at his house without my wife.

Any lack of warmth or congeniality Hayes felt from Hitchcock was certainly not due to anything the writer had done, nor was the director's behavior in any way unusual. It was just Hitchcock's way. David Selznick, Hitchcock's former employer, once remarked, "He's . . . not exactly a man to go camping with." In any case, Hitchcock was pleased with Hayes's work, and in the spring of 1954, while preparing *To Catch a Thief*, he had given Hayes a short novel by an English writer named Jack Trevor Story. The novel appealed to Hitchcock's English humor and appreciation for understatement. When he told Hayes that he wished to set the tale against the autumn colors of New England, this decision appealed to the writer's native sensibilities and his own appreciation for small-town eccentricity. The novel they both responded to was *The Trouble with Harry*.

The Novel

Jack Trevor Story's first novel was published in England in 1949. The novel concerns a small boy, Abie Rogers, and several adults who happen upon a dead man named Harry Worp in the woods near a tiny English village called Sparrowswick Heath. A retired seaman, Captain Wiles, believes himself responsible for Harry's death and wishes to dispose of the corpse. In the process, Captain Wiles befriends a local spinster, Miss Graveley, and a modern artist, Sam Marlow.

Miss Graveley has surprisingly little reaction when she sees Captain Wiles dragging a dead man by the ankles and invites him for afternoon tea. Other villagers pass through the woods and take even less notice of Harry. These include Mark Douglas, the landlord and local womanizer; Mrs. D'Arcy, with whom he is having an affair; Dr. Greenbow, the local surgeon and entomologist; and the spouses of the first pair, Cassy Douglas and Walter D'Arcy. The only others to come across Harry and take any notice are a wandering tramp, who steals Harry's shoes and socks, and later a cigarette from the corpse, and Abie's mother, Jennifer, who is delighted by Harry's earthly departure.

In the center of the village is Wiggs's Emporium, where the proprietress, Mrs. Wiggs, stocks groceries and, among other items, the paintings of Sam Marlow. Sam and Mrs. Wiggs spruce up Miss Graveley for her date with Captain Wiles, and later, Sam calls on Jennifer to find out what she thinks should be done about Harry.

Sam learns that Jennifer is the dead man's widow—and that Harry is a nuisance best forgotten.

Captain Wiles and Miss Graveley get to know each other over tea at the latter's cottage, while Sam and Jennifer, too, become quickly smitten. Together, the four try to decide what should be done with Harry. Each, with the exception of Sam, has reason to believe he or she killed Harry, and the body is buried and disinterred over and over again, as the responsibility shifts from one to another. When it is established by Dr. Greenbow that Harry died of heart failure, he is returned to the spot where he died in order to be found again, but not before his death helps to bring about several romances.

A reader in Paramount's story department passed on the novel when it was submitted to the studio in 1950, stating, "This is an engagingly uninhibited little story, in a highly amusing style. The humor is too fragile and whimsical and the story too fanciful for transportation to the screen. Although the characters are presented as real people, they belong to a slightly fey world, and the plot itself is much too tenuous for a screen comedy. Not recommended."

"To my taste," Hitchcock told François Truffaut, "the humor is quite rich." It was characteristic of him to reveal very little when discussing his reasons for making a film—as though concealing what attracted him to a given subject meant protecting the secret of his art. Nevertheless, Hitchcock had been delighted by Story's novel when he first read it in 1950 and thought enough of it four years later to instruct his agents to purchase the movie rights, which they did without divulging his name. This was standard practice for Hitchcock, so that he could avoid paying a high fee for literary material whenever possible. Unaware of Hitchcock's interest, the rights were sold for $11,000, out of which Story claimed he received only $500. Hitchcock, in turn, charged $78,000 to the production for the story rights. In truth, Story's short novel reads rather like a detailed film treatment, and his pithy dialogue and aural descriptions are evidence of his radio background.

Hitchcock first announced his plans to film *The Trouble with*

Harry while in New York in May 1954 en route to Cannes. To the press he revealed, "It's the story of a body found by a 4-year-old boy and what happens to it thereafter. It's set in England but I hope to shoot it in New England late this fall." Although Paramount had little faith in its commercial potential, the studio approved a $1 million budget in the hope that the commercial appeal of *Rear Window* and *To Catch a Thief* would help the new film as well.

Hitchcock initially planned to cast Cary Grant in *The Trouble with Harry*, but was frustrated by the deal the actor had worked out for *To Catch a Thief*. On that film Hitchcock saw his share of the profits only after Grant's percentage of the gross had been deducted. According to Hayes, "Hitch said, 'I'm not going to make another picture with him [Grant] and give him all this money up front and a percentage of the gross and ownership of the negative.'" Although Grant's name would have added to the marquee value of *The Trouble with Harry*, Hitchcock remained confident that, with his own name and a modest budget, he could make a success out of a small picture.

"It was a relief from the pressures of trying to make a big box-office success," remembered Hayes. "We were just trying to make a good picture and enjoy it. I don't think Paramount really wanted to make it because they didn't see much future in it commercially. But Hitch had done so well with them, they couldn't quarrel with him." Even if Paramount had doubts about the story material, the Hitchcock name brought prestige even to the most unconventional projects, and the possibilities of a film set against the autumn colors of New England aroused the studio's eagerness to exploit the VistaVision process.

By this time, Hayes's future at Paramount seemed pretty bright. *Rear Window* and *To Catch a Thief* had each been single-movie contracts. However, after starting *To Catch a Thief*, the studio had signed Hayes to three more pictures—*The Trouble with Harry*, *The Captain's Table*, and another Hitchcock production. In a June 8 memo from John Mock, head of the story department at Paramount, to studio attorney Sidney Justin, it was noted that a fourth film would be added to Hayes's contract. The writer's salary for the fourth production would be $1,500 per week, with a fifteen-week guarantee, extending his contract to thirty-two months for the four pictures. Although this meant Hayes was still far from receiving top dollar, his salary had nonetheless doubled—and *Rear Window* still hadn't been released.

The Screenplay

John Michael Hayes had officially gone on the payroll of Story Fund #89042, *The Trouble with Harry*, on June 14, 1954, while staying at the Carlton Hotel in Cannes for the location filming of *To Catch a Thief*. The screenplay he began to write remained very close to the original material. "It was rather faithful to the novel. I added touches of my own, but still wanted to deepen it somewhat," said Hayes. "But Hitch was always taken with that story and its simplicity, and feared that if we started tampering with it, we'd lose what was there."

Hayes's first draft, or yellow script, is dated July 12, 1954, with pages added through July 15. The script is 157 pages in length, with 245 shots—less than half the number of shots in the scripts for both *Rear Window* and *To Catch a Thief*. Almost religiously faithful to Story's novel, even in its dialogue, Hayes's first draft of *The Trouble with Harry* nonetheless includes several significant changes. While much of the first draft survives in the finished film, at least one major aspect of the story would be changed and one subplot involving four characters would be completely excised.

Hayes set his script against "the autumn foliage in State Line, New Hampshire," once the writer's hometown. An episode from the middle of the novel begins the action, as Walter D'Arcy bicycles across a meadow toward the home of Cassy Douglas, who is sitting on her porch shucking peas. Walter delivers a letter, which reads:

Dear Madam,
At the top of the wooded path at Farrington's pond stands a large oak tree, sometimes known as "the shot gun oak," for

reasons best left undiscussed. If you will be in the aforesaid place at dusk tonight you may hear something to your advantage.

Yours faithfully,
A friend.*

Both in the novel and in Hayes's first draft, the spouses of Walter D'Arcy and Cassy Douglas are having an affair. Walter, who at times is seen spying on his wife with binoculars, convinces Cassy to meet him at the Shot Gun Oak in order to catch their cheating spouses—Mark Douglas, the local womanizer, and Mrs. Walter D'Arcy, a trashy blonde. Story concludes this subplot by having the couples discover each other in the woods. On seeing his wife with another man, Mark Douglas runs home weeping, with Cassy following triumphantly. Reunited, the D'Arcys embrace and face the promise of a renewed marriage. In his treatment of the subplot, Hayes is a little less kind to the first cheating pair. "They deserve each other," says Walter D'Arcy. "They certainly do," replies Cassy Douglas. When Mrs. D'Arcy asks her husband what he intends to do, the script notes: "For an answer, Walter D'Arcy suddenly describes a brief arc in the air with his hand, ending with a resounding smack on Mrs. Douglas's pleasant but neglected derriere." And the two walk away, arm in arm, to teach their spouses a lesson.

Walter D'Arcy's letter makes for an intriguing opening, which Hayes follows by picking up where the novel begins, as four-year-old Arnie Rogers, changed from Abie, is seen "crawling on his stomach, Commando style," with a disintegrator ray gun held in his hands. A series of aural details follow in the script—the "loud roar of an exploding firearm" heard three times, "human exclamations and grunts of feminine indignation," and the sound of "wood hitting wood"—each breaking the silence and meant to be quickly forgotten by the audience.

As in the novel, young Arnie finds the body of a man in a patch

---

*Farrington was the name of Hayes's maternal stepgrandfather, with whom his family had lived in State Line, New Hampshire, during the early 1930s.

of trampled grass and hurries home. Captain Wiles is then introduced, polishing his shotgun following a morning of hunting. Feeling if he hasn't shot at least two rabbits he will return home empty-handed, Captain Wiles notes, "Blessed are they who expect nothing, for they shall not be disappointed." Hayes borrows the invented beatitude from his early play *Delaney and Sons*. After striding through the woods in the hopes of finding his kill, Captain Wiles also finds the body of Harry Worp and believes he must have shot him. Sticking closely to Story's novel, Hayes includes an insert (Scene 43) showing that "from every tree there seems to be suspended a hangman's noose waiting for the neck of Captain Albert Wiles." Hitchcock, however, wanted to remain understated in his treatment of the material and so expressive details like this would be dropped later.

Scene after scene in the first draft unfolds as they did in the novel. As Captain Wiles tries to dispose of Harry, he meets Miss Gravely—spelled "Graveley" in the novel—who invites him to her cottage for coffee and blueberry muffins. The parade of passersby continues, as Captain Wiles is prevented from moving away with the corpse, first by little Arnie returning with his mother, Jennifer; then by Dr. Greenbow, chasing butterflies; by a tramp who steals Harry's shoes; and, finally, by the libidinous Mark Douglas, walking with the trashy blonde, Mrs. D'Arcy.

As Story does in the novel, Hayes introduces the artist Sam Marlow as he is loudly singing on his way through the countryside to Wiggs's Emporium. The proprietress, Mrs. Wiggs, is a polite, insignificant widow, again as in the novel. In later drafts, Hayes would inject a bit of the bluntness from his Stella McCaffery character.

Upon meeting Jennifer, Sam says, "You're wonderful. You're beautiful. You're the most wonderful, beautiful thing I've ever seen." Here Hayes adds a moment between Sam and Arnie. Sam trades some baby possums he found for a dead rabbit that Arnie found. Arnie then asks to borrow the rabbit and leaves to make some more trades, wisely adding, "You never know when a dead rabbit might come in handy."

In Story's chapter "The Truth About Harry," Jennifer tells Sam all about the death of her lover, Robert, and how his brother, Harry, proposed to her when he discovered she was pregnant with Robert's child. On their wedding night, Harry placed a picture of his brother over their bed and told Jennifer to pretend she was making love to Robert. In Hayes's first draft, Jennifer explains that Harry put on his brother's clothes and told her to pretend he was Robert, at which point she left him. Harry's recent appearance was born out of loneliness. "He even offered to dress and act like himself, but it was too late," Jennifer explains, and so she hit him on the head with a milk bottle before he left.

In a scene between Captain Wiles and Miss Gravely, Hayes added the now familiar Hitchcockian black humor during a meal. When Captain Wiles compliments Miss Gravely's blueberry muffins, she tells him the berries were picked "where you shot that unfortunate man." Eager to change the subject, Captain Wiles admires the coffee cup Miss Gravely just purchased for him at Wiggs's Emporium. Miss Gravely says the cup had been in her family for years and was her father's before he died, adding, "He was caught in a threshing machine."

Captain Wiles and Sam bury Harry, dig him up, and rebury him as the responsibility for his demise shifts from character to character, finally ending up with Miss Gravely, who confesses that she struck Harry with her hiking shoe when he confused her for Jennifer and "demanded his rights" as a husband. These comic adventures all lead up to Hayes's most significant departure from the novel, which occurs when Sam sells his paintings to a millionaire. In the novel Sam receives £200 for his paintings, and the scene occurs offscreen. Hayes's Sam barters with the millionaire, obtaining gifts for his new friends. For himself he asks for only a bugle with the same tone as the horn on the millionaire's car.

As in the novel, Sam proposes to Jennifer, leading back to the complications the situation with Harry has created. Jennifer will have to prove she is not married, and so the quartet proceeds once more to the burial spot to dig up Harry. Once again Dr. Greenbow stumbles upon the body, angered this time because his butterflies get away from him. The doctor examines Harry, determining he had a heart seizure. The following morning Harry is laid out in the woods—to be found again by Arnie as the newly paired couples move down the woodland path.

Hitchcock and Hayes were once more bringing together characters that had somehow isolated themselves from the rest of the world. In *Rear Window*, L. B. Jefferies avoids intimacy by traveling the globe and keeping his camera lens between himself and his subjects. In *To Catch a Thief*, John Robie lives a quiet life at his villa with his housekeeper and cat. The characters in *The Trouble with Harry* also find themselves for one reason or another living alone. Where *Rear Window* and *To Catch a Thief* hinge on crime for their MacGuffins, *The Trouble with Harry* is perhaps the purest treatment of Hitchcock's romantic vision.

The straightforwardness of the plot and characters is like that of a fairy tale. Lacking the suspense elements that distinguish the majority of the director's works, *The Trouble with Harry* offers a tale of death and rebirth as natural occurrences. It is a pastoral comedy, rooted in the Greek and Roman traditions. Indeed, at one point in Story's novel, the tramp is heard by the main characters "mumbling something from Virgil"—a likely reference to the poet's *Bucolics* or *Eclogues*. Despite what the director has stated, the emphasis is not on the aspect of deadpan comedy but rather on the previously mentioned inevitability of death and rebirth as well as the sexual awakening and reawakening of its repressed characters.

Hayes and Hitchcock were still filming *To Catch a Thief* when they completed the first draft, so they discussed their work between setups and during lunches on the set. "He never went into the commissary," remembered Hayes. "After the script was done, he wanted me in the office every day for conferences and to have lunch with him." The script was frank in its discussion of sex and death, which is exactly what the director wanted, but it was still clouded by an element which interfered with the main theme. Hitchcock and Hayes quickly began revising the script, completely eliminating the subplot of the adulterous Douglases and D'Arcys. The scenes between the two pairs were richly drawn by Hayes, flavored with a charm and attention to eccentric detail not found in Story's novel, but were out of place among the other characters. Also cut was a scene at Sam Marlow's barnhouse studio among Sam, Jennifer, and Arnie, and the scenes at Wiggs's Emporium were tightened. The result was a 134-page preliminary green script dated July 27, which was submitted to the Production Code Administration on August 3, with the request that the script be evaluated as quickly as possible due to the September starting date for shooting.

Joe Breen responded to Luigi Luraschi's query on August 5, giving the PCA's general approval but noting that the illegitimacy of Arnie would need to be eliminated. Breen also called attention to specific lines of dialogue he found objectionable:

Page 51: The line "Do you realize you'll be the first man to cross her threshold?" together with the Captain's reproof and his subsequent line "You have to open preserves someday" all seem to contain an offensive sex suggestive implication. It should be either omitted or changed.

Pages 63 and 64: All this discussion about Jennifer's wedding night is totally unacceptable.

Pre-production

Hayes went to work revising the script while Hitchcock's production unit began making arrangements for the location production, which was set to begin in a little more than one month. Weather Services, Inc., of Boston, Massachusetts, issued to Paramount Pictures their autumn 1954 forecast for the New England area, predicting that for September "rainfall will be close to twice the normal" and that for October there would be "markedly improved conditions, starting near the beginning of the month." Hitchcock would try to schedule the location production to coincide with the improved weather.

By mid-August, Herbert Coleman, now Hitchcock's associate producer, and Doc Erickson departed to scout locations in New Hampshire and Vermont. On their arrival in New York, Erickson recalled:

We were on our way to scout locations in Vermont, and Frank Loesser, whom Herbie knew from past work in Hollywood, on musicals and so on, said, "Go see *The Pajama Game*, I'll see that you get into the house seats." Herbie and I both were at that matinee performance of *The Pajama Game*, and we were so taken with this girl, she was sensational. We thought we were watching Carol Haney—we didn't know any better. So at intermission when I opened the program, out fell this little notice saying, "Today's performance is by Shirley MacLaine, due to Carol Haney's inability to be here." Actually, she was just ill that day. She had broken her ankle earlier on, that's how Shirley had been in the play before and how Hal Wallis found her. So we ran out of the theater and went immediately to the phone to call Hitch, to tell him this is the girl we thought would be absolutely perfect for *The Trouble with Harry*. Well, of course, then he got into the act with Herman Citron and discovered they had test footage there at Paramount. The next morning when we called to inquire more about it, Hitch in his droll way put us down like "Where've you been? I've seen the footage. You fellows are late." But he was good-natured about that.

From New York, Coleman and Erickson traveled north and visited Wolfeboro, Bretton Woods, and Peterborough in New Hampshire, as well as Chittenden and Stowe in Vermont, where a short drive away they discovered the perfect settings for the film in Craftsbury Common, East Craftsbury, and Morrisville.

For the lead role Hitchcock selected John Forsythe to play the artist Sam Marlow. The actor was appearing in John Patrick's

Broadway hit *Teahouse of the August Moon* at the time, but he secured an eight-week leave so that he could make the film. For Captain Wiles nobody seemed more perfectly suited than Edmund
Gwenn, who is best remembered for his portrayal of Santa Claus in
Miracle on 34th Street and who had previously appeared in Hitchcock's *The Skin Game, Waltzes from Vienna,* and *Foreign Correspondent.* The wonderful character actresses Mildred Natwick and
Mildred Dunnock would round out the cast as Miss Gravely and
Wiggy.

Rewriting

Hitchcock and Hayes continued revising the "green" script, which
in the Hitchcock Collection is heavily marked and annotated, introducing a new character to the story. The personality of Deputy
Sheriff Calvin Wiggs can be traced to two characters who are mentioned in the novel but never actually appear. The first is Mr.
Grayson, an angry parent whose son was nearly shot by Captain
Wiles, and the second is Henry Wiggs, Wiggy's late husband, who
was the town's game warden.

Calvin Wiggs also had other possible origins. In *The Hitchcock
Romance*, Lesley Brill wrote of Calvin: "His first name, indeed,
might playfully allude to the gloomy theology of his famous Protes-
tant forebear." However, Hayes's text states: "Beyond [Mrs. Wiggs],
next to the Emporium, we see a gas pump, and a small lean-to
garage, with the usual garage items stacked around for sale. The
garage is run by her son, Calvin Wiggs—Calvin Coolidge Wiggs."

Calvin Coolidge, the thirtieth president of the United States,
was governor of Massachusetts when Hayes was a boy. Coolidge was
a popular president in spite of a reputation for being rather glum
and unsmiling. He had a laconic wit, common sense, and frugality,
all of which were admired as examples of sturdy New England
virtues. During his term, Coolidge was criticized for being ineffective in his handling of an oil-lease scam that became known as the
Teapot Dome scandal. The glum, unsmiling New Englander and

ineffective legal authority sounds rather like Deputy Sheriff Calvin Wiggs. As a boy, Hayes was a voracious reader who very likely followed the former president's syndicated series of articles on current events printed in 1930 and 1931.

Calvin Wiggs is the only character Hitchcock and Hayes added to the story. Calvin is unlike the other characters, possessing a suspicious and unfriendly nature, and like so many police figures in Hitchcock's films, he is completely inept. In addition to establishing a contrast, Calvin Wiggs gave voice to the puritanism that is only hinted at in the novel. Story describes an episode that ultimately cost Henry Wiggs his life, when the local womanizer, Mark Douglas, came into the shop and asked whether they carried "a certain commodity" (condoms). When Wiggs emphatically replied in the negative, Douglas suggested that he could guarantee a steady sale of the commodity if he would keep a small supply in a discreet corner of the shop. Incensed by the remark, Wiggs proceeded to chase Douglas through the countryside with his double-barreled shotgun. The experience strained the shop owner's heart, but Story concludes that "right to the end his shop retained a Catholic purity of stock."

On Saturday, September 4, Alfred Hitchcock boarded the 8:00 P.M. Santa Fe Super Chief at Los Angeles's Union Station, bound for Chicago, with a connection to New York. He had just wrapped principal photography for To Catch a Thief that afternoon. When he arrived at New York's St. Regis Hotel, the director met the twenty-year-old Shirley MacLaine for the first time; he later said of her inexperience before the cameras, "I shall have fewer bad knots to untie." The following Wednesday John Michael Hayes also flew from Los Angeles to New York, where he stayed a few days before journeying with Hitchcock up to Stowe on September 10. On their arrival the filmmakers set up base camp at the Lodge at Smugglers' Notch, located at the foot of Mount Mansfield, Vermont's highest elevation.

Together, Hitchcock and Hayes added their finishing touches to the July 27 script, which was completed on September 14. To appease the PCA, it had to be stated that Jennifer and Robert had been married before he was killed so that the question of Arnie's illegitimacy was no longer an issue. The first draft also remained close to the novel in Jennifer's retelling of her wedding night with Harry. In both instances Harry wanted Jennifer to pretend that he was Robert while he made love to her. But in the final draft Harry never shows up to consummate his marriage, having read a disagreeable horoscope in the hotel lobby.

In the novel, after stealing Harry's shoes, the tramp comes upon Harry on a second occasion and swipes a cigarette that Sam had put in his mouth. The tramp never returns in the first and revised drafts, but in the final script he is arrested by Calvin Wiggs when he is found with Harry's shoes. The tramp's description of the corpse matches the portrait of Harry drawn by Sam and causes Calvin to become suspicious. This adds for some hilarious moments as the quartet try to conceal the corpse from the baffled deputy sheriff.

In changing the character of Dr. Greenbow from the butterfly-chasing entomologist to a nearsighted poetry enthusiast, Hayes drew upon his love of reading from his boyhood in State Line, New Hampshire. In the final draft, Dr. Greenbow walks about the woods so engrossed in a book of poetry that he takes no notice of the corpse when he stumbles over it twice in broad daylight. The third and final time Dr. Greenbow comes upon Harry, it is nighttime and the doctor is reciting Shakespeare's 116th sonnet:

> Let me not to the marriage of true minds
> Admit impediments. Love is not love
> Which alters when it alteration finds,
> Or bends with the remover to remove:
> O, no! it is an ever-fixed mark,
> That looks on tempests and is never shaken;
> It is the star to every wandering bark,
> Whose worth 's unknown, although his height be taken.
> Love 's not Time's fool, though rosy lips and cheeks
> Within his bending sickle's compass come;

Love alters not with his brief hours and weeks,
But bears it out even to the edge of doom.
If this be error, and upon me prov'd,
I never writ, nor no man ever lov'd.

"It's my favorite sonnet from Shakespeare," recalled Hayes. "I had to put something in. I don't think the audience understood what it was all about, but it went with the theme. We had Shirley MacLaine and John Forsythe, and there were all sorts of things that prevented them from getting together. It was apropos that these two unlikely people end up getting together. They met and got to know each other under the strangest of circumstances, but they were destined to be a couple. Nobody got it in the audience, but I got it and I amused myself."

Hayes also added one of the film's most memorable lines. After Jennifer accepts his proposal of marriage, Sam kisses her. She warns him, "Lightly, Sam. I have a very short fuse." Hayes thought the line appropriate to the scene and character but never anticipated that it would bring about a huge reaction from the audience. "It rocked the theater," remembered Hayes, "and I looked up in total surprise. I had no idea. It was a fairly common expression. I didn't mean it the way it came out. I meant that she was very emotional. I didn't mean that she was climactic, but that's the way the audience roared with it, and I was genuinely surprised."

In the first draft, when bartering with the millionaire for his paintings, Sam asks for a bugle. At another point in the revisions, Sam asks for a $10,000 life-insurance policy, with Arnie as the beneficiary, adding, while looking at Captain Wiles, that he should "make the policy pay double if I'm accidentally shot." By the final script, Hayes had seized upon the idea of having Sam whisper what he wants for himself and then reserving the punch line for the film's tag, when it is revealed that he wants a double bed for Jennifer and himself. Also added to the final script was Sam Marlow's introductory song, "Flaggin' the Train to Tuscaloosa," composed by Raymond Scott, with lyrics by Mack David. Scott, a conductor for

NBC-TV's *Lucky Strike Hit Parade*, originally composed his tune as a jingle for the tobacco company.

The Location Shoot

Hayes incorporated the revisions to the final shooting script, the first ninety-seven pages of which were typed on September 20, the day principal photography on Production #10332, *The Trouble with Harry*, began in Craftsbury Common. The company, including John Forsythe, Mildred Natwick, and Mildred Dunnock, was scheduled for a 6:00 A.M. call that morning to begin shooting the Wiggs's Emporium scenes. Sam Marlow's abstract paintings were created by artist John Ferren, whom Hitchcock later engaged to design the nightmare sequence in *Vertigo*.

On September 22 the company moved to Morrisville for the Rogers cottage and porch scenes between Forsythe, MacLaine, and, as Arnie, young Jerry Mathers, who later starred in the title role of TV's *Leave It to Beaver*. While the company was busy shooting, Hayes continued churning out the final pages of script at the Lodge. The writer recalled:

> We stayed in the Lodge at Smuggler's Notch, and they had some great chefs from Switzerland and very sophisticated cuisine. It was a lovely inn, and must have been very popular, because they had unusual things on the menu like calves' brains and steak tartar, and elaborate European desserts which were pretty and chocolaty and fattening—things that you don't find on the average New England menu.

According to Doc Erickson, "Only the elite stayed there. Hitch's favorite few. They had a wonderful wine cellar, good food, and we had a great time."

As the final pages were completed, they were mimeographed and sent back to the studio for final typing, which, with revisions,

was completed by October 13. The final script was then forwarded
to the PCA and promptly approved without further objection from
Joe Breen.

Hitchcock intended to shoot the entire film in Vermont. The
main exteriors were to be shot in Craftsbury Common and East
Craftsbury, with a few scenes shot at Cabot and Greenwood Pond.
For the interiors, a makeshift sound stage had been created out of
the American Legion Barracks in Morrisville, which doubled as the
local high school gymnasium. The second unit took scenic shots at
locations throughout the state.

The area got a true glimpse of Hollywood moviemaking, as inhabitants of the surrounding towns were recruited to assist in the
production. Many Vermonters found themselves performing such
tasks as driving trucks, buses, and cabs to haul both equipment and
members of the company to and from the sets. Others were hired as
painters and carpenters or assigned clerical duties. A young Morrisville boy was even commandeered to catch a frog to be used in
the scene where Sam exchanges a frog with Arnie for the dead rabbit. Before long, the company was overcome by other eager boys
with frogs of their own. Several townspeople also got the chance to
pose before the camera and lights as stand-ins for the actors while
scenes were being set up for filming.

One afternoon, while the company was shooting, Hayes stayed
behind at the Lodge, where he was working on revisions. Alma
Hitchcock remained there as well and asked, "Would you like to
have lunch with me today?"

"I'd be delighted," said Hayes.

The two went to the restaurant at the Lodge, and Mrs. Hitchcock ordered calves' brains. "They looked like something from the
Harvard Museum, on a plate," recalled Hayes. "She's talking, and
we got along fine. Alma was a lovely person, and she began cutting
down. 'Squeak, squeak, squeak,' went the knife as it cut through the
brains." Hayes tried as best he could to avert his eyes.

"You know, I'm glad I'm having lunch with you," Alma told the
writer. "Because if Hitch were here, he'd be absolutely revolted."

Hayes, who could no longer control himself, finally turned away and looked out the window.

"Oh dear. You, too?" asked Alma.

Hayes apologized, "I'm sorry, it's just something that I can't get used to."

"Well, I'll hurry up, and eat it fast."

During the first few days of production, the company was forced to dodge the autumn showers and retreat to the cover set at the Legion Barracks, but it soon was clear they would not be able to complete the exterior scenes on location as planned. The continuous showers were stripping the trees of their colorful leaves. Much time was lost when they prepared to shoot exteriors, only to be forced indoors. Even scenes shot inside the Legion Barracks suffered from raindrops hammering on the tin roof. In some scenes rain can be heard in the background on the soundtrack.

Then, as if the weather problems were not enough, on the morning of October 12, while the company was filming in the Legion Barracks, a support arm mounting an 850-pound VistaVision camera to a crane broke and sent the camera crashing to the floor. The camera grazed the director's shoulder and pinned crew member Mike Seminerio to the floor. Fortunately, there were no serious injuries, and shooting resumed after the broken equipment was replaced with duplicates from the second unit.

Disenchanted by the inclement weather, Hitchcock decided to abandon the Vermont location. Morrisville's local weekly, *News & Citizen*, reported on October 14 that "Hollywood's experiment with making an entire motion picture in Vermont ended Thursday as director-producer Alfred Hitchcock and his cast leave for their home studios after bucking Vermont's unpredictable weather for more than a month." Hitchcock reportedly sent scouts to Virginia in search of a suitable location to complete the picture. Failing to find a satisfactory substitute, the company retreated to the more comfortable and controllable surroundings of the studio sound stage, but not before collecting an ample supply of Vermont maple leaves with which to create "fill-in" trees for the remaining scenes.

The Comfort of the Studio

Production resumed on October 18 on Stages 12 and 14 at Paramount. The cast and crew quickly made up the lost time, and principal photography closed on October 27. From a cast relatively unfamiliar to moviegoers, Hitchcock had gotten some wonderfully offbeat performances. Hayes remembered Hitchcock being especially taken by Shirley MacLaine's freshness. "When she came down on the set and read her lines, Hitch said to me, 'I'm not going to tamper with this girl. She has such an odd quality and it's delightful. I start giving her directions, and we're going to lose it.'" Of her experience working with Hitchcock, MacLaine recalled, "I remember the first script reading we had. Something came to me, like the mystery of acting does, and I just kind of invented this little part. And Hitch said to me, 'My darling, you have the guts of a bank robber.'"

John Michael Hayes remembered that Hitchcock had a theory that after two pictures he would have gotten all he could out of a writer, and so, as a rule, he frequently collaborated with a different writer on each new project. There may be some validity to Hitchcock's theory, in that after two projects a writer may have gotten to know the director's methods so well that any spontaneity of collaboration is no longer possible. With the exception of Alma, Hitchcock broke his rule with only three writers—Eliot Stannard during his silent period, Charles Bennett while at Gaumont-British, and John Michael Hayes at Paramount.

Stannard, Bennett, and Hayes were the only three screenwriters to work on more than two consecutive screenplays that Hitchcock actually filmed. More than a decade would pass between Ernest Lehman's screenplays for *North by Northwest* and *Family Plot*, as well as Samuel Taylor's screenplays for *Vertigo* and *Topaz*. Lehman and Taylor also worked on other projects for Hitchcock that never made it beyond the stage of pre-production. However, it is worth noting that Hitchcock also worked with Ben Hecht consecutively on *Spellbound* and *Notorious*, and Hecht also did some uncredited rewriting on *Lifeboat* and *The Paradine Case*.

Hitchcock and Hayes had now been working together for seven-teen months and, remarkably, had completed three films in that time, each very different from the one before. *Rear Window* was proving to be one of 1954's top box-office attractions, and their lat-est efforts had both been happy occasions. Throughout the writing of *The Trouble with Harry*, Hitchcock and Hayes had discussed nu-merous ideas and evaluated many literary properties that were sub-mitted to the director. One idea that Hitchcock had been toying with for a number of years was a chase across the faces of Mount Rushmore. Hayes recalled:

> In every spare moment we had kicked around ideas for something called *North by Northwest*. What Hitch really wanted to do was develop a story on which he could hang the Mount Rushmore scene and a few other unrelated ideas. That's not the way movies are normally created. He origi-nally wanted to start it at the United Nations and end in Alaska. I remember one idea involving an automobile pro-duction line that never made it into the completed picture. The hero would arrive to question a production foreman. As the scene would begin, the foreman would point out a frame coming on the line and talk for a minute about the wonders of the assembly line. Then the questioning would begin and the two men would start walking. In the background, we'd see this frame being built into a car. After a few minutes, the necessary dialogue would be finished. But before the scene ended, the foreman would point to this car that the audience has seen assembled from a frame. The hero would go over, admire it, open the back door and a corpse would fall out.

As many of his writers attested, Hitchcock was a genius at com-ing up with ideas for wonderfully original sequences that they somehow had to weave into the story logically. Hitchcock delighted reporters and exasperated his writers with situations such as this: "I once had an idea that I wanted to open a picture at the Covent Garden Opera, or the Metropolitan, or the Scala in Milan. And Maria Callas is on the stage singing an aria, and her head is tilted upwards and she sees in a box way at the back, a man approach the back of another man and stab him. And she's just in the middle of singing a high note, which now turns into a scream. And it's the highest note she's ever sung in her life. The result of which she gets a huge round of applause . . . I don't know the rest."

Before the writer and director could decide on their next project, Hayes had to go to MGM to do the final screenplay for *The Bar Sinister* and was scheduled to begin working for producer Sol Siegel on an adaptation of Richard Gordon's *The Captain's Table* for Paramount. Hitchcock, on the other hand, needed to turn his attention to supervising the post-production of *To Catch a Thief* and *The Trouble with Harry*. While Hitchcock's regular editor, George Tomasini, was busy with the former, veteran Paramount editor Alma Macrorie began assembling the film for *The Trouble with Harry*.

Shortly after completing production, Hitchcock received an unsigned letter dated November 3, 1954, from the author of *The Trouble with Harry*, Jack Trevor Story. In the letter Story expressed his feelings that although he was thrilled that his book was being filmed by a top-flight producer, he could not conceal his disappointment that the £100 he eventually received ended up going to creditors anyway. Unhappy with the deal his agent had worked out, Story wondered whether Hitchcock or Paramount would be able to increase his fee so that he could take his family to the premiere in some style.

A few weeks later, Hitchcock replied to Jack Trevor Story in a letter dated November 30, in which he wondered whether or not the unsigned letter had indeed come from Story. Unable to do anything about the deal that had already been made, Hitchcock indicated that he was still interested in seeing Story's sequel to *The Trouble with Harry*, which in a previous letter the author had said he would send to Hitchcock. The director closed his letter by telling Story that he would be in London around the Christmas holidays and that he would try contacting him then.

There is no indication as to whether or not Hitchcock ever contacted Story while in London or that Story ever submitted a *Harry*
sequel to Hitchcock. Many years later, in 1977, Story recalled his
experience with Hitchcock in the *London Sunday Telegraph*; he
stated that, even at that late date, Hitchcock's agents had approached him to sign over the renewal rights to *The Trouble with
Harry* in perpetuity and for no additional fee. "I have no intention
of maintaining Alfred Hitchcock in his old age," Story replied.

Hitchcock Scores Herrmann

In late November, while composing the score for *To Catch a Thief*,
Lyn Murray recommended to Hitchcock that Bernard Herrmann
compose the score for *The Trouble with Harry*. The composer and
director had met more than a decade earlier but had failed to come
together until this time, beginning what was perhaps the most significant composer-director collaboration in film. They would work
together for the next eleven years, until their relationship was severed over their collaboration on *Torn Curtain* in March 1966.* Because of its rural story and characters, *The Trouble with Harry*
lacked some of the visual panache for which Hitchcock was famous, and so depended on music to provide pacing and mood. Herrmann's score, composed in little over a month from December
1954 to January 1955, perfectly set the tone Hitchcock required. It
is both comic and warmly romantic, unlike the darker and bolder

---

*Pressured by Universal to commission a pop score for *Torn Curtain*, Hitchcock instructed Herrmann to compose a score that was not heavy-handed. But
Herrmann, who had customarily been given a free rein by Hitchcock, went
ahead and composed a score that he felt suited the film. When Hitchcock arrived at the recording session and listened to Herrmann's main title theme,
which included parts for sixteen French horns, twelve flutes, nine trombones,
two tubas, two sets of timpani, eight cellos, and eight basses, the director went
into a tirade and canceled the session on the spot. Without hearing the remaining cues that had been composed, Hitchcock removed Herrmann from
the project, and the two never spoke again.

musical statements Herrmann would provide for Hitchcock in films such as *The Wrong Man*, *Vertigo*, and *Psycho*.

Production reopened on December 2 and 3 for added scenes and retakes. Edmund Gwenn and Mildred Natwick were called in for a new scene in which Captain Wiles reveals to Miss Gravely that Sam asked the millionaire for a double bed. With the retakes and added scenes inserted, the picture was submitted to the PCA for its certificate of approval while Hitchcock left for a European vacation with Alma. On December 22, 1954, Geoffrey M. Shurlock issued the code seal to *The Trouble with Harry*.

For the film's opening, Hitchcock commissioned *New Yorker* cartoonist Saul Steinberg to create original drawings to be used as a background to the main title sequence. The drawings depict the autumn foliage of New England, finally coming to rest on the figure of a man, on his back, eyes closed—dead. The artist delivered his drawings in July 1955 and was paid the sum of $3,000.

The Release

The Trouble with Harry was premiered in Barre, Vermont, on September 30, 1955. In attendance were Hitchcock, Shirley MacLaine, and Governor Joseph Johnson. The film was very well received by Vermonters, who got to see some of their own back yard in the splendor of Technicolor and VistaVision. The film later opened at the Paris Theater in New York on October 17 to lukewarm reviews. Bosley Crowther complained, "It is not a particularly witty or clever script that John Michael Hayes has put together from a novel by Jack Trevor Story, nor does Mr. Hitchcock's direction make it spin. The pace is leisurely, almost sluggish, and the humor frequently is strained."

Penelope Houston wrote of the film in *Sight and Sound*: "Assimilating the black contours of the *comédie noire* into the gentler comedy of village eccentricity, Hitchcock and his scriptwriter, John Michael Hayes, have concocted an entertainment insidious in its charm." And she added, "The authentic gaiety that lightens this gallows humour comes somewhat unexpectedly from the latter-day Hitchcock . . . and John Michael Hayes's script, less coldly smart than his writing for *Rear Window* and *To Catch a Thief*, has an easy, sophisticated good-humour."

The mixed reaction to *The Trouble with Harry* was a great personal disappointment to Hitchcock. Although it had been enthusiastically received in England and France, it did not find a general American audience because the studio confined the film to first-run theaters in large cities. Hitchcock remained convinced that its disappointing performance at the box office was the result of Paramount's poor promotion and distribution of the film. "I'm afraid that the exhibitors, the people who run the cinemas, and those people who distribute films, my natural enemies, couldn't see it as an attraction for the public."

Years later, when asked if he had ever made a film without regard to any audience, Hitchcock replied, "Yes, I made one called *The Trouble with Harry*. It was a big loss. The film has lost, I suppose, about a half a million dollars. So that's an expensive self-indulgence."

5 / Into Thin Air

Alfred and Alma Hitchcock celebrated their twenty-eighth wedding anniversary and the Christmas holiday in 1954 with a trip to Europe that included visits to Paris, Frankfurt, and Zurich as well as their traditional stay at St. Moritz. Combining business with pleasure, the Hitchcocks also stopped at the London and Paris offices of Paramount, supervised the French dubbing of *To Catch a Thief*, and took a two-day excursion to Morocco, where the director found an exotic background against which he could set the opening of his next picture. The visit to Morocco and the stay at Claridges Hotel in London allowed Hitchcock to charge more than $7,000 of his expenses as a location survey for his next production, a remake of his 1934 success *The Man Who Knew Too Much*.

John Michael Hayes spent a more modest Christmas at his Encino, California, home with his wife, Mel; their three-year-old daughter, Rochelle; and his parents, who had come to live in California for two years. This was a happy time for the Hayeses, who were enjoying their success. *Rear Window* had been one of the year's biggest hits, and Hayes now had a multipicture contract with Paramount and found himself sought after by some of Hollywood's top producers. In November he began adapting *The Captain's Table* for Sol Siegel and expected to be back working with Hitchcock the following March.

Hitchcock and Hayes had discussed numerous properties while *To Catch a Thief* and *The Trouble with Harry* had been in production. Hayes recalled, "Hitch would say, 'Read this, and tell me what you think.' So I would tell him whether I thought it would make a good picture or not, or what I thought I could do with it, and he would take that under advisement."

Among the properties they had given serious consideration to was Ian Fleming's *Casino Royale*, Henry Cecil's *No Bail for the Judge*, Peter Fleming's *Brazilian Adventure*, Frank Owen's nonfiction telling of *The Eddie Chapman Story*, and an original idea for which Hitchcock envisioned a chase across the faces of Mount Rushmore. Hayes did not recall Hitchcock having mentioned a remake of *The Man Who Knew Too Much* as a possibility during any of their discussions.

The Original Film

Charles Bennett and D. B. Wyndham-Lewis wrote their original story in the spirit of H. C. McNeilie, better known as "Sapper" to fans of his adventure and spy stories. Bennett recalled, "British International owned the rights to a famous character in rather cheap British literature, Bulldog Drummond. And I was asked to write a story about him. So I wrote a story called 'Bulldog Drummond's Baby,' in which Bulldog Drummond's baby was kidnapped. And when Hitch left British International he took the whole thing to Gaumont-British, and it became *The Man Who Knew Too Much*."

In 1934 Hitchcock reunited with Michael Balcon, with whom he had earlier worked on silent films. Hitchcock pitched the story to his former employer, who was now head of production at Gaumont-British. Balcon was immediately interested and told the director to buy the rights from BIP. Hitchcock did, at a cost of £250, and shrewdly sold the rights to Balcon for £500. Leaving behind Sapper's Drummond character, the story was reworked to focus on an ordinary British family instead of a master spy. This of course became Hitchcock's stock-in-trade—taking ordinary people and putting them into extraordinary situations. The story by Bennett and Wyndham-Lewis was transformed into a screenplay over April and May 1934, with scenario credit going to Edwin Greenwood and

A. R. Rawlinson and with additional dialogue by the Welsh actor and playwright Emlyn Williams.

The plot of the 1934 film is well known. While vacationing in St. Moritz with their young daughter, Betty, Bob and Jill Lawrence befriend a French secret agent, Louis Bernard, who is assassinated. Before dying, Bernard reveals to the Lawrences that an assassination is to take place in London. To ensure the Lawrences' silence, Bernard's killers kidnap Betty and smuggle her from Switzerland to London.

The Lawrences return to London, and with only the slightest clue from Bernard's message and a telephone call traced to a seedy part of the city, Bob and his brother-in-law Clive strike out on their own to recover Betty. After confronting a dentist in collusion with the kidnappers, Bob and Clive stumble upon the anarchists' den, inside a seemingly legitimate chapel. Before long, the kidnappers hypnotize Clive and hold Bob at gunpoint. To fend off his captors, Bob begins throwing chairs, and a struggle ensues, during which Bob discovers a pair of tickets in the assassin's coat pocket, suggesting that the assassination will take place during a concert at the Royal Albert Hall. Bob manages to awaken Clive, who escapes and telephones Jill, who in turn rushes to the hall.

Abbott, the anarchist leader, plays a record for the marksman, Levine (changed to Ramon in the film), indicating the precise moment when his gunshot will be concealed by a crash of cymbals. Arriving at the Albert Hall, Jill is confronted by Levine, who tells her that her daughter's safety depends on her own silence. The concert begins and Jill wrestles over whether to remain silent and save her daughter or to cry out and save the diplomat. At the last moment, Jill screams, causing Levine to miss his mark.

Levine flees and is followed by the police to the hideout, where there is a shoot-out. When all the anarchists except Abbott and Levine are killed, Levine escapes to the roof, bringing Betty with him. A police marksman is reluctant to fire at Levine, fearing he might hit the child. Jill, who had earlier lost a shooting competition in St. Moritz, takes the rifle from the officer and coolly fires at

Levine, who falls from the roof. Inside, Abbott commits suicide, and Bob, Jill, and Betty are reunited.

Even before the Hitchcocks boarded the *Liberté* in Southampton for their return to New York, the director's production office at Paramount was busy making initial preparations for what promised to be a large-scale production—a remake of Hitchcock's own earlier film. By the time Hitchcock returned to Hollywood late in January 1955, a breakdown of the 1934 shooting script had been completed. The "one-line breakdown" of the original script, dated January 12, divided the picture into its key sequences, noting in a very broad sense location, character, action, and timing.

Remakes and Old Friends

"Hitchcock Plans Remake of Thriller," reported *The New York Times* on January 23. A. H. Weiler revealed that James Stewart would star in a remake of *The Man Who Knew Too Much* for Paramount and that "John Michael Hayes, responsible for the script of *Rear Window*, and Angus MacPhail, an editor on the original film, will do the adaptation." Since Hayes would be unavailable until early March and Hitchcock planned to commence production by the end of April, he engaged his old friend and associate Angus MacPhail to outline the scenario for the remake. MacPhail had been present during story conferences for the 1934 version while he was chief story editor at Gaumont-British and had worked with Hitchcock in a similar fashion, outlining a treatment for *Spellbound* before Ben Hecht wrote the screenplay. The Scottish writer, credited with originating the term "MacGuffin," was also responsible for the scenario of *Bon Voyage*, one of two short French films directed by Hitchcock in 1944 for the Ministry of Information.

The hiring of MacPhail was an act of kindness on Hitchcock's part. Nearly two years prior, MacPhail had initiated a correspondence with Hitchcock from the South of France, where the writer found himself ill and without means to pay his expensive hotel and restaurant bills or his return passage to England. But Hitchcock and

Alma were in Canada for the opening of *I Confess* when MacPhail's letters arrived in California. When he hadn't heard back from Hitchcock after several tries, MacPhail sent an urgent cable, which Alma received when she returned home. Alma contacted her husband, and in a matter of days, Hitchcock had come to MacPhail's rescue.

Later in 1953, a group of MacPhail's closest friends from the Ealing Studios in Britain, including writer-directors Frank Launder and Basil Dearden and producer Monja Danischewsky, sent a letter to friends and colleagues of the writer appealing on his behalf for anonymous donations so that he could be given a monthly allowance during his hard time. Hitchcock always had a fondness for MacPhail, whose last screen credits had been Ealing's *Whiskey Galore* and *Train of Events*, released in 1948 and 1949. When Hitchcock saw MacPhail in London during his 1954 trip, he decided a job would do more for the writer's esteem than a handout.

John Mock, head of the story department at Paramount, dispatched a memo to the legal department on January 24, 1955, requesting a starting notice for MacPhail, effective Thursday, January 20, "to work on a treatment of the Hitchcock untitled property" at a salary of $750 per week with an eight-week guarantee, pro rata thereafter, plus round-trip from London. MacPhail, who when hired was not yet a member of the Writers' Guild, resided at the Westwood Manor Hotel on Wilshire Boulevard while in Hollywood.

Constructing the Plot

Almost immediately, Hitchcock and MacPhail reviewed the original screenplay to see where it could be updated and how they could better adapt it to the stars of the new production. More than a decade earlier, David Selznick had urged Hitchcock to remake *The Man Who Knew Too Much*, but plans never went beyond preliminary story discussions. By the mid-1950s, however, Hitchcock was sufficiently confident that a remake would not be a "run for cover," but that he instead could genuinely do something more with the story. Hitchcock already had James Stewart in mind for Bob and was eager to secure Doris Day for Jill when story conferences began. MacPhail's overall function was to serve as a springboard for Hitchcock to bounce ideas at while waiting for Hayes to start on the script in early March. However, as MacPhail's notes reveal, he contributed both to the structure and several key episodes that made it into the finished film. The remainder of those notes are fascinating footnotes to Hitchcock's working method, as well as to a version of *The Man Who Knew Too Much* that might have been.

The earliest notes, dated January 31, reveal that MacPhail and Hitchcock were working closely with the 1934 script, still using character names from the original. The first set of notes was largely concerned with the Lawrences' search for the kidnappers' London hideout and established that the Lawrences were American and had a son, unlike in the original. For use in the scene involving Bob's capture at the chapel, MacPhail suggested that Philip pass an object to his father that he can later use to free himself from his bonds. "A routine setup of course," wrote MacPhail, "but it might be redeemed if the object passed to Lawrence by the boy is some absurdly ingenious kid's toy."

Even at this stage, the mechanics of the film's final moments were established. MacPhail wrote that Abbott and his accomplices abandon the chapel for the embassy after their hideout is discovered. The ambassador becomes extremely irritated when he learns that the assassination has failed and that "the gallant intended victim is going to keep his date as the guest of honour at the embassy party when the concert is over." Backstage at the Albert Hall, Bob and Jill learn that Scotland Yard cannot intervene at the embassy due to extraterritoriality but that a blind eye would be turned if the couple acted on their own. Jill gets herself invited to the embassy reception by the would-be victim, where she—a professional singer—sings in order to attract her son's attention. This device was inspired by the well-known legend of King Richard I (Richard the Lionheart), who on his return from the Crusades was captured and imprisoned by Leopold of Austria. Richard's troubadour, Blondel de Neale, went about singing his friend's favorite song outside every castle until he heard Richard chiming in with the second verse, revealing his whereabouts. Like Richard, Philip sings a response to his mother. MacPhail commented, however, "Very unnatural to me that the kid should not be gagged. How inefficient can these Commies be?"

Holding story conferences daily, Hitchcock and MacPhail plotted the opening sequences, which had been relocated to Marrakesh. Notes dated February 1 sketched in the bus ride of the vacationing Lawrences. When the bus jolts on the bumpy road, eight-year-old Philip grabs at an Arab woman's *yashmak* (veil) and hell breaks loose. A Frenchman, Louis Bernard, comes to the rescue, and the grateful Lawrences invite him to dine in their suite. Over cocktails, Louis stands alone on the balcony, listening as Jill sings Philip's favorite song before bedtime—setting up the payoff for the finale. A gunshot is heard, and Louis calmly moves back indoors. Passing the noise off as the backfire from a car, Louis says, "They dope the gasoline around here with coconut oil."

The notes from February 2 again adhered closely to the original film, detailing the substitution of Jill for Clive in the dentist's office and chapel sequences, although Hitchcock and MacPhail omitted the use of hypnosis that was featured in the original. In the 1934 film Bob discovers a concert ticket in the assassin's coat pocket during a struggle. MacPhail wrote: "The manner in which Bob gets the clue about the Albert Hall is monstrous. We'll try and think up something a little less corny."

By February 7, Hitchcock and MacPhail had completed a three-page, single-spaced "skeleton," outlining the story and beginning with the Lawrences on a bus bound for Marrakesh. Bob, an architect in this early draft, is described as "quick-tempered, impulsive, emotional." Jill, a professional singer, "trusts her hunches and her impulses." The Lawrences are determined that their eight-year-old son, Philip, will not be spoiled—so of course he is. On arriving at the hotel in Marrakesh, the Lawrences become acquainted with the

Reverend Hugh Abbott and his wife, Agnes, "a delightful English couple." In the 1934 version Abbott is accompanied by a fake nurse named Agnes, who later turns out to be the hypnotist in the chapel. This is the first mention of the Abbotts being a couple; Hayes would later develop them into a complex pair of characters when he wrote his screenplay.

The events of the evening followed the previous days' notes, with the Lawrences entertaining Louis in their suite, Jill singing Philip's favorite song, and Louis excusing himself after a gunshot is fired at the balcony. In this version the Lawrences depart for a sightseeing expedition with the Abbotts the following morning, which climaxes tragically in the death of Louis. While being questioned by the French police, Bob gets a mysterious telephone call telling him that Philip has been kidnapped.

With the clue of Louis's dying words—which had not yet been determined by the filmmakers—the Lawrences arrive in London to recover their boy and are greeted at the hotel by Gibson of the Foreign Office, who reveals that Louis was an agent of the Deuxième Bureau. The Lawrences refuse to divulge what Louis told them and set off for a chapel in Notting Hill. Arriving at the chapel, Jill joins in a hymn to "draw Bob's attention to Mrs. Abbott at the organ," as well as to Mr. Abbott in the pulpit. On seeing the Lawrences, Abbott feigns an asthma attack and sends the congregation home. A struggle ensues, during which Bob gets a clue about the Albert Hall and Jill manages to escape. Following the marksman Levine's musical instruction for the assassination, the criminals depart for the embassy. MacPhail indicates that Jill's arrival at the Albert Hall should be cross-cut with Bob making his escape from the chapel and the Abbotts arriving with Philip at the Russian embassy. The events from the Albert Hall sequence onward remained as previously outlined.

Having established the basic structure, Hitchcock and MacPhail tossed about ideas reminiscent of the gags and twists that made the director's British thrillers famous. The Scotsman's humor is also revealed in his notes. Suggesting a hymn they could use for the chapel scene, MacPhail wrote: "I will sing it to you, if not forcibly prevented." The idea was now for the Lawrences to misinterpret the dying words of Louis, which would continue to change until the final script was written. In MacPhail's notes of February 8, Louis's dying words are "London, Contact Champion Barman Urgent. Service. Choral. Sunday. Premiere."

The words "Contact Champion Barman" set the Lawrences on a frantic search through a series of pubs with the name Champion, which leads them to a bizarre funeral procession leaving the Champion pub in Notting Hill. The Lawrences learn from the pub owner that the deceased was the best bartender he ever had, and that if he were alive he would be reading Scripture in the little chapel that afternoon. Bob and Jill proceed to the chapel, where they determine through Louis's dying words and the word "festival" in a hymn that the assassination will occur in the Festival Hall. Jill leaves Bob behind in the chapel and hurries directly to the concert hall. Still trying to capitalize on the hypnosis angle, MacPhail wrote: "Bob, I will now reveal to you, is a psychiatrist in good standing. He hypnotizes his captor and makes his getaway."

MacPhail continued brainstorming, suggesting in his February 9 notes that the revelation of Abbott as a cleric might be delayed by introducing the Abbotts in the hotel swimming pool with Philip. When the Abbotts and Lawrences meet the next day for sightseeing, Abbott would then be wearing his collar. MacPhail also suggested that Bob's captor in the chapel be a former heavyweight prizefighter, whom Bob hypnotizes into believing he is Joe Louis engaged in a battle for the World Heavyweight Championship. Bob is then able to escape while his captor boxes an imaginary opponent.

Also introduced in the notes of February 9 is the first indication that Mrs. Abbott could be a sympathetic character, when she is discovered by her husband knotting the sheets that Philip uses to escape. Abbott stabs his wife, who is later discovered by Jill. Mrs. Abbott's dying words are "I told him to run as fast as he could across the park to the American Embassy." At this point MacPhail suggested that following Louis's death, Bob, a surgeon in this version of the outline, should comment that the knife was incompetently handled and that the "victim should never have lived to speak," so that in the final clash between Bob and Abbott their struggle over a knife is especially dramatic. Bob gets the upper hand, causing Abbott to say, "Go ahead. Finish me off. But you'll hang for murder." Bob replies, "Even the greatest of surgeons sometimes slip up on a difficult operation. And I'm a very average surgeon." Bob uses the knife on Abbott, and death is instantaneous.

By February 12 Hitchcock and MacPhail had completed a revised skeleton four pages in length, incorporating many of the changes in construction as well as more character detail. For instance, Louis Bernard asks the Lawrences many questions about their background, to Jill's annoyance. The outline indicates: "Jill's feminine intuition tells her that Louis is not the simple charming boy he seems." It also reveals that Jill gave up a career on the stage when she married.

The death of Louis was also described in detail for the first time. Hitchcock told François Truffaut that the murder of Louis was based on part of an idea he had long hoped to realize.

The idea was to show a ship from India sailing into the London docks, with a crew that was three-fourths Indian. One of the sailors was being chased by the police and he'd managed to get on a bus that was going to St. Paul's Cathedral on Sunday morning. He gets up into what's called the Whispering Gallery. The police are up there and he runs to one side while the police run around the other way. Then, just as they nearly catch up with him, he jumps over and falls in front of the altar. The service is interrupted as the congregation rises and the choir stops its singing. Everyone rushes over to the fallen man's body, and when they turn it over, they discover a knife in his back. Then someone touches his face and the black comes off, showing white streaks. It turns out he wasn't a real Indian.

In the outline, the sequence begins with an Arab man pursued by the police. After putting the police off his trail, the Arab leans against a white wall, but "The shadow of a knife looms. It strikes." The Arab continues on with the knife in his back until he comes upon the Lawrences and the Abbotts, in front of whom he collapses. "The Arab's dark hue streaks with sweat and blood. Bob wipes the dying man's face. It is Louis."

The outline concludes with the events leading up to the finale at the embassy, where Jill is asked to sing. Jill sings the lullaby she sang for Philip, whose voice is heard chiming in faintly from upstairs. Jill continues singing to divert attention from Bob's movements as he follows Philip's voice.

Returning to Louis Bernard's dying words, MacPhail suggested in his notes of February 15 that one of the words uttered is "sorter." But Bob dismisses the word insignificantly as "sorta." Later, Gibson asks Bob if Louis mentioned a contact at Mount Pleasant. When Gibson departs, Bob and Jill learn from a hotel waiter that Mount Pleasant is the main London post office—where the mail gets sorted. They depart for Mount Pleasant immediately. Posing as a correspondent from *The Washington Post*, Jill manages to get an official to show them the inner workings of the British Postal System's miniature railways. The mini-rail cars carry mail, but the last one contains the corpse of the mail sorter Louis was speaking of, Lajos Vassily.

Bob and Jill go to the dead man's flat in Notting Hill to search for clues. They meet Vassily's landlady, an eccentric breeder of Siamese cats, who is not surprised to learn of her lodger's demise. "Queer sex, that was the trouble with him," she says. As the Lawrences disentangle themselves from the cats that are leaping onto their shoulders, they question the landlady further and discover she means "one of those queer religious sects." She tells them that Vassily regularly attended services at a chapel on Portobello Road, for which they depart.

Almost daily, it seems, MacPhail concocted elaborate and wild devices to weave into the story, sometimes to the detriment of the previous day's work. Exactly how much of this material was the sole work of Angus MacPhail, or the combined work of MacPhail and Hitchcock, or the sole work of Hitchcock with MacPhail taking notes, is unknown. However, as many of these suggestions bear little resemblance to the finished film, it seems safe to say that most of the ideas rejected by Hitchcock were not those which he conceived himself.

On February 17 Hitchcock and MacPhail paused to analyze the background of the plot thus far, which MacPhail's notes reveal was derived from events in Communist-ruled Hungary, where the new premier, Imre Nagy, had adopted such liberal policies since taking office in 1953 that with the political climate in Moscow becoming more hardline, Nagy's removal seemed imminent. In fact, even before a treatment for *The Man Who Knew Too Much* was completed, Nagy was removed from office. Although the nationality of the prime minister is never mentioned in the final film, MacPhail suggested that the Russians intend to "put the Western Allies in the wrong" by arranging the assassination of the Hungarian prime minister while on an official visit to London. The Abbotts—Communist operatives in London—are instructed to meet an expert assassin from Morocco and smuggle him into England. But the Deuxième Bureau has gotten wind of the scheme and send their best agent, Louis Bernard, to identify the agents, who are only known to be traveling as a married couple. Louis initially suspects that the Lawrences may be the agents he is after, until he sees the Abbotts, who are apparently already on to him and arrange to have Louis killed in the marketplace.

In another set of notes, also dated February 17, MacPhail reconsidered Louis's dying words for the third time; they now read: "London . . . London . . . Barmaid Collins . . . Chapel Front . . . Rhapsody . . . Sunday . . . deadline . . . deadline." After meeting with Gibson, Jill is on the edge of a breakdown. Bob takes her to see a colleague of his in London, who extrapolates from Louis's dying words that they must contact the barmaid at the Collins Music Hall, where, the doctor explains, weekly music revues "of a sexy type" are held. Bob leaves Jill in the doctor's care and proceeds to the Collins Music Hall, where a revue called *We Couldn't Wear Less* is doing brisk business. Bob is unable to get the barmaid's attention until the crowd of factory workers flocks into the stage area, where a striptease is about to begin. The killer has followed Bob and now observes him questioning the barmaid, a retired French burlesque queen named Marie. After Bob learns the address of the chapel from Marie, he manages to evade the killer when the crowd charges back into the bar after the raunchy musical number has finished.

Still trying to work in the use of hypnosis, on February 21 MacPhail elaborated on a character named Dr. Craig, a wise and sympathetic former teacher of Bob's. In this version, following their meeting with Gibson, Jill is again close to a breakdown, and Bob brings her to see Dr. Craig, who uses hypnotherapy to help illuminate some of the clues embedded in Louis Bernard's dying words. Bob leaves Jill with Dr. Craig and is again followed by the killer.

The notes reveal that Hitchcock and MacPhail strove to devise a satisfactory sequence to replace the dentist's office episode from the original. After establishing that Bob would venture alone, Hitchcock required that there be a "continuous physical menace to Bob" throughout the sequence. MacPhail suggested that in order for there to be a continuous menace, Bob should be tailed by Louis's killer, and so the audience would have to get a glimpse of the killer back in Marrakesh. "I can't see any other practical means of achieving what you want here," wrote MacPhail, "perhaps J.M.H. will be able to think up a way of capitalizing on this weakness."

MacPhail's last set of notes before Hayes started on the project, dated February 24, described for the first time a sequence to be set in a taxidermist's workshop. And so Louis's dying words were changed yet again, and Bob interprets them as "London, London. Ambrose Chappell. Contact him." MacPhail wrote: "What he really means, poor fellow, as we discover later, is the chapel in Ambrose Street used by the enemy to communicate with subsidiary agents by means of a hymn which contains a code of instructions."

Bob discovers the name Ambrose Chappell in the telephone book while Dr. Craig treats Jill. In his notes MacPhail recalled, "There is, I believe, in Camden Town an establishment which is the last stronghold in Britain of taxidermy. They will stuff you anything from an elephant to a gnat. It was given a splash in a *Picture Post* or an *Illustrated* a couple of years ago."

Bob visits Ambrose Chappell, the taxidermist in Camden Town, whom MacPhail suggested could be played by Alastair Sim. MacPhail wrote that as Bob explains his predicament, "Ambrose unhappily gets an impression that Bob has murdered a Frenchman in Marrakesh and wants him stuffed." No doubt this typically British penchant for the macabre delighted Hitchcock. The taxidermist moves to telephone Scotland Yard, when Bob realizes he has been misunderstood. Chappell is sympathetic to Bob's story and tells him of the chapel on Ambrose Street. Bob rejoins Jill and Dr. Craig, and the Lawrences set out for Ambrose Chapel.

Pre-production and Location Scouting

While Hitchcock and MacPhail held story conferences, the director's production team prepared for the extensive location shooting which would have to commence in less than four months. In a letter dated January 31, 1955, associate producer Herbert Coleman referred to the project as "A Hitchcock Untitled" when he requested assistance from Richard Meland, an executive at Paramount's London office. Coleman needed to know whether it would be possible to film at night somewhere in the outskirts of London, where the principal foreground set would be a building from four to eight stories high with adjoining shops, and with the additional requirement that the background contain something that would immediately identify the location as London. Coleman added, "Hitch thought perhaps there would still be a partially bombed-out area that we could use as our basic requirement and put up our own small shops if they do not exist." Coleman asked Meland to have photographs taken of any locations he thought suited their purposes, and to send them to Hollywood along with an April–May schedule for the Royal Albert Hall, which they also hoped to use as a location.

Coleman's mention of putting up "our own small shops" indicates a restaging of the Sidney Street siege, which concluded the 1934 version of the film. However, by early February Hitchcock had already decided on the musical climax at the embassy over a shoot-out on a London street. That same day, Hitchcock dispatched a letter to Edward de Segonzac of the Paramount office in Paris regarding his plans to film in Marrakesh. Of primary importance to Hitchcock was when the Hotel de la Mamounia closed for the season and whether the hotel would be willing to stay open an extra few weeks to accommodate the cast and crew for the location shoot. Hitchcock's second question concerned filming in the Arab quarter of Marrakesh itself, where he hoped to be able to photograph the narrow streets and alleys and atmosphere of the marketplace. Hitchcock had found on his recent trip that some of the natives resented being photographed and wondered whether it would be feasible to hire extras while in Marrakesh. On February 5 Hitchcock received de Segonzac's report that the Hotel de la Mamounia closed for the season on May 16 and was already booked for the Easter holidays between April 7 and 12. Production would have to commence in mid-May.

The story rights to *The Man Who Knew Too Much* had been optioned by David Selznick in 1941, while the producer had Hitchcock under contract. Selznick then teamed Hitchcock with producer John Houseman, and together they attempted to relocate the story to Sun Valley, Idaho; moving to a South American location; and ending in New York, where the villains plan to assassinate the Brazilian president while attending a performance at the Metropolitan Opera. The Houseman-Hitchcock collaboration had never gotten beyond preliminary discussions, and so there had been some question as to whether the story rights were still held by Selznick or by the 1934 film's current American and British distributors, United Artists and Rank. Hitchcock was naturally anxious to purchase *all* the rights to his earlier film, not only for the purpose of securing the copyright to his new production but also to prevent anyone exhibiting the earlier film from capitalizing on the publicity garnered by the remake. Acting on Hitchcock's behalf was his friend and former Transatlantic Pictures partner, Sidney Bernstein, who cabled Hitchcock from London on February 10 with the information that Rank could not legally contract to sell all the rights to the 1934 film but that they could sell the story rights. Rank was also willing to turn over the negative and have all its prints of *The Man Who Knew Too Much* withdrawn from distribution. The story rights were eventually purchased for $45,000, after which Hitchcock, James Stewart, and Lew Wasserman set up a corporation for the production called Filwite, Inc.

Back with Hitch

On February 12 the Academy Award nominations for 1954 were announced live on NBC-TV. Hayes and his family watched as he and Hitchcock were each nominated for their work on *Rear Window*. Hayes's older sister, Ellen Walsh, who still lived in Worcester, recalled her parents telephoning from Hollywood with the happy news. "They were all pretty excited," Walsh told a correspondent from the *Worcester Telegram*, the local paper for which her brother had been a reporter. "Of course he won't get it, but it's pretty wonderful that he was nominated." She also revealed that Hayes would soon be on his way to Africa with Hitchcock and that he would also be writing scripts for a "39-week series of television dramas to be produced by Hitchcock, starting this Fall."

Hitchcock valued Hayes's talents, which developed significantly under his tutelage. Even at the earliest stage of negotiations for *Alfred Hitchcock Presents*, the director wanted Hayes to be involved in the creative aspects of the series. At roughly the same time—the end of February—Hayes had been taken off *The Captain's Table*, the major non-Hitchcock film he had contracted to write for Paramount, which allowed Hayes to continue his close collaboration with Hitchcock. "I was going to do the screenplay," Hayes recalled, "and Spencer Tracy was going to play the lead. But Sol Siegel left Paramount and moved over to Metro, and they just stopped the picture."

On February 23 John Mock sent a memo to the legal department assigning Hayes to Story Fund #89048:

> Will you kindly put through a closing notice for the above writer effective as of Saturday, February 26, 1955, which will be a total of thirteen and a half weeks out of fifteen-week guarantee for the work on THE CAPTAIN'S TABLE. Mr. Hayes will report to Mr. Alfred Hitchcock Monday, February 28, 1955 to do the screenplay on THE MAN WHO KNEW TOO MUCH . . . A guarantee of fifteen weeks at a salary of $1,150,00.

"Hayes on Hitchcock Pic," announced *The Hollywood Reporter*. The teaming of Hitchcock and Hayes, embarking on their fourth movie, now warranted headlines in the industry trades. When he reported to begin work on *The Man Who Knew Too Much*, Hayes recalled, "I never saw the original script and never saw the original picture, except for the Albert Hall sequence at the end, which was pretty much the same as it was in the original. Hitch called me in and said, 'What I'm going to do is tell you the story, and you take notes and write the story I tell you, your way.' So we talked about a lot of things. I picked out the best ideas I could and made a screenplay out of it."

Out of discussions between the writer and the director, Hayes had a pretty solid idea of the story and began fleshing out the characters. Very quickly he had decided to transform the female lead into a composite of Doris Day and another world-renowned American singer, Jo Stafford.

In the early 1950s Jo Stafford had reached the height of her popularity when she prepared more than four hundred broadcasts for Radio Luxembourg, which transmitted her voice to an international audience of more than 350 million people. Stafford had become so popular that she caused a huge sensation in England during her engagement at the London Palladium in 1952. Stafford could not fathom the intensity of the reception she received from the British audience. "I'd never heard a roar like that—I wasn't prepared for it. It really startled me. But when I realized it was approval, I felt a lot better!"

The Treatment

Throughout March, Hitchcock and Hayes quickly gave shape to the characters and outlined the story in a detailed treatment, which they began setting to paper on March 14. Once again, Hayes concentrated on character development over plot construction. The key conflict in the treatment is not the assassination plot or the kidnapping of the child but the troubled marriage of the principal characters, whose names had been changed to Ben and Jo McKenzie in early March (and to McKenna by the final shooting script in May). With the original plot by Bennett, the inventive ideas by MacPhail, and the warm characterizations by Hayes, The Man Who Knew Too Much was shaping up to be one of Hitchcock's masterworks.

The central conflict between Ben and Jo McKenzie was something Hayes alluded to in Rear Window and witnessed to a degree in his own family. Hayes's father had been forced to give up his career as a vaudeville performer, and it is this aspect that Hayes drew upon in developing the relationship of the principal characters. Rear Window and To Catch a Thief explored the fears associated with marriage and intimacy. The Man Who Knew Too Much would probe the effects of marriage on a woman subjugated by her husband. L. B. Jefferies and John Robie were bachelors whose self-imposed isolation is broken down through the course of the narrative. At the beginning of The Man Who Knew Too Much, Ben appears firmly planted in the patriarchal roles of husband, father, and doctor. But it is quickly revealed that each of these positions is threatened when his family is faced with a crisis. Jo's value as wife, mother, and career woman is taken for granted by Ben, and it is their interdependence that he needs to understand.

In developing the antagonists, renamed the Addisons, Hayes drew a parallel relationship to that of the McKenzies. In characterizing Mrs. Addison, Hayes sought to make her a sympathetic figure. She is ultimately dominated by her husband and is an unfulfilled mother. "The wife of the minister was sort of ambivalent," explained Hayes.

> She envied Doris Day and Jimmy Stewart and their family relationship. It made her more interesting as a villainess that she has feelings which begin to come out. She begins to like the boy and doesn't want anything to happen to him. She's seen happiness, and a nice family blown apart, and suddenly it's too much for her.

While the director and writer were busy at the studio, preparing the treatment, Herbert Coleman and Doc Erickson were arriving at the Savoy Hotel in London amid snow flurries to begin a location survey and to secure permission from the various trade unions and authorities abroad. In a matter of days, Coleman reported on the locations he and Erickson had surveyed thus far, including the Connaught Hotel, the Royal Albert Hall, the Foreign Office at 11 Downing Street, the airport, two taxidermy shops, a variety of chapels, and several buildings to be used as an embassy, each of which would be covered with photographs so that Hitchcock could make his selection and adjustments to the script as necessary.

Coleman had located two taxidermists operating in London and reported that the taxidermist mentioned in the *Illustrated London News* "was most cooperative," while the other was "most disagreeable, but finally agreed to allow us to photograph his work room next week." As for finding a suitable location for the chapel sequences, Coleman anticipated little difficulty in obtaining permission to use any of the churches he surveyed, but in consideration of the fact that the chapel was to be used as the kidnappers' hideout,

Coleman felt, "we probably should not disclose here at this time what takes place in the chapel."

In addition to securing permission to film inside the Royal Albert Hall and its lobby, Coleman had also attended concerts at the Festival Hall in order to advise Hitchcock on the selection of an orchestra and conductor to be used in the film. Between the Royal Philharmonia and the London Philharmonic Orchestra, Coleman preferred the latter, adding that he was also impressed by the Philharmonic's conductor, Basil Cameron, "a small white-haired, bushy eye-browed, dapper and extremely pleasant man. The audience brought him back for bow after bow." In the end, Hitchcock chose neither the Philharmonic nor the Philharmonia, instead engaging the London Symphony Orchestra. Finally, Coleman reported that the British motion-picture unions were being so cooperative that they even agreed to allow Doris Day to bring her own hairdresser from Hollywood.

Following a brief visit to the Paramount office in Paris, Coleman and Erickson proceeded to Marrakesh. In a handwritten letter on Hotel de la Mamounia stationery, Coleman reported on March 17 that the restaurant in which they dined on their first night in Marrakesh, which had been recommended by the hotel, was not worth mentioning, but that on the second night, they were taken to a place called Dar É Salam, which Coleman believed was exactly what Hitchcock had in mind.

In a fashion typical of the kind of pre-production work Hitchcock had come to rely on from his company, Coleman described everything in minute detail—from the route traveled to get to the restaurant, to its small tiled entry, to the beautifully domed mosaic dining room with its low couches that extended toward the center of the room, and to the low inlaid wooden tables in between. As for the actual dining experience, Coleman continued:

It went like this. The table has been covered with a plain white plastic table cloth. At each place there was a pottery bowl on a small pottery plate with a plaid napkin tucked into each bowl. A small glass and a plain tablespoon completed each setting . . . Soon a dark native waiter wearing a fez, long dark robe, white shirt and four-in-hand tie appeared with a silver kettle, basin and towel, and all washed.

Next a large white wicker basket with a high coned top, three feet high, was brought in and placed on the floor. The top removed, he took out a covered pottery bowl from which was served a soup, similar in appearance to pea soup, but not as good! It was ladled into our bowls with a wooden ladle. Having finished the soup, the bowls were placed in the wicker basket, covered and taken away.

The second basket appeared, and inside was a large pottery bowl with whole roast chickens, called Poulet en Citron. As we're about to dive into this, the owner's French wife, in modern dress, came over to greet us and to remind us we must tear the chicken only with the thumb and first two fingers of the right hand. Messy, but good. During the above, heavy white biscuits were served from a smaller basket, similar to the larger one . . . Finishing the chicken, the ritual of burying the remains in the big basket was repeated and taken away.

Coleman's description of the first two courses suggests a virtual dry run for the restaurant scene that takes place in the film, so that all Hayes needed to do was add the characters and dialogue.

With information gathered from the survey trip, Hitchcock and Hayes began making the necessary alterations and revisions to the treatment, along with Angus MacPhail, whom Hitchcock kept on salary. "Hitch had to have somebody to talk things over with and keep notes," remembered Hayes. "But it was left up to me to finally write it. Angus was a perfectly nice man. He was a friend of Hitchcock's from the 1920s, and Hitch wanted to give him credit because he said, 'He needs a credit. He needs the work.'"

But Hayes recalls MacPhail contributing very little during any of these discussions, a criticism which has often been attributed to

MacPhail's prolonged battle with alcoholism—which both Hayes and Herbert Coleman mentioned to biographer Donald Spoto. Screenwriter Diana Morgan, one of MacPhail's closest friends and collaborators during his days at Ealing, remembered: "Angus wasn't a very good writer, but he had great ideas. He drank an awful lot and that was his downfall." However, this is an oversimplification of MacPhail's problem. MacPhail suffered frequent bouts of neuralgia, which often rendered him unable to work and which may explain why, from the time Hayes came on board in late February until the first section of the treatment was submitted to the budget department in late March, MacPhail was mysteriously silent.*

Notes from a March 26 story discussion appear to be MacPhail's sole contribution following the prodigious amount of story notes he provided Hitchcock with in February. These notes detailed the events from the arrival of Ben and Jo in London through the finale, but again, a number of these ideas never found their way into the script. For example, MacPhail continued to try to work in the character Dr. Craig, Ben's old friend and former teacher. Concerned over his wife's mental health, Ben brings Jo to see Dr. Craig, and together the trio discuss the last of Louis Bernard's dying words, which were changed by MacPhail yet again to: "Try Aeneas Ryecroft." Ben finds a single listing in the telephone directory for a taxidermist named Aeneas Ryecroft and departs, leaving Jo in Dr. Craig's care.

By this time, all the ideas of Ben being followed by Louis's killer had been tossed out. In this version of the events, Ben simply fears that he is being followed by an elderly gentleman of "slightly sinister appearance" and manages to lose his alleged pursuer. Ben arrives at the workshop of Aeneas Ryecroft, who, it turns out, is the

---

*A year after working on *The Man Who Knew Too Much*, Hitchcock engaged MacPhail to do an adaptation of Laurens van der Post's novel *Flamingo Feather* at a weekly salary of $1,000. But MacPhail's neuralgia had become so severe that after fourteen and a half weeks all MacPhail had been able to accomplish was a three-page outline and fourteen pages of letters to Hitchcock and Herbert Coleman in which MacPhail occasionally mentions his poor progress due to his attacks.

man that Ben believed was following him. After a series of misunderstandings, Ben appeals to Ryecroft, whose colleagues assist Ben in locating a place called the Aeneas Ryecroft Hall.

Ben and Jo reunite and, while en route to the hall, recognize Mrs. Addison peering into a shop window. They confront Mrs. Addison, who acts as if she had never met Ben and Jo. Mrs. Addison quickly dodges the McKenzies by going into a pub through which she is able to enter the Aeneas Ryecroft Hall by means of a secret passage. Even MacPhail admitted, "My mind is poison against this incident, so cannot do it justice."

The chapel and Albert Hall sequences remain virtually unchanged in these notes, but the embassy sequence begins to take shape. Inside the embassy, it is the ambassador who determines that, since the assassination attempt failed, Hank must be gotten rid of. Noting that the "odor of burning flesh" would make the incinerator impractical, the ambassador contrives a plan in which the child "can be easily strangled" and stuffed into a diplomatic mail bag, which would not be subject to search by the authorities. Ben and Jo arrive at the embassy, and Jo is asked to sing. As she sings, Ben searches the embassy for Hank and is confronted by an embassy official "whom he is compelled to render unconscious." When another official arrives, Ben explains that he is the doctor who has been called to treat the first official. The final moments and the reunion of the McKenzies were still to be sorted out.

Even before finalizing the treatment, Hayes started scripting the opening sequences on March 25, while Hitchcock met with the art, costume, and music departments, which were busy preparing their contributions to the production. Hitchcock also began compiling extensive casting notes with suggestions for types. In early April, Herbert Coleman ordered more than a dozen prints for the director to view the work of actors who had been suggested for supporting roles. Hitchcock rarely tested actors, preferring instead to screen their work in private so he would not have to reject them face-to-face if he was not satisfied.

Doris Day remembered that the director exerted the same control over her wardrobe. "The first time I saw Hitchcock, I was with Edith Head, talking about my costumes."

> Hitchcock came in, wanting to see the sketches and discuss them . . . On that day he threw out some of the sketches and was very precise about exactly what he wanted for my wardrobe. Hitch's office on the Paramount lot was right next to Wardrobe so he'd often drop in during my fittings to keep an eye on just what they were creating for me.

A studio memorandum indicates that Paramount agreed to sell Doris Day all costumes created for her in the picture at 50 percent of cost.

Hitchcock feared that the story might be familiar to a large portion of the audience and hoped to counter that by showing off the exotic locales in Technicolor and VistaVision. Director of photography Robert Burks had just completed *The Vagabond King* for Michael Curtiz. The art director on that film was Henry Bumstead. "Hitch asked Bob Burks if there were any young, talented art directors that he would enjoy working with," recalled Bumstead, "so he chose me as the young art director."

> I met with Hitch, he liked me, and I was assigned to *The Man Who Knew Too Much*. Naturally I was surprised and thrilled that I was going to be working with Mr. Hitchcock. I had admired his work for many years, but in my wildest dreams I never expected I would ever work for him.

Bumstead became a happy addition to the Hitchcock troupe, and went on to do the production design for *Vertigo*, *Topaz*, and the director's final film, *Family Plot*. (Bumstead also worked on *No Bail for the Judge* with the director during much of 1959, but the film was never produced.)

The Academy Awards ceremony in 1955 was held on March 30 at the Pantages Theater, and Hayes attended with his wife, Mel.

Hayes remembered that neither Hitchcock nor Paramount took out ads in *Variety* for voters to consider *Rear Window* for any of its five nominations. Instead, the studio concentrated its campaign on the Perlberg-Seaton production of *The Country Girl*, for which Grace Kelly won as best actress and George Seaton won for his screen adaptation of Clifford Odets's play. Paramount also earned an Academy Award for technical achievement that year, for developing the production and exhibition process VistaVision.

Following the Academy Awards, changes to the story continued, as Hayes was not satisfied with the character of Dr. Craig (Ben's former instructor) and, along with Hitchcock, invented instead a group of Jo's theatrical colleagues, two of which were based on real people. Val Parnell was the managing director of the London Palladium and had been responsible for bringing to England such performers as Jo Stafford, Judy Garland, and Danny Kaye.* Described as "a carnival spieler in Savile Row finery," Parnell had come to epitomize the British theatrical manager, a man whose rough manner was still evident despite his elegant tailoring. Parnell's wife, Helen, had been a music-hall dancer, and so their addition to the script brought some authenticity to the British theatrical milieu. Hitchcock even obtained permission to use the Parnells' names in the film, as well as an anecdote told by Val involving British comedian Bud Flanagan.

The introduction of Jo's friends added a dimension to her character, stressed the value of her career, and provided much-needed comic relief after the harrowing scene of Ben telling a sedated Jo that their boy has been kidnapped. To play up the comedy at this point in the story, Hitchcock indicated in a series of handwritten notes how the scenes in the London hotel should be laid out. Jo

---

*In the treatment Hitchcock and Hayes proposed that one of the bouquets in the McKennas' suite be from Danny Kaye, should he be appearing at the Palladium at the time. Although in the finished film Danny Kaye didn't send flowers to Jo, there is a reference to him in the script. During the scene where Jo's friends are trying to figure out what the McKennas are up to, Val Parnell says, "It must be a new American gag, I'll ask Danny about it."

tells Ben he had better destroy the scrap of paper bearing Louis's dying words. Just as Ben burns the piece of paper in an ashtray, the Parnells and friends enter. "Even if Ben doesn't burn his fingers," Hitchcock writes, "at least the encounter from Val's point of view starts Ben behaving a little oddly."

Hitchcock then suggests that Ben has difficulty venturing out of the hotel room to keep his appointment with Ambrose Chappell without appearing rude. First Ben claims he does not have any English money, so he says, "I'll, er, just go downstairs and cash a traveler's check." Val produces a fat wallet and offers, "How much do you need, old boy? Name it." Thwarted, Ben asks for ten pounds. Hitchcock milks the situation for suspense, as Ben tries to come up with another excuse, finally saying he has to telephone a colleague and does not want to disturb anybody. Helen Parnell foils this by saying, "There's a phone in the bedroom, Mac." Ben goes into the bedroom and finally somehow makes his exit, unknown to the others. In the film these ideas were dropped and Ben simply makes an awkward exit, leaving Jo to entertain her guests.

Rather than Ben learning of the chapel from one of the workers in the taxidermist's shop, Hitchcock indicates that Jo arrives at the conclusion herself, continuing the theme of feminine intuition established in *Rear Window* and *To Catch a Thief*. Hitchcock accomplishes this by giving Helen Parnell a fancily tailored poodle and having Helen ask Jo whether she thinks his collar is becoming. Jo says, "His collar. I don't think it suits him somehow. It's not his character." The association with Addison as a minister suddenly clicks—she realizes Ambrose Chapel isn't a man, it's a place. Jo departs for the chapel, leaving the Parnells and company bewildered. "Ambrose Chapel," worries Val aloud. "You don't think he'd be an American theatrical agent, do you?" This too would be treated more simply in the final script and film.

By mid-April, Hitchcock still hadn't cast the supporting roles, nor had Hayes completed a first draft script; yet production was still scheduled to begin in Marrakesh on May 12. Hitchcock forged ahead, however, seeing to the all-important musical selections for

THEY MADE THE HEADLINES
by Phillips. '52.

In the 1950-51 season, Mr. Hayes had more suspense shows to his credit than any other writer for radio. Among the scripts Mr. Hayes authored were "Sam Spade," "Night Beat," "Suspense," "Richard Diamond" and many others.

When? Where? who did it? why? IDEAS?

Mr. Hayes now lives in Burbank, Calif., where he is a successful author of screen plays. He is a graduate of Worcester's High School of Commerce and the University of Massachusetts. At one time, Mr. Hayes was a Telegram reporter.

John Michael Hayes, author of 1500 radio dramas and many screen plays. Mr. Hayes was born in Worcester.

LEFT: A page from the March 29, 1953, *Worcester Telegram & Gazette*—John Michael Hayes's hometown paper. Reprinted with permission of the *Worcester Telegram & Gazette*

BELOW: Hayes (*left*) at a Massachusetts State College broadcasting studio, Amherst, Massachusetts, 1941. Photograph courtesy of John Michael Hayes

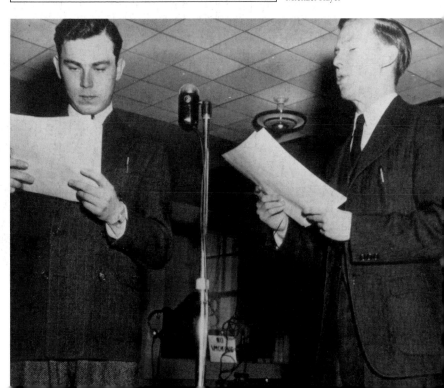

Hitchcock and Hayes on the set of *Rear Window* on Paramount's Stage 18, December 1953. Photograph courtesy of John Michael Hayes

John Michael Hayes, during the filming of *Rear Window*. Photograph courtesy of John Michael Hayes

LEFT: Anita Colby, "The Face": model, actress, beauty expert, ad executive. Hitchcock named Colby as one of the inspirations for the character Lisa Fremont in *Rear Window*. Movie Star News

BELOW: Hayes's wife, Mildred Louise Hicks. As a model she went by the name Mel Lawrence and was Hayes's own inspiration for the character Lisa Fremont in *Rear Window*. Photograph courtesy of John Michael Hayes

Grace Kelly in the casual attire worn by Lisa Fremont at the end of *Rear Window*.
Movie Star News

John Michael and Mel Hayes at their home in Burbank, California, April 1952. The Siamese cats Ting and Ling were a gift from James Mason and his wife. Photograph courtesy of John Michael Hayes

Grace Kelly signs a model cast for James Stewart. *Movie Star News*

Wendell Corey and James Stewart reading the script for *Rear Window* in their flight gear for a photograph of Doyle and Jeff that appears on the wall in Jeff's apartment, November 1953. Photograph courtesy of John Michael Hayes

ABOVE: Cary Grant and Hitchcock on the set of *To Catch a Thief*. Grant lent oil paintings from his personal art collection for the film. *Movie Star News*

OPPOSITE: Hitchcock, Hayes, and Grace Kelly in the stunning gold dress on the set of *To Catch a Thief*, August 1954. Photograph courtesy of John Michael Hayes

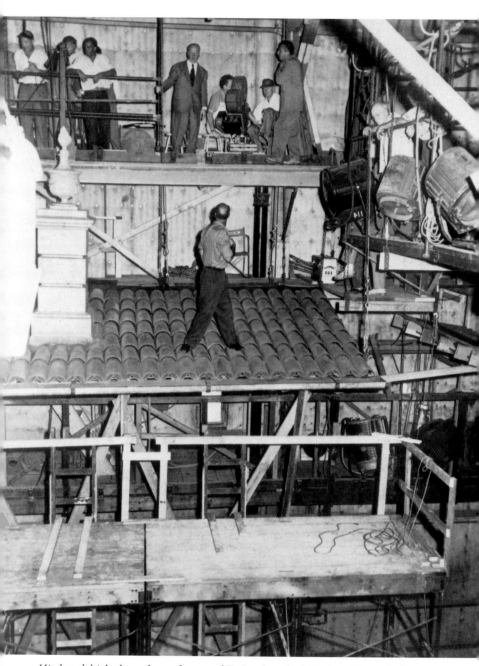

Hitchcock high above the rooftop set of *To Catch a Thief*. Hitchcock brought Hayes here just to see if the writer was as afraid of heights as he was himself. *Movie Star News*

Hitchcock, Grace Kelly, and Alma on the set of *To Catch a Thief*. This was Kelly's third and final film for Hitchcock. *Movie Star News*

Hitchcock celebrates his birthday with the company of *To Catch a Thief*, August 13, 1954. Moments earlier a secretary had invited everyone to "have a piece of Mr. Hitchcake's cock." *Movie Star News*

LEFT: John Michael and Mel Hayes holding the Edgar Allan Poe Award presented by the Mystery Writers of America for his screenplay of *Rear Window*, April 21, 1955.

Photograph courtesy of John Michael Hayes

BELOW: Hitchcock, Mildred Dunnock, and Hayes on location in Craftsbury Common, Vermont, for *The Trouble with Harry*, October 1954.

Photograph courtesy of John Michael Hayes

Mildred Dunnock and John Michael Hayes on location in Craftsbury Common, Vermont, for *The Trouble with Harry*, October 1954. Dunnock also appeared in Hayes's *Peyton Place* and *Butterfield* 8. Photograph courtesy of John Michael Hayes

Doris Day and Hitchcock going over the script for *The Man Who Knew Too Much*.
Early in the filming Day feared the director was unhappy with her performance,
since he offered little comment. *Movie Star News*

LEFT: James Stewart and Hitchcock on the set of *The Man Who Knew Too Much*. *Movie Star News*

BELOW: Art director Henry Bumstead, Doc Erickson, Hitchcock, and Herbert Coleman. Hitchcock inscribed the photo "You were saying Hank?" Photograph courtesy of Henry Bumstead

Flora Clarabella (Mrs. Marcello Mastroianni), Mastroianni, Carroll Baker, and Hayes at the Golden Globes ceremony, 1965. Photograph courtesy of John Michael Hayes

Hayes, Carroll Baker, and producer Joseph E. Levine. Baker appeared in three Hayes films: *But Not for Me*, *The Carpetbaggers*, and *Harlow*. Like Hayes's, Baker's career suffered under Levine. Photograph courtesy of John Michael Hayes

the film. Delighted with the score Bernard Herrmann had just
recorded for *The Trouble with Harry*, Hitchcock asked the composer
if he would like to write an original concert work to replace Arthur
Benjamin's "Storm Cloud Cantata" in the Albert Hall sequence. "I
didn't think anybody could better what Benjamin had done," Herrmann later said. The piece was a great showcase, and Herrmann
simply reorchestrated the cantata and expanded several sections.
Hitchcock then invited Herrmann to make an on-screen appearance conducting the London Symphony Orchestra and the Covent
Garden Chorus, which the director planned to film inside the Albert Hall.

To create Jo's songs for the picture, Hitchcock commissioned
the Paramount songwriting team of Jay Livingston and Ray Evans.
Livingston and Evans wrote two songs specifically for *The Man
Who Knew Too Much* — "We'll Love Again" and "Holy Gee." But
when they were asked if they could write something that fit the international flavor of the film, they played "Que Sera, Sera," which
they had already written after seeing Joseph L. Mankiewicz's *The
Barefoot Contessa*. Hitchcock selected "Que Sera, Sera" at once,
but because another song had already been titled "Che Sera, Sera,"
the Livingston-Evans title was changed to "Whatever Will Be." The
lyrics to all three tunes were approved by the Production Code Administration on April 18.

The First Signs of Trouble

The third week in April 1955 was cause for celebration for both Alfred Hitchcock and John Michael Hayes. On the morning of April 20 Hitchcock allowed himself a few hours away from the office
to become an American citizen. A brief celebration was held at the
Paramount studio after the ceremony at the Los Angeles County
Court. Over champagne and cake, the company congratulated
Hitchcock, who had at last officially embraced his adopted nation.
The other celebration was for an achievement both the writer and
the director could be proud of.

For his script for *Rear Window*, the Mystery Writers of America presented an Edgar Allan Poe Award to John Michael Hayes. The Southern California chapter of the MWA held its annual dinner and awards ceremony at Richlor's restaurant on April 21. Hayes and his wife, Mel, were in attendance, but Hitchcock declined an invitation to see the writer accept his award. As reported in the MWA newsletter: "Asked what it's like to work with Alfred Hitchcock, Hayes gave an amusing description of that complex character: gourmet, wine connoisseur, martinet, perfectionist, and amazing authority on such unexpected matters as the origin of waterfalls." According to one member who attended the event, "John Michael Hayes was so clever in his Edgar acceptance speech that he even managed to stifle envy in the assembled peons like yours truly."

Hayes later told Hitchcock biographer Donald Spoto that the following morning, when he brought the statuette to show Hitchcock, the director had ungraciously dismissed it and, by implication, Hayes's achievement by saying, "You know, they make toilet bowls from the same material." What may have been said in jest by Hitchcock appeared to Hayes to be an act of resentment and jealousy. Hitchcock, Hayes felt, was unable to muster up the generosity of spirit to acknowledge someone else's accomplishment. Shortly thereafter, Hayes was asked to write a piece for *The New York Times* about working with Hitchcock. The article, Hayes remembered, praised the director's methods and included a grateful acknowledgment of how much he had learned from Hitchcock. However, the article was never published, because according to Hayes, Hitchcock tore it up after Hayes showed him the manuscript, saying, "Young man, you are hired to write for me and Paramount, not for the *New York Times*."

The Screenplay

The revised treatment, dated April 22, was seventy pages in length and was a detailed visual representation of the finished film. With the story officially laid out and the characters and motivations decided upon, Hayes immediately set to work finalizing his first draft script while Hitchcock insisted that all matters regarding the roles of Scotland Yard and the Foreign Office be checked at the "highest level possible" for detail and accuracy. True to his reputation as "the fastest writer in Hollywood," Hayes turned in the first 165 pages of the first draft in three days' time.

Hayes's April 25 draft followed the construction of the treatment, but in terms of character and dialogue seemed far off the mark of Hitchcock's expectations. The McKenzies of the first draft are rougher around the edges than the McKennas that finally made it to the screen. Ben and Jo are more argumentative, although the cause of the tension between them does not surface immediately. Even their seven-year-old boy, Hank, is somewhat insolent. In the hotel suite in Marrakesh, Hank remarks to his mother about his dinner, "I thought I was gonna get Arabian food. This looks like something you'd cook." Jo retorts, "Just eat it and consider yourself lucky." Later, in response to Ben's suggestion that the baby-sitter might teach him the native language, Hank replies, "Oh boy. How do you say 'Drop dead' in Arabic?"

For the restaurant scene between the McKenzies and the Addisons, Hayes wrote the scene to contain two separate conversations between the men and women. Addison and Ben discuss their work, with Addison seeking free medical advice from Ben: "I have something of a weight problem . . . I can eat nothing for days and gain weight. What do you think I ought to do?" (Was Hayes getting back at the director for his derogatory comments?) Jo tells Mrs. Addison of the incident on the bus and the strange Frenchman they met that day. Hayes finally reveals the cause of the tension between the McKenzies when Mrs. Addison asks, "Don't you approve of the stage, Mr. Conway?" Ben corrects her, "*McKenzie.*"

Hayes uses the marketplace sequence to develop further the conflict between Ben and Jo. Excited about a new Broadway musical she's been offered, Jo exclaims, "The book is brilliant. Almost written for me!" Reminding Jo of her commitments at home, Ben asks, "Sign the contracts yet? Suppose the show's a hit? . . . Then one season will stretch into two and maybe a picture offer." Finally, Ben agrees to read the script, but he also makes Jo promise to stop encouraging Hank's interest in show business. "He has a good mind," Ben says, "give him a chance to develop it." Ben hopes Hank, too, will become a doctor.

Ben's attitude toward Jo's profession is rather like Jeff's dismissal of Lisa's fashion work in *Rear Window*. In that film, however, Lisa's profession was never really a central issue to be resolved—just a point of mild contention throughout. But once Ben begins to bend his position, Jo lightens the mood by promising, "For every time step he'll learn a new muscle—and for every chorus, three bones."

Following the scene in which Ben informs Jo of the kidnapping, Hayes includes a lengthy sequence between Ben and the concierge in Marrakesh. The concierge wants to telephone the police when Ben tells him the Addisons may have taken his boy. Ben stops the concierge, who is surprised by his attitude and says, "I never had a child, Monsieur, but if I had one and he was stolen, I'd find it hard to be indifferent as you seem to be." Together Ben and the concierge search the Addisons' room, but find nothing.

In general, Hayes's first draft suffers from being overwritten. The incomplete script is 165 pages in length and ends at Scene 286 (in the chapel before the Albert Hall sequence). Scene 286 in the final shooting script occurs forty-five pages earlier. The length of the complete final shooting script is 167 pages in total. In addition to being heavy on dialogue, the first draft is also weighed down with weak dialogue or, as Hitchcock's notes suggest, dialogue which is often "too much on the nose."

Hitchcock's Notes

There was no time for lengthy discussions about changes required in the script, so Hitchcock dictated his notes on Hayes's incomplete first draft on April 27. For nearly every page of incomplete script there is a corresponding notation—the notes are often very specific, indicating the need to change a single word, an entire speech, a description of action, or a camera direction. At other times, the notes are more general, indicating an alteration required for characterization or for scene length. These notes illustrate just how much control Hitchcock asserted, in addition to demonstrating that he did indeed, at least privately, express more interest in motivation, dialogue, and character than he cared to admit publicly.

For the opening sequence Hayes wrote that the Arab woman cries out loudly when her veil is pulled off by Hank. Of this sequence Hitchcock reminded Hayes that the emphasis on the woman's cry should be eliminated so that it is the outburst of her indignant husband that sends Hank backing away. To achieve this, Hitchcock directed Hayes to remove all references to the woman's cry and Hank's reaction to it, as well as having Hayes insert a medium shot of Hank and the woman in favor of a close shot of the woman alone, which was called for in the first draft.

For the scene in which Jo sings the lullaby to Hank in their hotel suite, Hitchcock suggested that Hayes insert "a whistling obbligato by Hank," which should be "paid off at the end of the picture." Also part of the hotel sequence is the moment when the assassin, who has now been given the name Rien, comes to the door of the McKenzies' suite. This moment was particularly important because the story required that Jo recognize Rien later when she sees him in the lobby of the Albert Hall. Hitchcock instructed Hayes that Ben and Jo should advance toward the door simultaneously, but that she should beat him to it. When Jo opens the door, she should see a silhouetted figure standing in the corridor, which for a brief moment would appear to be sinister. "A set will be designed so it will have a bright day-lit window behind the figure," Hitchcock explained. "We should establish that the light in the lobby between the bedroom and the door to the corridor is out, so that Jo opens the door and sees this figure. Ben switches on a light and we are able to see the man's face."

Although the Addisons are first seen outside the Hotel de la Mamounia, they are introduced during the restaurant sequence. Mrs. Addison, the script indicates, stares at Jo both in front of the hotel and, later, inside the restaurant. Jo becomes very nervous about this, until it is revealed that Mrs. Addison has simply recognized Jo as a celebrity, recalling that she had seen Jo in a musical along with Broadway leading man Alfred Drake. (In fact, Jo's duet with Hank in the first draft is of the song "People Will Say We're in Love," which was one of Drake's numbers when he led the original cast of Rodgers and Hammerstein's *Oklahoma!*) However, Hitchcock had second thoughts about Mrs. Addison's characterization, feeling they had given her far too great a knowledge of the New York stage while also trying to portray the Addisons as a stuffy English couple. "I'm afraid this needs a whole new fresh idea," wrote Hitchcock, who suggested that perhaps Mrs. Addison should mention having seen a photograph of Jo wearing a Salvation Army uniform. It turns out that Jo had worn such a costume when she appeared in *Guys and Dolls*. "This is just a crazy idea," Hitchcock continued. "But it would help to keep Mrs. Addison from being quite so worldly, and on the other hand give Jo an opportunity to explain what she is." In the final draft, though, all the business about Alfred Drake and *Guys and Dolls* would be dropped.

Although it had been agreed that the key conflict of *The Man Who Knew Too Much* was to be between Ben and Jo, Hitchcock wanted to avoid including a scene in which the couple have a direct argument over her show-business career. Hitchcock felt what Hayes had written was "very old hat" and asked that it be rewritten completely "in some form that will be a little more satirical and more comic."

Always eager to avoid movie clichés, Hitchcock expressed concern over foreign characters who speak English, this time pointing out the awkwardness of the scene between the McKenzies and the police commissioner in Marrakesh. At one point in the first draft the commissioner says, "Speaking as I do perfect English." Having recently screened so many films for the purposes of casting French actors for *To Catch a Thief* and *The Man Who Knew Too Much*, Hitchcock noticed this line in practically every one and felt this was too obvious a way of getting around the problem of having foreign characters speaking English for the audience's benefit. Hitchcock decided that the commissioner speaking English would be self-evident and that no explanation would be needed.

For the scene where Ben receives the telephone call telling him that Hank has been kidnapped, Hitchcock indicated that he wanted to change the setting in the script to avoid the "conventional head of an Arab, and a telephone, and a shadow" by instead showing the back of a chair in an an elaborately decorated Moorish house, suggesting that whoever is behind the kidnapping is in well-to-do circumstances. "The dialogue makes no difference," wrote Hitchcock. "Maybe the arm of the speaker could be seen sticking out on the arm of the chair, and this arm would not be in a business suit, but might be in a robe or something."

Hitchcock was also very concerned about the scene in which Ben sedates Jo and then tells her their son has been kidnapped. Hitchcock felt that some of Jo's dialogue—"I could kill you!"; "He's my child more than yours! I had him"; and "I'll never, never forget this! Drugging your own wife!"—was too melodramatic and asked Hayes to keep it "meaty," while eliminating some of Jo's more histrionic lines. Although it had followed the sedation scene in the treatment, Hitchcock now realized that the sequence between Ben and the Hotel de la Mamounia concierge added nothing to the story and felt that any pertinent information in the scene could be put into the following scene between Ben and Jo. Hitchcock also feared that if information of Hank's kidnapping had gotten back to the police through the concierge, "it would open up a whole can of peas for us." Even though he asked that the scene be thrown out, the well-traveled Hitchcock couldn't help commenting that "the concierge's attitude is quite impertinent."

On their arrival in London, the McKenzies are introduced to Frederick Buchanan of Scotland Yard's Special Branch. Hitchcock expressed much concern over Hayes's handling of the characterization of Buchanan, to the point that he felt the whole scene might need to be rewritten. To Hitchcock, Buchanan needed to come off as a typical English Secret Service man—impressive, sympathetic, and full of understatement—which meant that his dialogue should have the utmost economy. "I know, John, this is a very difficult job to do and I think we should possibly try to find some examples to guide you. Buchanan is not at all a John Williams type, that is to say, not what we would call a silly-ass type," sympathized Hitchcock. "To show you how difficult this character is, I remember when we made the original film, I had a very famous actor, Sir Lewis Casson, the husband of Dame Sybil Thorndike. When I started to rehearse him I found he was a little on the 'hammy' side and the scene suffered from this. Although it was a daring thing to do, I had the nerve to remove this distinguished actor from the part and get somebody else who was more subtle, but still distinguished."

Following the sequence between the McKenzies and Buchanan at the airport, Ben and Jo check into a suite at Claridges and are soon joined by Jo's friends—Val and Helen Parnell, and two actresses, Cindy Fontaine and Jan Peterson. Thinking ahead to the film's tag, which still hadn't been written, Hitchcock noted that when Ben is asked about Hank, his answer should remain ambiguous, "so that when we come to the tag, it does not call for a big explanation."

For comic relief, Hayes had also written a scene in which Jo's friends are bewildered by Ben and Jo's odd behavior of abandoning them in their hotel suite, in search of either a man or a place called Ambrose Chapel. Val concludes that Ben and Jo must be playing some sort of game, perhaps an international scavenger hunt. But Helen reminds Val that the object of a scavenger hunt is to bring home what you find. "How could they bring home a chapel?" asks Helen. "Ever hear of William Randolph Hearst?" replies Val, who suggests that they have another drink so they can dream up a more outlandish explanation. "If it's good enough, maybe Graham Greene'll buy the plot," says Val. Hitchcock wondered, although not seriously, whether this scene might provide an opportunity for him to be self-referential, writing, "Could Alfred Hitchcock buy the plot instead of Graham Greene?" He ultimately concluded that no matter who bought the plot, the reference should be eliminated since it would draw the audience's attention to the writers of the film they were seeing.

Hitchcock felt that as written in the first draft, the scene where Addison explains the mechanics of the assassination to Rien—playing the record to demonstrate how the cymbals will conceal his gunshot—was a little flat. Lines such as "This is how the shooting is planned" or "It is a good box which we chose for its advantageous position opposite the target," wrote Hitchcock, were "awfully on the nose." The incomplete first draft ended with Ben's capture in the chapel, and so Hitchcock closed his notes by writing that he and Hayes should discuss the remaining scenes the following day, April 28.

Angus MacPhail also turned in notes on Hayes's first draft script to Hitchcock on April 25. MacPhail's notes were mainly concerned with the characterizations of the Addisons and Buchanan. "I'm afraid I think the Addisons in the restaurant sequence emerge as rather boring characters, for which we are all three to blame," wrote MacPhail. "One trouble is that we can't capitalize on the normal stuffy nature of the bourgeois English tourist because of Addison's alleged professional occupation and his wife's being a fan of shows amongst other things." He then suggests, "Another angle which might be worth exploring is that Mr. Addison is henpecked . . . He would be meek and nervous, always hanging on her latest word. This would be consistent with their 'real' relationship later on." Buchanan, MacPhail felt, "is just plain bad."

Without time for Hayes to complete his first draft, Hitchcock left for New York and London on April 29, along with Herbert Coleman and Angus MacPhail. Before departing, Hitchcock had laid out the Albert Hall sequence for Hayes, which was submitted to the PCA as pages A through S. The director also decided at the last minute to call the film *Into Thin Air*, and initiated a search to clear the title. Character names were also checked and changes were required to avoid conflict with living persons. Thus, the McKenzies became the McKennas and the Addisons became the Draytons.

That same day, the PCA sent a letter to Paramount censorship liaison Luigi Luraschi, detailing its concerns about the script.

Geoffrey Shurlock warned that strict enforcement of the code would prohibit a story in which a child is kidnapped. However, Shurlock stated:

> We feel the danger of running afoul of this provision can be obviated by making it absolutely clear that the child is held merely as a hostage, with no actual threat to his life.
>
> As to the scenes near the end of the picture in which Addison is shown definitely threatening the life of the boy by holding a gun to his head, I would like to urge and recommend that the threat be directed at the father rather than at the boy. We believe this switch in emphasis will help materially with the overall problem, and we believe not do serious damage to the structure of the story.

Although the script never explicitly states whether or not Addison is a genuine minister, Shurlock expressed reservations, suggesting "it would be well if some means could be found earlier to put more emphasis on the fact that he is not actually a minister." Along with the usual PCA objections to words like "damn," Shurlock pointed specifically to the details concerning the murder of Louis Bernard:

> Page 59: Some means should be found of indicating that the police either apprehended or killed the Arab whom they are chasing in scene 104. Such an indication might be brought out in dialogue in subsequent scenes in Buchanan's office. Also we assume of course that scene 105 will be handled with proper care and restraint to avoid offensive gruesomeness.

On his arrival in London on May 1, Hitchcock cast the remaining roles. For the villainous English couple, whose names had been changed to Edward and Lucy Drayton, Hitchcock engaged Bernard Miles and Brenda de Banzie. Daniel Gelin was chosen to portray the mysterious Louis Bernard, and for the assassin, Rien, Hitchcock went for the openly sinister look of Reggie Nalder.

Although Angus MacPhail was taken off salary on May 2, Hitchcock wired John Mock on May 5, informing him that MacPhail would be rehired for two weeks in Marrakesh, beginning May 9, to edit and make notes on the script pages as they were sent by Hayes. With Hitchcock's detailed notes in hand, the new character names cleared, and the PCA's objections duly noted, Hayes began writing the final shooting script under the new title *Into Thin Air*. Hayes recalled:

> Hitch went off and the script wasn't even finished. We only had maybe a third of it, and gaps in that too, because he'd scheduled it before we were ready. They went to Marrakesh, and I was sending pages by Pan American pilot to the set. Then I flew to London, wrote on the airplane in the lounge, and then wrote all day and mimeographed at night, and brought the script to the set in the morning until we caught up.

By May 7, Hayes had completed the first seventy-four pages of the final shooting script, which were sent to the director. On May 10 the first section of the shooting script arrived in Marrakesh with a title page bearing only the name of John Michael Hayes; this irritated Hitchcock. That same day, at Hitchcock's instruction, Herbert Coleman sent a memo to John Mock indicating that the "script cover page should not contain the word 'FINAL.'" Hayes was unaware at the time that Hitchcock intended to give shared screenplay credit to Angus MacPhail.

Hayes continued writing, and rewriting, as Hitchcock was still unsatisfied with the scene between Ben and Jo in the marketplace, where they have a discussion about Jo's desire to resume her singing career. But Hayes was soon inspired, and on May 11 he turned in a revision of this scene in addition to a whole new version, which focused on Ben's career in a very humorous way. Hayes remembered:

There were two sets of dialogue, because Hitch wanted something lighter. Ben and Jo were in the marketplace and were going to face a bad situation, and Hitch didn't want a scene with a family argument over her going back on the stage. It didn't seem to fit the mood, nor the walk they had to take, so they cabled me and asked for some other dialogue to fit the scene. So I went home and I wrote all that stuff about how Ben's patients had paid for their trip and their new clothes, and so forth: "I'm wearing Mrs. So-and-So's appendix." I sent it to them and I remember John Mock saying, "Oh, this is so good!" And he got a cable back from Marrakesh saying how delighted they were with the dialogue.

Both marketplace scenes were approved by Geoffrey Shurlock on May 13 and inserted in the script labeled versions A and B. A day earlier Hayes had turned in pages 75 through 139, and with the script still incomplete, he departed for London, where he registered in a suite at the Savoy Hotel on May 17.

On Location in Africa

Principal photography on Production #10336, *The Man Who Knew Too Much*, began in Morocco on May 13, 1955. Doc Erickson recalled:

On *The Man Who Knew Too Much*, we did divide our attention between London, Morocco, and the studio. Hitch's wonderful notion of shooting movies was to take the principals to location so that you knew you were actually there, and then get back to the studio where it was more comfortable.

The location production proved to be more problematic than anyone anticipated, with delays caused by rioting mobs. Under a French protectorate from 1912 to 1956, Marrakesh had been administered by the Glaoui family for many years, the last of whom, Thami al-Glaoui, had been the chief instigator in the deposing of Sultan Mohammed V in 1953. Since then, antagonism between the French and Arabs had been escalating in Morocco and seemed to be coming to a head at about the same time *The Man Who Knew Too Much* began filming. In a letter to Hugh Brown, Erickson gave a progress report on the first week's shooting:

> Saturday, May 21, 1955
>
> Hitch keeps saying, 'who wrote this sequence into the picture?' As usual he was ready to go home as soon as he arrived. He's not even keen about going to London, but he's committed himself to those damned interiors up there now. Poor Bob has his work cut out for him lighting those rooms. But you know how that set construction figure keeps scaring Hitch.
>
> I know you people are in the dark about a lot of the things regarding our schedule and cast and planning, but so are we. So, as we said when I left, we'll just plow along and hope for the best.
>
> As a personal favor, Bob Burks asked me to mention to you that he is very dubious of his chances to do Hitch's next picture in N.Y., and wants you to be thinking about a possible show for him at Paramount.

Erickson's reference to "Hitch's next picture in N.Y." is, of course, *The Wrong Man*, which was to be made for Warner Bros.

The Wrong Man was based on the true story of Christopher Emanuel Balestrero, a musician from New York who had been wrongly accused and tried for armed robbery. The story had been chronicled in *Life* magazine by Herbert Brean as "A Case of Identity," and had already been dramatized on television for *Robert Montgomery Presents* as "The Identified Man." Before departing for

Marrakesh, Hitchcock had given the story to John Michael Hayes to get his opinion of the material. Hayes remembered Hitchcock was not pleased when he told him he disliked the story and believed it wouldn't make a successful picture. Furthermore, Hayes maintains that Hitchcock wanted the writer to forgo his salary, since Hitchcock himself was to receive no director's fee as a gesture of goodwill he promised Jack Warner in 1952 (although he was still to receive his percentage of the profits). Hayes's apparent rebellion, by not being equally enamored with either the story or business arrangements, added to the sense of friction growing between the writer and director. Doc Erickson sensed that Hitchcock and Hayes were drifting apart. Erickson recalled:

> I felt that there was perhaps tension developing after the first two or three films, where John was getting a lot of attention and more money. He was beginning to cost Hitch extra. Hitch was responsible for it in a way, but he also resented it, I think.

The London Shoot

On May 23 the company finished shooting at the Marrakesh location and the following day set out for London, where Hayes was still hammering away at the script in his suite at the Savoy. Erickson remembered:

> We were all very nervous because of the situation in Marrakesh at the time with the French and the Arabs. We used to hear the cracking of gunfire at night, and there were mini riots going on where you saw police hammer people over the head. So we were very happy to get out of there. Shortly after we got back to London Thami al-Glaoui had been shot, and that shook us up a bit too.

Production resumed on May 26, in the lobby of the Royal Albert Hall, continuing into June with interior and exterior scenes filmed at the taxidermy workshop of Edward Gerrard and Sons, which was located in Camden Town, and with exteriors of a chapel in Brixton.

Hayes completed the script in London on June 6 and left for Los Angeles, where he turned in the remainder of the script to the studio typing pool on June 11, when he closed on the picture. By this time, the title *Into Thin Air* also proved unavailable, and so all script pages dated June 13 forward bore the original title, *The Man Who Knew Too Much*. That same day, John Mock cabled the London offices of Paramount to ascertain from Hitchcock whether Hayes should begin adapting Laurens van der Post's South African adventure novel *Flamingo Feather*, which the studio had acquired for the director in March. A reply was cabled back stating that it was "too soon" to assign Hayes to *Flamingo Feather*. Hitchcock still wanted the writer to begin work on *The Wrong Man*, which, according to the director's agreement with Warner Bros., would commence production after completion of *The Man Who Knew Too Much*. Work on *Flamingo Feather* would be at least six months to a year away, so just as he had done on *The Man Who Knew Too Much*, Hitchcock wanted to assign the initial plot construction to Angus MacPhail, whose employment on *The Man Who Knew Too Much* had ended on June 7.

Hitchcock must have been relieved that, after three weeks of filming, he finally had a completed script and that he would soon be returning to the studio, where Henry Bumstead's sets were already being constructed. According to a letter dated June 7 from Doc Erickson to Frank Caffey:

Bumstead plans to leave here Friday night and so will be in the studio Monday morning with all the plans and information necessary to complete the sets for Hollywood shooting. He has done a splendid job throughout and Hitch is very happy with his work. Poor Bob Burks has really taken a beating on this location and I doubt whether he will ever want to see a natural interior again. I think Hitch may have had enough of natural interiors also.

Production continued in London, with the company working short days because of the Albert Hall's concert schedule.

Meanwhile, Geoffrey Shurlock responded to the final changed pages 73 through 167 on June 16, stating, "You will recall from a telephone conversation some time ago, it was agreed that in the telling of the story, references to 'kidnapping' shall be omitted." Although Schurlock requested the omission of the word "kidnapped," which was used twice in the script, one of these references remains in the finished film and the second was replaced with the equally pointed phrase "Don't you realize Americans dislike having their children stolen?" The PCA seemed more concerned with the portrayal of Drayton as a minister, with particular attention given to his sermon, so that it would not include any references to Christ. Oddly, no further mention had been made of the final scenes, in which, in the finished film, Drayton has a gun leveled at Hank's head.

Returning to Paramount

The company completed location shooting in London on June 21 and returned to Hollywood for the studio filming. Second unit director Basil Keys remained in London, shooting background plates, and on June 27 production resumed at the Paramount sound stages with the sequence inside the Arab restaurant.

After more than a month of location shooting was completed, Doris Day had become considerably distressed by what she saw as Hitchcock's lack of direction. "Hitch never spoke to me before a scene to tell me how he wanted it played, and he never spoke to me afterward," Day remembered. "On those evenings when we all had dinner, he was chatty and entertaining but we never spoke a word about the picture we were doing."

The leading lady became so concerned over what she had interpreted as Hitchcock's disenchantment with her that she at last confronted him in his office. "I really feel like I'm not pleasing you," she told Hitchcock.

"What makes you say that, my dear?"

"Well, you're not telling me what to do and what not to do and I just feel like I've been thrown into the ring and left to my own devices. We all have our big scenes coming up and I want to please you."

"But, Doris, you've done nothing to elicit comment from me," said Hitchcock.

"What do you mean?"

"I mean that you have been doing what I felt was right for the film and that's why I haven't told you anything."

With that, Doris Day returned to work with confidence. James Stewart sympathized with his co-star and later recalled:

> I knew Hitch pretty well, from having made *Rear Window* and *Rope* with him. He didn't believe in rehearsals. He preferred to let the actor figure things out for himself. He refers to this method as "planned spontaneity." Of course, this is confusing to an actor who is accustomed to a director who "participates" in the scene. In the beginning, it certainly threw Doris for a loop. Hitchcock believe[d] that if you sit down with an actor and analyze a scene you run the danger that the actor will act the scene with his head rather than his heart, or guts.

The Breakup

Production continued well into July as John Michael Hayes waited for word of his next assignment. He hadn't spoken with Hitchcock since he'd returned to Hollywood in early June. Meanwhile, according to Herbert Coleman, Hitchcock and Alma made changes to the script as needed. With very few exceptions, these changes were minor editorial ones. The only major changes were made on July 8, when Hitchcock referred to the dialogue from the 1934 film for the scene when Drayton instructs Rien, the assassin.

When John Mock called Hayes, it was not with news of another

assignment but to inform him that he had just received from Hitchcock's office a title page for the script bearing the words "Screenplay
by John Michael Hayes and Angus MacPhail." When it became
clear to Hayes that Hitchcock intended to give screenplay credit to
MacPhail, he sought the advice of Mock, who in his position as
head of the story department instructed him to send a formal
protest, which he did in a Western Union telegram on July 27:

> JOHN MOCK
> PARAMOUNT STUDIOS
> I HEREBY PROTEST THE TENTATIVE SCREEN CREDITS FOR
> "THE MAN WHO KNEW TOO MUCH." I DO NOT FEEL THAT
> ANGUS MACPHAIL IS ENTITLED TO SCREENPLAY CREDIT.
>
> > JOHN MICHAEL HAYES

According to Hayes, Hitchcock threatened never to speak with him
again if he persisted in a credit arbitration. Convinced he was in the
right, Hayes went ahead with the protest. The matter would now be
settled by a credit arbitration committee according to rules established by the Writers' Guild of America.

This was not the first time MacPhail's contributions to a Hitchcock picture had been called into question. A decade earlier, *Spellbound* producer David Selznick wrote in a memo: "It is something
of an injustice to Ben Hecht to credit Angus MacPhail but, as to
this, I will gladly abide by Mr. Hitchcock's judgment." Hitchcock
did give screen credit to MacPhail on *Spellbound* even though
Hecht's script had been substantially revised from MacPhail's outline.

Hitchcock continued shooting, completing the interior scenes
on the bus, which included the incident with the Arab woman, on
July 30. On the afternoon of August 4, Hitchcock sent a memo to
John Mock indicating that submission of script materials for the
WGA arbitration should be delayed because the picture was still in
production and changes were still being made to the script. The
relationship between Hitchcock and Hayes had now officially

become a battle. Ironically, that very evening the second of their collaborations, *To Catch a Thief*, was to have its world premiere at the Paramount Theater in Hollywood.

Production continued into August, with the scenes inside the McKennas' Marrakesh hotel room still to be filmed. On August 5 Doris Day and Christopher Olsen's a cappella duet of "Whatever Will Be" was shot, and the critical episode of Ben sedating Jo was filmed on August 9, the latter requiring more takes than any other scene in the production. Hitchcock rarely shot more than three or four takes, often getting just one "good" take and one for protection. But Scenes 146A and 147E, in which Ben sedates Jo and then tells her that their son had been kidnapped, were taken eleven and ten times each, until Hitchcock was satisfied with the performances of the film's stars. Years later, Doris Day claimed that for her it was the most difficult sequence in the film.

Principal photography ended on August 24, with the production thirty-four days behind schedule. The following day Angus MacPhail's Hollywood agent, Reece Halsey, who was then head of the literary department at the William Morris Agency, sent a letter to the Writers' Guild supporting Hitchcock's actions by stating that MacPhail felt that he was entitled to at least first screenplay credit.

Even with principal photography completed, Hitchcock added two scenes that required special care to the script on August 26. "Hitch loved trick shots," recalled Henry Bumstead.

> In each of the four films I did with Hitch, he always had a few scenes or sets that he insisted on doing a certain way. Each film, throughout his career, he came up with new ideas or tricks that got the film industry's attention. Just think of what he could have done if he had all the tools we have to work with today. The scene in *The Man Who Knew Too Much* where the heavies come out of the back door of the chapel was filmed part on location, part on the backlot, and the rest was a matte. [A matte shot combines live-action elements with a pre-photographed or painted background.] Not

spectacular, but good use of the tools available to us at that time.

In the finished film, the trick shot appears twice. The first time is when the assassin, Rien, exits the rear of Ambrose Chapel, while in the distant background Jo is standing on the other side of the street, waiting for Ben to arrive. The set and matte are used a second time later on as the Draytons flee the chapel with Hank. (Bumstead would also use this technique on *Vertigo* for a splendid shot in which a priest and two nuns are seen climbing to the roof where the woman's body has fallen at the same time that James Stewart is shown on the opposite side of the frame exiting the church. The tower in the foreground of the image is a matte.)

During September, while the Writers' Guild arbitration committee considered the drafts and notes, Hitchcock directed the added scenes and retakes for *The Man Who Knew Too Much*. At this time, Hitchcock also completed the main title background shot, which involved filming a wide shot of an orchestra with the camera moving closer and closer to single out the cymbalist, who crashes his cymbals and holds them up to the camera. To emphasize the significance of the cymbals to the plot, Hitchcock engaged James Allardice to write an appropriate prologue to superimpose on the tail end of the main title shot. Allardice, whose services the director had already found useful in writing the prologues and epilogues for *Alfred Hitchcock Presents* (which was set to premiere on CBS-TV on October 2, 1955), received $250 for the six versions of the prologue he turned in on September 23.

On November 1, after considering the drafts, treatments, notes, and changes, the arbitration committee of the Writers' Guild of America handed down their decision that for the screenplay of *The Man Who Knew Too Much* John Michael Hayes was entitled to sole on-screen credit. Angus MacPhail's name would appear only in the screen achievement records as "contributor to screenplay construction."

The Release

The Man Who Knew Too Much received its certificate of approval (#17717) from Geoffrey Shurlock on February 27, 1956. On the morning of March 12, James Stewart made himself available to film his introduction for the theatrical trailer, and later that day a black-and-white television promo was filmed with Doris Day. "Alfred Hitchcock strikes the highest note of suspense the screen has yet achieved!" boasted the ad campaign.

A preview for *The Man Who Knew Too Much* was held at Paramount Studios on April 23, 1956. On May 1 *The Hollywood Reporter* called the picture a "first-rate suspense yarn," and *Variety* noted that Hayes's "dialogue is particularly good." For the Hollywood premiere on May 22, Hitchcock was joined by James Stewart, Doris Day, and the honorary hostess, Hedda Hopper, at the Paramount Theater. Proceeds from the event—approximately $18,000—were donated to the University Religious Conferences to help finance the group's "projects for brotherhood and racial and religious understanding." The picture was well received by critics and fared exceptionally well at the box office. "Whatever Will Be" received the Academy Award for best song, the only category for which *The Man Who Knew Too Much* was nominated.

No one could have foreseen that the circumstances under which *The Man Who Knew Too Much* was written would be the cause of controversy and, ultimately, the dissolving of a superb collaboration. The process by which the writing took place went as follows: Hitchcock used MacPhail as a sounding board to construct a plot based on a story credited to Charles Bennett and D. B. Wyndham-Lewis from the 1934 film. After constructing the initial plot with MacPhail, Hitchcock filtered this material to Hayes in conference, from which a detailed treatment emerged. As each section of the treatment was finalized, Hayes fleshed out the corresponding section of the screenplay, adding dialogue and full character action until the screenplay was completed.

If the nature of MacPhail's employment seems to have been left vague, Hitchcock was at fault. MacPhail was officially engaged for a guaranteed eight-week period for the purposes of writing a treatment. Yet during that period, the only work that appears to have been done by MacPhail is a series of notes—albeit some thirty pages' worth, including some quite detailed ones—that establish the basic structural differences between the remake and the original screen story for the 1934 film.

Interestingly, although MacPhail was being paid a weekly salary, his note-writing mysteriously ended on February 24, a few days before Hayes began working on the project. It is also apparent that no work was done on setting a treatment to paper until March 14, two weeks *after* Hayes's arrival at Hitchcock's office. By March 25, Hayes had completed the first third of the treatment, and at that time, MacPhail resumed his note-writing on March 26, when he provided Hitchcock with a detailed summary of a story conference concerning the arrival of Ben and Jo in England. By this time Hayes had begun writing the screenplay for the section of the treatment that had been completed. And again, there was nothing further from MacPhail.

A 70-page treatment was completed on April 22, and on April 25 Hayes turned in the first 165 pages of the first draft script. MacPhail then provided Hitchcock with two pages of comments on Hayes's incomplete draft. On April 27 Hitchcock dictated detailed page-by-page notes on the screenplay, addressing some of MacPhail's concerns, so that Hayes could make revisions while the company departed for location filming, which would commence in two weeks' time. On April 29 Hitchcock and MacPhail left for England, and Hayes remained in Hollywood, where he continued working on the script. Hayes completed pages 1 through 74 of the final white script on May 7, and pages 75 through 139 on May 12, before departing for London, where he wrote the remainder of the script as the production wrapped location filming in Marrakesh and began shooting in London. On June 6 Hayes turned in a completed script, returned to Hollywood, and his services on *The Man Who Knew Too Much* ended.

Based on the circumstances, Hayes was entirely right to be surprised when (more than a month later) Hitchcock submitted to the Paramount story department the tentative screen credits with MacPhail sharing credit for the screenplay. John Mock must have been equally surprised, since the only official starting notice the story department received concerning MacPhail was for his assignment to work on a treatment.

Article 8 of the WGA's 1955 Motion Picture Basic Agreement states that a writer and the head of the studio's story department must be informed by the producer of the assignment of any writers to a project. This rule is meant to prevent any writer from being surprised upon receipt of the tentative writing credits by providing an awareness of the writers assigned to a project and the services they are hired to perform. While Article 8 does not explicitly state that story material created by the prior writer must be made available to subsequent writers, it is presumed by the WGA that any subsequent writer will have had access to prior material whether firsthand or communicated verbally by the producer. Although it was not a determining factor in the arbitration, none of MacPhail's materials were made available to Hayes, nor are they listed among the inventory of written material in the Paramount story files. MacPhail's notes remained with Hitchcock.

"I was told that there were pages sent to the Guild that Hitch said Angus worked on," recalled Hayes. "But if that was true, he never showed them to me and never mentioned them to me. I heard that Hitchcock got reprimanded by the Guild for it. But why he did it is still a mystery." Three other writers had a similar experience with Hitchcock, although theirs did not result in a credit arbitration. In 1961 *Psycho* screenwriter Joseph Stefano was the first writer engaged by Hitchcock to adapt Winston Graham's novel *Marnie*. Stefano made extensive notes and wrote a 161-page treatment, but the project was set aside when Hitchcock's first choice for the female lead, Grace Kelly, dropped out and the director began work on *The Birds*. When work on *Marnie* resumed, Hitchcock hired *The Birds*' screenwriter, Evan Hunter, without informing him that Stefano had written a treatment a year earlier. Hunter recently confirmed that he was not provided with any of Stefano's materials and that he did not actually learn of the other writer's involvement in *Marnie* until more than twenty years later. Coincidentally, when Evan Hunter was replaced on *Marnie* after writing an early draft script, Jay Presson Allen was also never informed that she was the third writer assigned to the script or provided with the work of her predecessors.

Hayes maintains that he alone wrote the screenplay for *The Man Who Knew Too Much*, and with the exception of the changes made to the screenplay after Hayes left the production, documentation supports this. Hitchcock's April 27 notes on the first draft script of April 25, 1955, seem written for the purposes of guiding Hayes alone in his writing of the final shooting script. The only references to MacPhail in those notes are to instruct Hayes to discuss with MacPhail the English characterizations in the script. Also supporting Hayes is the fact that MacPhail also made notes on the April 25 script, offering his opinion and suggestions.

Angus MacPhail's departure for London with Hitchcock and Coleman on April 29 is further evidence that Hayes was left alone to begin the final shooting script in Hollywood. The first seventy-four pages of that draft are dated May 6. Production records indicate that MacPhail went off salary on May 2, although he went back on salary on May 9, while in Marrakesh with the company.

Correspondence from personnel such as censorship liaison Luigi Luraschi and story department head John Mock regarding the script are addressed either only to Hayes or to Hitchcock and copied to Hayes but not MacPhail. None of this is to suggest MacPhail did not contribute to the picture. But Hitchcock was being especially generous to MacPhail by offering him screenplay credit.

Years later, Hitchcock complained about the allocation of credits in Hollywood, harking back to the methods he was able to employ at Gaumont-British. "I miss the things that one did in England, where you could work with someone who was a very good writer of melodrama, but who wasn't necessarily the best dialogue writer. I would go through all the donkey work with him and then, having completed the theme, hand it over to the dialogue writer. This won't work in this country, because of the screenplay credit situation. It won't. I've tried it. Now if there's any dispute, a committee reads all the material and allocates the credits."

In the end, as with any credit arbitration, the written material prevailed. Had MacPhail written the treatment as he was hired to, he might have earned an "Adaptation by" credit and might even have been entitled to share in the screenplay credit. But of the pages finally submitted to the WGA by Hitchcock's office, a great many of the ideas were not incorporated into the script, leaving the credit arbitration committee to reach but one conclusion: that Angus MacPhail contributed to the construction of the screenplay, but that the screenplay was that of John Michael Hayes.

Although Hayes had won the arbitration for sole screenplay credit, it was, in a sense, a mixed victory. Hayes knew the moment he challenged Hitchcock that there was no going back, that he had outgrown Hitchcock's ego, and that the partnership of Alfred Hitchcock and John Michael Hayes had been forever severed.

6 / Un-Hitched

The years following the breakup of the collaboration of Alfred Hitchcock and John Michael Hayes were tumultuous ones in the industry. The studio system had been in decline since the late 1940s owing to the advent of television, the forced divestment of theaters by the major studios, and the increasing control of independent artists no longer under long-term contract to the studios. Under such conditions, *auteur* directors flourished. The industry, as always, was less kind to writers.

Hitchcock had been fortunate in having John Michael Hayes as his collaborator on his first four films at Paramount. Audiences of the 1950s had come to expect a high level of excitement, wit, and sophistication from a Hitchcock movie. *Rear Window*, *To Catch a Thief*, *The Trouble with Harry*, and *The Man Who Knew Too Much* conditioned audiences to light comic thrillers, each presented in wide screen and Technicolor (the latter three in VistaVision). But the director's first production after his four-film collaboration with Hayes was *The Wrong Man*, made for Warner Bros. in black-and-white, with a dark and gloomy script based on actual events—and it failed at the box office.

When Hitchcock returned to Paramount to make *Vertigo*, advance publicity boasted of a return to Technicolor and VistaVision, as well as the reappearance of a tried-and-true Hitchcock star, James Stewart. How could they go wrong? What Hitchcock and the studio had not reckoned was that his lighter features and enormously popular television series, *Alfred Hitchcock Presents*, had left audiences unprepared for the emotional realism and deeply personal statement Hitchcock made in *Vertigo*. Hitchcock had returned to the darker vision he expressed in the 1940s and early 1950s. The rounded characters of the Hitchcock-Hayes films, which shared an optimistic viewpoint, were shoved aside in favor of the emotionally haunted characters who occupied such films as *The Wrong Man*, *Vertigo*, *Psycho*, *The Birds*, and *Marnie*. Even the wonderfully comic *North by Northwest* is rooted in some of the distasteful elements of *Notorious* and *Vertigo*: in all three, a woman is used as a sexual pawn in some grand confidence scheme, twice by agencies of the United States government.

The six films Hitchcock made immediately following his collaboration with Hayes have gained in critical estimation since their initial release—and thus so has Hitchcock's reputation. Of those titles, *The Wrong Man* is generally considered the least successful; perhaps Hayes had been right about it. The story had been told in *Life* magazine and filmed for television; what more could Hitchcock have done with it? *Vertigo*, on the other hand, is hailed by many as the director's masterpiece, although it did not fare well at the box office in its first run. *North by Northwest* was a genuine hit from the start, and *Psycho* became the director's highest-grossing film.

The Birds and *Marnie* were Hitchcock's first two efforts at his new studio, Universal. The move to Universal made Hitchcock an incredibly wealthy man. But at what price? Here was a producer-director who had consistently made his own films or, when working with David Selznick, had fought to make his own films, but who was now speaking of "financial ethics" when asked about his choice of subject material in interviews. Had Hitchcock sold out? After *Marnie*, it could be argued that the director allowed MCA to take over and sell Hitchcock the product, while Hitchcock the artist had quietly gone into retirement.

Torn Curtain and *Topaz* followed, but both films were uninspired. In spite of the tired efforts, accolades from the critical community in America had finally come to Hitchcock, beginning with a retrospective by the Museum of Modern Art in 1963. Scores of books and monographs followed, and the Academy presented its coveted Irving Thalberg Lifetime Achievement Award to Hitchcock in 1968.

At the age of seventy-two Hitchcock returned to form with *Frenzy*, made in his native London, with an English cast headed by Jon Finch, Alec McCowen, and Anna Massey, and a witty and well-structured script by Anthony Shaffer. The film is rich in dark humor, yet, oddly, is one of the director's coldest films in that its protagonist isn't any more likable than the serial rapist-murderer who frames him. Then, reunited with his *North by Northwest* scenarist, Ernest Lehman, Hitchcock turned out the light *Family Plot* as his final motion picture, released in 1976. Hitchcock died on April 29, 1980, in his Bel Air home, with his family beside him. Up until a few short months before his death, Hitchcock was still doing the work he loved best: preparing yet another script, with yet another writer.

And what of John Michael Hayes? After leaving Hitchcock's entourage and trusted inner circle, what was his position within the industry? Hayes had to prove that he could do it on his own. Of his years with Hitchcock, Hayes explained:

> The collaboration got my writing the notice of the critics, the public, and the studios. It provided an opportunity to show that I had something to say, that I had a viewpoint and a unique way of working, and it was recognized. But that was my downfall, because it was too recognized, and Hitch resented it. It moved my career from "B" pictures into "A" pictures. You know, when you walk with Hitchcock, Jimmy Stewart, Cary Grant, and Grace Kelly, you walk with the first team. So, it did a lot for my career. It lifted me right out of the ordinary journey of the screenwriter's life, and there were a lot of good writers who never got the chance. So I was lucky. Working with Hitchcock can add to your career.

When it was clear that he was persona non grata in the Hitchcock entourage, with a credit arbitration pending, his relationship with Paramount was temporarily halted. Hayes went over to Twentieth Century–Fox, where he began working on a story called *Solo* for producer Buddy Adler. The movie was intended as a vehicle for Cary Grant and Frank Sinatra, but Hayes was unsatisfied with the characters and the story, and left the project after writing three drafts.

While *Solo* did not take flight, Hayes remained eager to find a property that would separate him from Hitchcock's name. He might have teamed up with another superstar director, this time Billy Wilder, on a romantic comedy loosely based on events from the life of Maurice Chevalier called *A New Kind of Love*, but Wilder was so caught up in the runaway production of a Charles Lindbergh biopic, *The Spirit of St. Louis*, that plans for the Chevalier film were ultimately scrapped. Hayes was eventually offered the job of adapting what was to become a scandalous bestseller, Grace Metalious's *Peyton Place*. "I asked my agent to find me a story about a small town," remembered Hayes.

> *Peyton Place* came up in galley form, and I agreed to do it. I had no idea that it was going to cause the scandal and sensation it did. But I went out and had a successful picture, a very talked about picture, and it made me feel good that I could do it without Hitch. It wasn't just Hitchcock, it was John Michael Hayes, too. That was important professionally, for me to show the Hollywood community, and the producers and the directors, that on my own, without Hitch, I was still good.

Hayes spent the better part of 1956 writing *Peyton Place* for producer Jerry Wald. Eight drafts later, *Peyton Place* went before the cameras in the spring of 1957 in Camden, Maine. Hayes's script retained the sensational elements of the novel—rape, suicide, illegitimacy, and small-town gossip, to name a few—but he tastefully reworked those elements into a sensitive drama about the stifling effects of small-town life.

When *Peyton Place* opened in December 1957, it was a hit with audiences and critics alike, becoming the top-grossing film of the year. Hayes wrote another article for *The New York Times*—one Hitchcock did not have the opportunity to tear up—conveying the difficulties of adapting a bestseller. *Peyton Place* earned seven Academy Award nominations, including one for best picture and one for Hayes's screenplay. Hayes was also honored with a nomination for best American drama by the Writers' Guild of America.

Following his success with *Peyton Place*, Hayes was engaged to do a series of adaptations for various producers at different studios. When Don Hartman set up his own independent production company at Paramount, where he had previously been head of production, he took out a full-page ad in the industry trades announcing, "I have always believed that good writing is the basis of good picture making. This is what prompted me to select as my first three independent productions for Paramount Enid Bagnold's *The Chalk Garden*, Thornton Wilder's *The Matchmaker*, and Eugene O'Neill's *Desire Under the Elms*, and to sign as the screenwriters, John Michael Hayes and Irwin Shaw." Hayes had been hired to adapt the first two, beginning with Thornton Wilder's stage success *The Matchmaker*, which starred Shirley Booth, Paul Ford, Shirley MacLaine, and Anthony Perkins. *The Matchmaker* was well received and later was successfully transformed into the stage and screen musical *Hello, Dolly*.

In the summer of 1957 Hayes traveled to England with two purposes. One was to meet with Ingrid Bergman to discuss the possibilities of her starring in Don Hartman's production of *The Chalk Garden*, and the second was to research small inns in Bournemouth for an adaptation of Terence Rattigan's *Separate Tables* for Hecht-Hill-Lancaster, with whom he had signed a two-picture deal. *The Chalk Garden* was ultimately delayed due to Hartman's untimely death at the age of fifty-seven.

Separate Tables originated on the stage as two one-act plays about a group of diverse characters, most of whom are living in some kind of self-imposed isolation. Hayes's task was to meld the two storylines; the first involved a divorced couple who, in spite of their volatile relationship, are inexorably drawn to each other, and the second concerned a retired Army officer whom the others learn was recently convicted of lewd behavior. Hayes completed his first draft very quickly and was completing his second draft at the end of September 1957 when he found himself in the uncomfortable position of having to deal with three strongly opinionated producers who didn't always see eye to eye. The writer recalled:

> Trying to please three egotists was very difficult. I sat through endless story conferences with Harold Hecht, James Hill, and Burt Lancaster, where it was almost as if they were trying to write the scenes for me. The rewriting got so tiresome. Two of them would like a scene, and one of them wouldn't like it. I'd rewrite the scene, and then a different two would like it. Finally I said to Harold Hecht, "I can't work this way. Somebody's got to be in authority." I didn't want anything more to do with the operation and told them I didn't even want my name on the picture. Now, I had another commitment with them, and I gave it up. My agent almost fell over dead. He said, "You can't! You're just giving away money." I said, "Ned, if I continue to work here, I'll go crazy."

The producers then brought in another writer, John Gay, to complete the script. Ultimately, Gay and Rattigan shared credit for the screenplay, which received an Academy Award nomination, although very few changes were made from Hayes's adaptation. The cast included David Niven, Deborah Kerr, Wendy Hiller, Gladys Cooper, and two American stars, Rita Hayworth and the film's co-producer Burt Lancaster. The film did very well at the box office and earned seven Oscar nominations, including one for best picture, but it was an experience that did not end happily for Hayes, who, in retrospect, should have retained his credit.

Hayes remained in demand in 1958, when he adapted Bernard V. Dryer's novel *The Image Makers* for producer Charles Schnee at Columbia. Difficulty in casting the North African adventure prevented its going before the cameras. Hayes then returned to Paramount, where he did uncredited work on the William Perlberg–George Seaton film of Garson Kanin's *The Rat Race*, which starred Tony Curtis and Debbie Reynolds as a struggling jazz musician and a dance-hall hostess. Hayes continued his association with Perlberg and Seaton, for whom he wrote the screenplay of *But Not for Me*, which he completed in early 1959. The film was the third screen adaptation of Samson Raphaelson's play *Accent on Youth*, which in this version involved a successful Broadway producer played by Clark Gable, who finds inspiration in his personal secretary, who is thirty years his junior and played by Carroll Baker.

It was during the production of *But Not for Me* that Hayes had an opportunity to come face-to-face with Hitchcock. The writer and director had not spoken since their falling-out over *The Man Who Knew Too Much* three years earlier. While attending the Bolshoi Ballet with Gable, Hayes happened to be seated next to Alma and Alfred Hitchcock. The former partners cordially exchanged greetings, and Hayes recalled that during an intermission Alma leaned toward him and whispered, "You know, John, I'm going to talk to Hitch. You and he should work together again."

Whether or not Alma ever spoke to her husband about Hayes, years after their breakup, the mere mention of his name was still a sore subject with Hitchcock. When hired to write the screenplay for *Psycho*, Joseph Stefano was specifically instructed *not* to inquire about Hitchcock's falling-out with Hayes. Years afterward, Stefano experienced a different kind of resentment from Hitchcock. Following *Psycho*, Stefano was engaged to draft a treatment of *Marnie*, but the project was put off before he could begin the screenplay. When Hitchcock resumed development of *Marnie*, nearly two years later, Stefano was busy writing and producing the television series *The Outer Limits* and had to turn Hitchcock down. Although *Marnie* was a box-office failure, Stefano admired the picture and conveyed his opinion to Peggy Robertson when he saw her at a charity function. Stefano's comment was met with a coolness that he felt belonged more to Hitchcock than Robertson when she intimated that *Marnie* might have been different had Stefano not abandoned the project to work on his own television series.

Other writers suffered similar consequences from their own perceived betrayals. Ernest Lehman remembered Hitchcock refusing to speak with him for days when he turned down $100,000 and a percentage of the gross to script the director's ill-fated *No Bail for the Judge*. Evan Hunter was dismissed from *Marnie* after expressing misgivings about the film's rape scene. George Tabori quit *The Bramble Bush* after he and Hitchcock could not come to terms on the story, writing in a letter to the director: "Perhaps I am too old to be told how to write, or really incompetent to fit into the discipline of a big studio . . . I know you are chagrined, but I hope it'll turn into a recognition that as I felt unable to give you my best, it was better to give nothing."

As 1959 drew to a close, Hayes found himself increasingly disenchanted with the Hollywood lifestyle. The disappointment inherent in writing projects that were then shelved or canceled; the pressures of working at a studio; the constant prodding by his agent, Ned Brown, that he should try his hand at directing; and a prolonged and bitter strike by the Writers' Guild* helped Hayes make the decision to move with Mel and their children—Rochelle and Garrett—to Maine, where their youngest children, Meredyth and Corey, were born. In a village called Grindstone Neck just outside Winter Harbor, John and Mel purchased a three-story, fourteen-room house that had been built in 1892 and sat on twenty-seven acres. Yet in spite of his being some three thousand miles from Hollywood, the offers continued to pour in, and Hayes spent nearly half the next two years in Hollywood and Europe.

---

*In October 1959 the West Coast branch of the Writers' Guild of America began a prolonged and hostile strike against independent producers over residuals from the sale of films to television. The strike lasted eight months with the producers giving into the screenwriters' demands.

In December 1959 Hayes completed his script of *Un Carnet de Bal* for Perlberg and Seaton, based on a 1937 French film of the same name about a self-centered woman brought back to reality when she visits the men she danced with at a ball in her youth. Once again, difficulty casting a large-scale production led to the film being canceled. Hayes was then asked to script-doctor an Elizabeth Taylor vehicle for MGM based on John O'Hara's *Butterfield 8*. "The script was written by Charlie Schnee, who was a friend of mine, but it was just unshootable," remembered Hayes.

> The producers hoped it would be just a polish job, since the director, Danny Mann, and the cast were already on location in New York. But it had to be completely rewritten. So they left me alone in a hotel and sent secretaries over twice a day to pick up pages to type up and bring them back to have me proof, and bring them down to the set, where everybody was waiting for them.
>
> Now, when it came to the credits, the producers were initially going to give me sole writing credit, or credit over Charlie. Now, years earlier, if Charlie hadn't stepped in when the blacklisters at MGM had me confused with someone else, my career in pictures might have ended and I'd have never known why. So I insisted that Charlie should get first credit, and that's the way it reads on the picture.

Because of his sensitive handling of *Peyton Place*, Hayes seemed the ideal scenarist for a new adaptation of Lillian Hellman's *The Children's Hour*. The play concerned two young women, Martha and Karen, who run a girls' school and find themselves the subject of a witch-hunt and scandal when one of the students, Mary Tilford, says that she saw the women display an unnatural affection for each other. The lie causes Mary's grandmother, Mrs. Tilford, to remove her from the school and to influence the other students' parents to do the same. Martha and Karen initiate a libel suit against Mrs. Tilford, but ultimately lose the case. Mrs. Tilford eventually learns that her granddaughter had been lying all along and hopes to remedy the situation, but it is too late. The school is ruined, Karen's fiancé has broken off their engagement, and tragically, Martha commits suicide when she realizes that she does indeed have romantic feelings for Karen.

With the loosening of the production code and the more accepting public attitude toward homosexuality, director William Wyler had hoped not only to bring a more faithful version of *The Children's Hour* to the screen but also to push the envelope by bringing it up-to-date. Wyler had made a film from Hellman's play more than twenty years before as *These Three*, which eliminated the lesbian theme by having Martha and Karen find themselves in love with the same man. But while the updated filming of *The Children's Hour* was more faithful to its source material than *These Three*, it was also less successful.

Wyler and Hayes initially agreed that, in modernizing Hellman's play, they should concentrate on the effect the lie has on the main characters rather than on the hysteria it causes in the town. In this way, the story would become more of a psychological drama as Martha becomes aware of her feelings for Karen. Shirley MacLaine, who played Martha, regards *The Children's Hour* as the biggest disappointment of her early career. "John Michael Hayes had not pulled any punches in the script," MacLaine recalled.

> But after the shoot was completed, Willy got cold feet about the lesbian subject. He cut out all the scenes that portrayed Martha falling in love with Karen. Scenes where I [Martha] lovingly pressed Karen's clothes, or brushed her hair, or baked her cookies ended up on the cutting-room floor. The audience was supposed to be aware of the growing love Martha developed for Karen, which is what gave the film tension, because Karen was not aware either. In eliminating those scenes, Willy gutted the intention of the film.

"It was an unhappy picture for me," Hayes recalled. "I had a very turbulent relationship with Willy Wyler. He had hired me to do it differently and then wouldn't let me. Finally the frustrations were so great that one day I collapsed and had to be taken to the hospital." In spite of a fine cast, which in addition to MacLaine included Audrey Hepburn, James Garner, and Miriam Hopkins (who had also been in *These Three*), the production was criticized for being a "cultural antique" rather than the taboo-breaking film intended by its producer-director.

In late 1962 Hayes began one of the most significant associations of his career when he met Joseph E. Levine. Levine had made a name for himself and his company, Embassy Pictures, through the distribution of foreign-made exploitation films, and he set up a production office in New York when he purchased the rights to Harold Robbins's steamy bestseller *The Carpetbaggers*. "He had a big office full of people waiting for their first movie," said Hayes of the distributor-turned-producer.

> I could not think of how to start *The Carpetbaggers* and I called Joe Levine and said, "I'm going to send back all that nice money you gave me, because I can't figure a handle on it." Instead of being discouraged, he said, "Well, it's only been a couple of weeks. Take your time." And I went to bed that night. In the middle of my sleep, I remembered a quotation from Seneca, who was a Roman writer at the time of Nero, and the quote was "Who knows what pain lies behind virtue, and what fear behind vice." Suddenly I had a Christmas tree on which to hang all of the decorations of the characters I had.
>
> When I write, I have to have a viewpoint. Some people call it a spine, or framework, or skeleton. Something that I'm aiming for right from the beginning that holds my story together. That's why you can't tamper with the script and the story in the middle of it, on the set, because you lose that progression, that spine. You can't get off this track.

After reading the script, Joe Levine sent a telegram to Hayes: "I READ THE SCRIPT AND I THINK IT'S GREAT. I AM GLAD YOU TYPED IT ON GREEN PAPER BECAUSE THIS PICTURE WILL MAKE NOTHING BUT

MONEY." Levine's telegram couldn't have been more prophetic, for although critics found *The Carpetbaggers* an easy target, the film was a tremendous financial success. After *The Carpetbaggers*, Levine went about making plans and buying up literary properties, almost repeating the actions of the film's fictional Jonas Cord.

In an era where long-term contracts were a thing of the past, Levine enjoyed having complete control over a person's career. His projects were big and expensive, but too often relied on lesser material. Still, with the promise of greater control and financial compensation, Hayes entered into a long-term contract that, over the next few years, Levine continued to update, add to, and amend. What Hayes didn't know was that most of Levine's plans would never come to fruition. Like Hayes, Carroll Baker, who had starred in *The Carpetbaggers*, suffered under the egomaniacal Levine. In her autobiography, *Baby Doll*, Baker quotes actor Peter O'Toole as calling Levine "the producer of a thousand broken promises."

In 1962 producer Ross Hunter and Universal Pictures obtained the rights to Enid Bagnold's drama *The Chalk Garden*, which Hayes had adapted years earlier for Don Hartman at Paramount as a vehicle for Ingrid Bergman. Production had been canceled because of Hartman's untimely death, but Hunter brought Hayes back on board to draft a new script for director Ronald Neame. Starring Deborah Kerr, Dame Edith Evans, John Mills, and his daughter Hayley Mills, *The Chalk Garden* is the story of a love-starved teenager and a governess who puts herself at risk to see that the child is reunited with her mother. *The Chalk Garden* received a Golden Globe nomination for best picture in 1965 and is perhaps Hayes's finest achievement of the 1960s.

Again with Harold Robbins providing the source material and Levine producing, Hayes adapted *Where Love Has Gone*, which he completed in late November 1963. It was another tawdry tale, this time loosely based on the stabbing death of Lana Turner's gangster-lover Johnny Stompanato by her teenage daughter. Levine then agreed to allow Hayes the opportunity to produce a film from his own original story and script, *Isabel and Burton*. The story of Sir

Richard Francis Burton—scholar, poet, explorer, author, diplomat—and Isabel Arundell, daughter of an aristocratic English Catholic family, who fell in love with Burton after reading of his adventures, then set out against the odds to meet him, seduce him, and marry him. *Isabel and Burton* was an epic story, which Levine promised would be filmed in 70mm at locations in England, Africa, and South America. But in spite of Levine's announcements to the press, which included a two-color, two-page spread in *Variety*, he never fully committed to the project.

While waiting for Levine to set up the production of *Isabel and Burton*, Hayes was named vice president in charge of literary properties for Embassy, where he adapted another Harold Robbins novel, *The Adventurers*, and wrote an original screenplay, *Nevada Smith*, based on a character from *The Carpetbaggers*. Meanwhile, Levine turned his attention to producing a bio-pic of Jean Harlow when he purchased the rights to a recently published biography by Irving Shulman. At the same time, another version of Harlow's life story was going into production in a cheap and short-lived method called Electronovision. While the other version could not match the production values that Levine and Paramount would bring to their *Harlow*, the producer began to sacrifice quality for speed in a frantic rush to beat the other production to the theaters. When the first script proved unfilmable, Levine and Carroll Baker, who was to play Harlow, brought in Hayes to completely rewrite the script as it was being shot.

"I wrote night and day, and they started shooting when I was on page 18," recalled Hayes. "I hadn't even finished the script, and they shot it in sequence, because they agreed to deliver it to the theaters by a certain date, and they cut it and scored it reel by reel." The script did not follow the life of the real Jean Harlow, but instead gave the essence of the buildup and tragic fall of a screen goddess, but in a very sensationalistic way. In spite of the lavish sets and costumes, one of the few highlights of *Harlow* is the title sequence, the concept for which came about from the need to start the production. Hayes recalled:

The director, Gordon Douglas, and the studio said, "What are we going to do while you're writing?" I said, "You know what I have always wanted to see was a studio waking up. It's dark and the first grips arrive and everybody's sleepy and having doughnuts and coffee, and then the girls come in and get made up and one thing and another." So I sketched out all these scenes of a studio waking up, and Neil Hefti composed this wonderful music, and Gordon Douglas did this brilliantly. I still think it's one of the most interesting openings in a movie, and it was done to give the cast and crew something to do until I got to the character and dialogue.

After *Harlow*, which had been unanimously panned by critics, Hayes allowed Levine to persuade him to consider another rewriting assignment for the Sophia Loren vehicle *Judith*. Hayes recalled:

I got called in as a script doctor. They'd been working on *Judith* a year and a half, were on location seven months, and never shot a single scene. So I went down to New York to see the head of Paramount. I flew down from Maine in the morning and planned to take the afternoon plane back home, but I never got back. They gave me the screenplay and offered me a lot of money and said, "We want you to go to Italy tonight." And I said, "I can't. I don't have anything to wear." They said, "Buy whatever you need in Rome and we'll pay for it."

I got into Rome at two-thirty in the morning, and it was about five o'clock by the time I got into the Excelsior Hotel. I had to be up at seven, because we were going to have a meeting at eight-thirty at Sophia Loren's apartment, where I was supposed to tell them what I was going to do. I went over to Sophia's apartment, and it wasn't just Sophia. It was her sister, her agent, twelve relatives, and a half-dozen other people. There's a whole room full of people who have been

working a year and seven months on a picture, and I'm supposed to tell them what to do. I started spinning a tale and
everybody thought it was wonderful.

So we flew El Al at night to Tel Aviv and then drove
miles and miles and miles to Naharia, on the Jordanian
border, where they had the location, and from the time I
landed, I worked night and day. They started shooting when
I was on page 21, and I finished the script in eighteen days.
Carlo Ponti wrote a letter to the head of Paramount and said
this was a creative miracle.

It was at this time that Hitchcock was busy preparing *Torn Curtain*, which was being celebrated as the master's "50th motion picture." But *Torn Curtain* was turning into a hackneyed attempt to
re-create something along the lines of *Notorious* and *North by
Northwest*. The script lacked the glamour and wit audiences had
come to expect from Hitchcock. While executives at Universal were
suggesting numerous writers to the director, those closest to Hitchcock tried to persuade him to call on John Michael Hayes. Hayes
recalled being approached about working on the project:

I said, "Look, I will go and help Hitch, all he has to do is call
me. But I'm not coming through the back door, hat in hand,
for the purpose of working for him. He said he would never
speak with me again. So just have him call up and say, 'I
haven't seen your ugly Irish face around for a long time.' Or,
'Is it true that you're still alive? I heard you were dead.'" I
mean any dumb thing.

But it was a gesture he couldn't make. He didn't have
that kind of sense of humor to just invite me for a drink and
say, "Would you do this?" Because Hitch would have to use
the words "help me" or "rewrite," and it would confirm the
fact that he needed me. I understand he had ego and pride
in an exaggerated form. Not that he didn't deserve it. But it
was so tremendous that it was impossible. It's like Caesar ad-

mitting he made a mistake, and he'd rather execute his critics than admit the mistake. Which is what Hitch did.

I understand that three or four times they asked him to
call me up, and he wouldn't do it. If he had, there would
have been no question at all that I would agree to repair my
relationship with Hitchcock, and go back and work with
him.

Sadly, a reconciliation between Hitchcock and Hayes was not to
be, and Hayes's script for *Nevada Smith* finally went into production in 1965. It would remain his last theatrical on-screen credit for
nearly thirty years. Hayes continued to write, adapting Irving Wallace's bestseller *The Plot* and Martin Caidin's action novel *Almost
Midnight*, but neither was produced.

In the 1970s, while still serving out his contract with Levine's
Embassy Pictures—which had since become part of the Avco Corporation and which, for all purposes, had crippled him creatively—
Hayes turned to writing and producing for television, including a
TV movie, *Winter Kill*, and the series pilot for *Nevada Smith*. In
1973 Bing Crosby Productions and Mort Briskin approached Hayes
to write *Walking Tall*, based on events in the life of Sheriff Buford
Pusser. Hayes took the assignment but not the screen credit, believing the project would do little for his reputation. Hayes continued
writing into the 1980s and came very close to going into production
on a number of projects, including *Indira Gandhi*, a mini-series
based on the life of India's third prime minister; *The Toma Story*, a
film about the life of David Toma, who was the inspiration for TV's
Baretta; and *Jane Brown's Body*, which was based on the true story
of a man who was convicted of murdering his wife, was later retried
and acquitted, and subsequently admitted that he had murdered
her after all. Following that, Hayes scripted *Pancho Barnes*, a TV
movie about the colorful life of the aviatrix that starred Valerie
Bertinelli.

In 1994 Disney released *Iron Will*, which began as an original
screenplay by Hayes in 1971, when he was commissioned by

Crosby and Briskin to write a script called *Hartman*, based on the true story of a boy who entered a dog-sled race in order to win money to attend medical school. Years later, when the rights were picked up by another company, Hayes was hired to write another draft. He changed the boy's name from Hartman to Stoneman — after the Army camp he was first stationed at during World War II — and retitled his screenplay *Iron Will*. After nearly thirty years, Hayes was once again in the spotlight.

Following a Supreme Court ruling in favor of Sheldon Abend, the literary agent who had purchased the rights to Cornell Woolrich's story "It Had to Be Murder" (the basis for *Rear Window*) and who successfully challenged MCA, James Stewart, and the Hitchcock estate in a copyright-infringement suit, there had been talk of a possible remake or sequel to Hitchcock's *Rear Window*.* Except in the unlikely event that an agreement could be reached between parties, the court's decision would prohibit an actual remake or sequel from being made, since the elements original to the motion picture *Rear Window* would be controlled by the film's owners. For example, the characters Lisa Fremont and Stella McCaffery — which were created expressly for Hitchcock's film — would not be available to anyone creating another screen adaptation of Woolrich's story.

Nevertheless, Abend continued trying to get a story developed that would interest producers. For years John Michael Hayes had been approached about participating in such a venture — including being offered as much as $500,000 and a percentage of the producer's profits — but he had always declined. Finally, in 1993, Hayes relented and began collecting his ideas for a proposed sequel to *Rear Window*. In a series of handwritten notes, Hayes roughed in a

---

*The lawsuit was initiated by Abend in 1984 following the re-release of *Rear Window* to theaters, television, and home video. A previous suit, brought by Abend in 1974 when the film was televised without his permission, was settled out of court.

number of suggested plot lines, characters, and devices, all with the object of building a story in the Hitchcock tradition of having suspenseful things happen to ordinary people.

From the start, Hayes knew that he wanted the primary setting of the story to be New England and, ultimately, the town of Deep Harbor, Maine—"*Rear Window* and *Peyton Place* combined," wrote Hayes—where it is stated that Jeff had grown up. In Hayes's notes, Jeff is sometimes referred to as L. B. Jeffries (using the spelling from the Woolrich story rather than Jefferies, as in his earlier treatment and screenplay) or LBJ, and one time as Errol B. Jeffries. Jeff's marriage to Lisa has fallen apart, and he has been remarried for a year when he decides to take his wife, Phyllis, on vacation to the town where he grew up. Phyllis is a painter, and although she prefers painting more sophisticated subjects, Jeff hopes that she will find subjects in the town that will inspire her, just as they inspired him when he first developed an interest in photography as a boy.

Where in *Rear Window* Jeff had been reluctant to get married, Hayes establishes that Jeff is now doing all he can to dampen Phyllis's desire to start a family. Jeff keeps telling her that he's not ready to become a father. While the details surrounding the murder in this projected sequel are rather sketchy—revolving around either an unsolved murder that took place in the town years earlier or an idea based on an actual incident that took place in Missouri, in which an entire town participated in the killing of a suspected murderer and covered it up—Hayes does introduce elements that Hitchcock might have used in one of his own films. For instance, in a possible scene at a cemetery, Jeff notices that a patch of grass above one grave is growing in a different direction from the rest. When he moves closer to investigate, we see a funeral taking place. The heads of the mourners are all bowed in prayer—that is, all but one, and that man is staring at Jeff.

Hayes also incorporates some of the sexual tension from *Rear Window*, noting that Phyllis becomes more and more frustrated when Jeff begins sitting up nights pondering the mystery in the town. Finally she determines that unless she can help Jeff solve the mystery, she may never have a baby. "Perhaps her painter's eye could help him with color clues," Hayes wrote. "She finds something, but won't tell him until after they make love." Eventually Phyllis's involvement puts her in mortal danger, and Jeff has to save her and get the villain at the same time.

For the ending Hayes proposed a tag reminiscent of *Rear Window*, in which Jeff is looking out the window of their apartment as Phyllis sits nearby reading a magazine about parenting. She mentions something about the article she is reading. "What did you say?" asks Jeff. "Oh, nothing," replies Phyllis. "Nothing that can't wait—for a month, or two." Jeff looks at her with a certain curiosity and wonder. Phyllis just smiles, privately.

Initially, Hayes thought to develop a plot that, like the original, would have Jeff suspect that a murder had taken place and then conduct his amateur sleuthing while drawing those close to him into the mystery, putting them and ultimately himself in harm's way in order to solve the crime. But Hayes soon realized that audiences might be interested to know what had happened to Thorwald and would wonder how Jeff would react if Thorwald had an opportunity to turn the tables. "Must connect the original *Rear Window* with the sequel *directly*," Hayes wrote in a note to himself. And that is the direction taken in his twenty-page outline dated August 20, 1993.

In the outline, Jeff is recently married to Phyllis Carlyle Jeffries, an interior decorator with high-profile clients. It's four years after the incidents surrounding the Thorwald murder, and Jeff decides to take his wife on a delayed honeymoon to the Jeffries' family home in Deep Harbor, Maine. Before departing, however, Jeff gets the feeling that somebody is watching him and believes that Thorwald is behind it, despite the fact that he's in a federal prison serving a life sentence for murder.

In Deep Harbor we learn more about the Jeffries family history through encountering a series of small-town New England characters, and Phyllis reveals her desire to have a family of her own with Jeff. Meanwhile, Jeff learns that someone pretending to be a reporter has been asking questions about him around town. Jeff telephones his New York detective friend, Thomas Boyle, to dig up what he can to see if Thorwald could be behind this snooping. Eventually Boyle learns that Thorwald hired a private investigator to follow Jeff and learn everything he can about him. But Boyle tells Jeff not to worry because Thorwald is suffering from congestive heart failure and couldn't harm him even if he wasn't in prison.

But Jeff remains suspicious, and it turns out that Thorwald has not only been feigning illness but has managed to escape from the prison ward at a hospital in the city. A series of suspenseful scenes follow, as Thorwald and Jeff play a cat-and-mouse game that leads to a climax on a rocky ledge jutting out into the ocean. As one reads the outline, it is easy to visualize a film starring James Stewart, Wendell Corey, Raymond Burr, and even someone along the lines of Grace Kelly, but owing to the legal complications it seemed best to drop the notion of doing a sequel and instead do an updated version of the story.

Not long after Christopher Reeve's 1995 riding accident, John Michael Hayes was again contacted, this time about the possibility of scripting a new adaptation of the Woolrich story as a vehicle for the actor. Hayes declined, but the picture was made in 1998 as a television movie for ABC starring Reeve and Daryl Hannah. While Reeve did an admirable job in this comeback role, the picture was a disappointment, lacking the wit and sophistication of a Hayes screenplay and the gripping direction of a Hitchcock.

In recent years John Michael Hayes has been a professor of film studies and screenwriting at Dartmouth College in Hanover, New Hampshire, where he and Mel relocated in 1988. In addition, Hayes has lectured around the country—at the Telluride Film Festival, the University of Oklahoma, and the University of Massachusetts—on screenwriting and on his work with Alfred Hitchcock.

The following analyses reveal four distinctly different approaches to the craft of screenwriting. In each script the focus is on a different aspect of story construction. *Rear Window* is often considered Hitchcock's most "cinematic" picture, but the director's visual language had to begin on the page before it could be put on celluloid. *To Catch a Thief* has been largely dismissed because of the sheer enjoyment it provides the viewer. Could there be any artistry at work in such fluff? Indeed there is, if one looks at the care with which the filmmakers injected the script and screen with recurring visual and verbal motifs. *The Trouble with Harry* reads and plays like a fable, a pastoral comedy that is essentially a character piece. The strength of *The Man Who Knew Too Much* lies in the rigorous insistence of its structure. Any one of these screenplays can be studied as a model for their story type.

In describing Hitchcock's technique of storytelling, John Michael Hayes observed:

There was a book written by Stendhal called *Le Rouge et le Noir* [*The Red and the Black*], in which there's a quote, "The truth about life is only told in its details." And Hitch believed in the philosophy that small things told big stories. He would move a camera across a ballroom, over the dancers, to a band, to a man in blackface, his eyes blinking, because he was the man we were looking for. In *Rear Window* Mrs. Thorwald's wedding ring became an important detail. He said, "If you want a fight, you don't have to have a big ballroom fight. You can achieve more by showing the hands clenching and twisting and the veins standing out." He believed that you could tell a story in details, and the small details revealed the larger picture.

Look what he did with the shower scene in *Psycho*. Seventy-eight different shots actually made a much more horrendous picture than if you'd just seen the stabbing and the full impression. So details are a very important part of the suspense technique and were very important to Hitchcock. I also believed in that philosophy, so we got along very well.

The Cinematic Language of Rear Window

The screenplay for *Rear Window* is as thorough a blueprint for a motion picture as a screenplay can be. Its visual design is structured upon what Hitchcock called subjective treatment. "Subjective treatment," the director has stated, "is the close-up of the person and what they see. *Rear Window* is purely subjective treatment—what Jimmy Stewart sees . . . and how he reacts to it." The basic rhythm of that design is structured in a series of triads—one, the subject; two, what the subject sees; and three, the subject's reaction.

While an argument can be made that the screenplay for *Rear Window* contains the best dialogue in any Hitchcock film, the director was also entirely correct when he said it was the most cinematic of his movies. Going beyond subjective treatment, Hitchcock had at his command a wide vocabulary of cinematic devices that he employed in *Rear Window*. Subjective treatment, camera movement, mise-en-scène, montage, sound, and transitional devices all come together to tell the story cinematically and support the narrative. "At all times the director must be aware of his intention," Hitchcock said. "What is his purpose, and how can he effect it in the most economical way? Not only must he provide images that add up to a language; he must also know what it is that makes it a language."

What follows is an examination of Hitchcock's cinematic language in the screenplay and film *Rear Window*. The opening shot establishes in one swift and purely cinematic gesture the world of our characters in the midst of a heat wave. Their mood is illustrated through details of discomfort and frustration. The forehead of L. B. Jefferies drips with sweat, a thermometer registers 84 degrees, the Songwriter searches for a pleasing radio station, the Childless Couple awaken on the fire escape from a restless night, and in a cage, two lovebirds appear to be arguing. All of this, the script notes, is taking place at 7:15 A.M., which tells us that the temperature, discomfort, and frustration are only going to get worse. Scene 1 begins with a precisely detailed description of the courtyard, establishing the setting, then, without a cut, offering a brief glimpse of the protagonist before introducing some of the supporting players.

The camera first moves to the apartment of the Songwriter, then continues on to a fire escape, where an alarm clock is ringing vigorously. There we see a man rise to a sitting position to switch off the alarm. He then leans forward and shakes somebody beside him. The head of this other person—his wife—rises where his feet are. The script notes through their sweaty pajamas and weary expressions that they enjoyed very little sleep in the heat of the night. The camera moves on to another building, still without a cut, where we see a small fan oscillating inside a window. Beside the fan sits an automatic toaster, and behind the toaster stands a full-bodied young woman, who the script notes is naked save for a pair of black panties. Throughout this little vignette, the woman's breasts remain hidden, first by the shadow of her curtains, then through the careful placement of her automatic coffeemaker and the movement of the oscillating fan.

What Hayes has begun, and will continue to do in the following sequences, is to introduce the minor characters in such a way that they become more than flat, one-dimensional caricatures. Through an idiosyncratic detail or two—the surprise revelation of the couple waking on the fire escape, the manner in which the ballet dancer's bare breasts remain hidden—these smaller characters leave an in-

delible mark on the reader and viewer. After the camera completes
its survey of the courtyard, it retreats through the protagonist's window and continues its movement inside his room. Our introduction
to L. B. Jefferies is a flawless example of economy in storytelling. Visually we learn his name (it is written on the cast that covers his leg
from hip to toe) and the cause of his injury, and through a collection
of action-packed photographs we also learn that if Jefferies were not
in a wheelchair, he wouldn't be passing the time in his apartment.

Rear Window is a masterpiece of construction and planning.
The first dialogue sequence is also the first time subjective camera
work is used in the film. In effect, two narratives are taking place —
Jeff's dialogue with his editor, Gunnison, and Jeff's point of view
and reactions to what he sees outside his window are conveyed simultaneously. Frequently, the dialogue taking place inside Jeff's
apartment (or on the telephone) either complements or parallels
the action he sees out his window. For example, when Jeff discusses
his views of marriage with his editor, he says:

```
                 JEFF
     Can you see me—rushing home to a hot
     apartment every night to listen to
     the automatic laundry, the electric
     dishwasher, the garbage disposal and
     a nagging wife.
```

Gunnison is quick to point out that wives no longer nag their hus-
bands — the proper term is *discuss*. Watching the Salesman's apartment, however, Jeff sees a nagging wife. Hitchcock and Hayes use
this technique several times, varying the pattern by using traditional
dialogue scenes — usually as separations, cutting from character to
character — as well as subjective sequences without dialogue, one of
the director's trademarks.

Lisa Fremont's entrance is both theatrical and mysterious. The
sequence begins with a big close-up of Jeff's sleeping face, upon
which the shadow of another figure soon appears. As filmed, the

first two shots of this sequence have a dreamlike quality. That dreamlike quality, both in the direction and in James Stewart's expression, is emphasized in the lyrics of one of the popular songs chosen for the film, "To See You," and in the lyrics of the original song "Lisa," heard in the film's final moments.

```
INT. JEFF'S APARTMENT—SUNSET—CLOSEUP
The two big profiles filling the screen. The
girl kisses Jeff firmly, but not passion-
ately. Then her head moves back an inch or
two. She speaks.

                    LISA
                 (Softly)
            How's your leg?


                    JEFF
            Mmmm—hurts a little.


                    LISA
            And your stomach?


                    JEFF
            Empty as a football.


                    LISA
            And your love life?


                    JEFF
            Not too active.


                    LISA
            Anything else bothering you?
```

> JEFF
>
> Uh-huh. Who are you?

Hitchcock and Hayes give Lisa a wonderful entrance: the camera follows her along in close-up as she moves to turn on the first of three lamps. The scene continues:

> LISA
> (As she moves)
> Reading from top to bottom —
> (Light on)
> Lisa—

The CAMERA FOLLOWS HER quickly to another lamp. She gets a little farther away from us so that we now see her down to her waist. She turns on the second lamp and the light shows us that her beauty is not alone in her face.

> LISA
> Carol—

The CAMERA PANS HER over to a third lamp which she turns on. She is now in full fig-ure, beautifully groomed and flawless. Her dress is high-style fashion and dramatic evening wear.

> LISA
> Fremont.

The camera direction and the precise indications of framing—big close-up, waist shot, full shot—are crucial to building up a dramatic introduction to Lisa. The theatricality of Lisa's entrance—her posing, her setting of the lights—is emphasized in her dialogue as she likens the evening to an opening night at the theater.

Hitchcock abhorred what he called pictures of people talking. Yet so often in his films one might regard sequences as just that if one fails to note the director's syntax in his choice of camera position and image size. In *Rear Window,* a clear example of Hitchcock's signature cinematic language occurs when Jeff tries his antimarriage campaign on Lisa by attacking the three things he said were most important to her—food, clothes, and the latest scandals.

There is an extraordinary variety of shots in this sequence as written. Each shift in camera position and image size—medium shot, semi-close-up, and so on—creates a pattern of emphasis within the sequence, indicating to whom we should be paying attention at a given moment. As written, semi-close-ups and close-ups dominate the sequence. In the execution, however, Hitchcock used such angles sparingly and only for dramatic impact. In the film the sequence begins with a medium shot of Lisa as described in Scene 71, which notes that the camera is shooting over the shoulder of Jeff.

Lisa argues that people aren't all that different, and that they share a common need for food, clothes, and entertainment. But Jeff counters her argument, expressing his view that Lisa couldn't possibly live his carefree and adventuresome lifestyle. In the script, the verbal sparring continues with alternating semi-close-ups of Jeff and Lisa. In the film, though, Hitchcock used the complementary medium shot of Jeff as described in Scene 76, this time shooting over Lisa's shoulder. This alternating of medium shots establishes a pattern that continues for nineteen shots, until Lisa sarcastically remarks that Jeff is being noble by being so brutally honest. Hitchcock then breaks the pattern with a close-up of Jeff, and for good reason. Lisa has touched a nerve, and for the remainder of the sequence—another seventeen shots in all—Lisa and Jeff do not share the frame together.

Scene 83 is the first moving shot in the sequence that begins as a close-up of Lisa, who then rises from the divan and moves to the center of the room, with the camera following her action. Agitated by the direction the conversation has taken, Lisa cannot sit still. She now sees what she's up against—Jeff is not willing to settle down, and he won't allow her to go with him.

In the film, Scenes 84 and 88 retreat to semi-close-ups, as opposed to the close-ups in the script. Again, Hitchcock is reserving his close-ups for dramatic effect. Scene 89 is a shot of Lisa standing in the doorway and is the first semi-long shot in the sequence, which is also used for dramatic purpose. Jeff has pulled away from Lisa, and Hitchcock's distancing of the camera illustrates Jeff's fear of commitment. This distance is still held in the following shot of Lisa, Scene 91, instead of cutting to a close-up as indicated in the script.

Jeff asks when he and Lisa will see each other again, to which Lisa replies, "Not for a long time. At least, not until tomorrow night." The script makes Lisa's exiting line appear lighthearted, calling for her to smile as she closes the door behind her. As portrayed by Grace Kelly, though, the smile is replaced by a pained expression, and there is no doubt that, for her, waiting until she can be with Jeff again *is* a long time.

Having just witnessed a lengthy separation and dialogue sequence, the audience is primed for a cinematic tour de force. In a sequence of purely subjective means, we observe with Jeff the nocturnal behavior of his neighbors on a rainy summer night. Several times during the night, Jeff sees the Salesman leave his apartment and return carrying a suitcase. The Salesman's odd behavior, along with the howl of the dog—in the film, this was changed to a woman's hushed cry and a shattered glass—have planted the seed in Jeff's mind (and the audience's) that something is not right. The punctuation of this sequence—an objective shot, or one that is not from any character's point of view—is one of the most significant in the film and epitomizes visually much of what Woolrich's story is about.

```
INT. JEFF'S APARTMENT—DAWN—CLOSEUP
A big head of Jeff. He is still in his
wheelchair, sound asleep. The CAMERA PANS
off his face, out through the window. The
rain has stopped, and the general light of
dawn is coming up. The CAMERA COMES TO
REST on the salesman's apartment and
corridor, which is still dimly lit by the
electric lights. We see the salesman
emerge into the corridor, pause a moment
to allow a woman to proceed him. Her back
is to the CAMERA and we do not see her
face. They move away, down the corridor.
The CAMERA PANS BACK onto Jeff's sleeping
face.
```

Hitchcock and Hayes provide the audience with privileged information, showing Thorwald leaving his apartment in the company of a woman whose face remains hidden and, more important, letting the audience know that this is *not* Jeff's point of view, for as we see, Jeff is sound asleep.

Woolrich relied on the literary device of first-person narration, having his Jeffries wonder if he misread the actions played out across the courtyard. But through this one visual, Hitchcock and Hayes shifted the point of view away from Jeff, planting a seed of doubt in the audience's mind and not, as Woolrich had, in his protagonist's. Had Hitchcock and Hayes shown this event through Jeff's point of view and allowed him to doubt his own convictions, he would have become a weak character. Instead, we are eyewitnesses to the account that Thorwald did leave at 6:00 A.M. with a woman, which will figure significantly when we later hear his alibi. We feel that we have been given more information than Jeff. But, in fact, we are being led up the garden path.

Hitchcock believed that camera movement fell into two categories—movement to follow a character or action and movement toward or away from a character or object. The latter Hitchcock defined as "dramatic movement," which is used for the purposes of making a statement. As the story unfolds, Jeff becomes more and more convinced that something has happened to the Salesman's wife and is determined to make Stella and Lisa believe him. After arguing with Jeff about his growing obsession with watching his neighbors and the conclusions he's drawn from doing so, Lisa sees Mrs. Thorwald's empty mattress and a large trunk in Thorwald's bedroom, and becomes convinced Jeff is right. To emphasize Lisa's reversal at this point in the story, the script calls for a tracking shot:

```
INT. JEFF'S APARTMENT—NIGHT—MEDIUM SHOT
Jeff lowers the glasses. His look is
sober. Lisa stands behind him, one hand on
the back of the wheelchair. She, too, is
serious. The CAMERA MOVES IN until Lisa's
head fills the screen. She says, slowly:


                  LISA
     Let's start from the beginning again,
     Jeff. Tell me everything you saw—and
     what you think it means.
```

This scene begins Lisa's transformation in Jeff's eyes. Lisa now takes an active part in the investigation, which will endear her to Jeff.

Later, when Detective Thomas J. Doyle arrives to report that Thorwald is innocent, he smugly bursts Jeff's and Lisa's enthusiasm with a lecture on rear window ethics. Disappointed and somewhat embarrassed, Jeff and Lisa lower the blinds and turn away from the window.

Lisa changes into her nightgown, which Jeff is about to compliment her on when a woman's scream is heard from the courtyard. The Siffleuse's dog is dead. Here Hitchcock uses a wide comprehensive shot of the entire courtyard. It is the first time such an angle is used in the film. The Siffleuse stands on her fire escape, and hearing the news that her dog has been strangled, she cries out.

Hitchcock and Hayes call attention to the entire courtyard. All the neighbors have come to their windows, except, as Jeff notes, Thorwald, whose presence in his darkened apartment is given away by the glowing tip of his cigar. Now Jeff and Lisa know they're right— Thorwald is guilty.

The following day, as Thorwald prepares to vacate his apartment, Jeff discovers that the zinnias in Thorwald's flower bed are shorter than they were before. This discovery is shown in a special-effect shot comparing the still image of Jeff's 35mm transparency to the live image of the courtyard. Jeff believes something is buried in the flower bed, which is the reason the inquisitive dog was murdered, and decides to send Thorwald an anonymous note and watch his reaction. Hitchcock also shakes things up at this point by bringing the camera up high, directly above Jeff, Lisa, and Stella, introducing another dramatic angle not used before in the film.

```
THE CAMERA RUSHES DOWN over Jeff's
shoulder, just in time to catch the last
word as he finishes writing the message.
The envelope is addressed to "LARS
THORWALD." The message reads, simply,
"WHAT HAVE YOU DONE WITH HER?"
```

In addition to introducing new angles at dramatic moments, Hitchcock and Hayes have also noticeably increased the rhythm and pacing of the film. There are nearly as many written scenes in the last third of the script as there are in the first two-thirds combined. "It's what I call the drive to the finish," Hayes explained.

You start your suspense, the pace gets a little more frantic, the noise increases, the conflict gets greater, and suddenly you're building to this finish. You start suspense, you drop it, you build it up again, you drop it until you get relief from it, you build it up, and each time, as you get closer to the end, it builds up more quickly and you have fewer interrupt-

WRITING WITH HITCHCOCK

ing interludes. Nothing. No distractions. You're now in pure suspense. You've built up your audience. You've teased them. You've let them know what's important and what isn't important. You've enlisted their aid on the hero's side and you go with it.

This is precisely the approach taken in the final moments of *Rear Window*.

Thorwald's startled reaction to the note makes Jeff even more curious to see what is buried in the flower bed, so he telephones Thorwald and, pretending to blackmail him, arranges a meeting in the bar of a local hotel. When Thorwald leaves, Lisa and Stella search the garden but find nothing buried there. Lisa then climbs into Thorwald's apartment via the fire escape and searches for Mrs. Thorwald's wedding ring. Lisa finds the ring but is caught when Thorwald returns suddenly. Jeff rescues Lisa by summoning the police. To get out of immediate danger, Lisa allows herself to be arrested, but not before signaling Jeff by flashing the wedding ring toward his window. The most terrifying moment in the film is prompted by this action:

```
We get a closer view of the waving hand.
She stops waving and holds her fingers
spread out. With her other hand she points
to the wedding ring on her left hand.

                  STELLA
       Mrs. Thorwald's ring!

THE LENS PANS UPWARD AND ACROSS until
it brings Thorwald's profile into the
picture. He is looking down directly at
Lisa's hands. His head slowly turns and
he looks right up — directly into the
lens. Suddenly he becomes aware that
```

> Lisa is signaling to someone who is
> watching him.

It is a startling moment in the film, as Thorwald looks right into the camera. The wedding ring has a second meaning—exclusively to Jeff—and so the two strands of the plot have come together.

The finale is one of the most ingenious and terrifying in the Hitchcock canon. The wheelchair-bound hero is left alone and helpless, with no means of defending himself from Thorwald except by improvising the use of some flashbulbs, which he employs to temporarily blind his attacker. The police arrive in time to save Jeff's life, but are unable to prevent him from being pushed out his rear window by Thorwald, in full view of the neighborhood he once watched so closely.

In the end, Jeff is able to admit his need and love for Lisa, and for a moment we are even given the impression that he has changed her. Lisa, now dressed in jeans, looks over at Jeff, sees he is sleeping, and reaches for a copy of *Harper's Bazaar*. Well, she hasn't changed all that much—and why should she?

Visual and Verbal Motifs in To Catch a Thief

After the extraordinarily structured screenplay for *Rear Window*, the final shooting script of *To Catch a Thief* may seem a little less disciplined. Whereas Hitchcock and Hayes concentrated on creating "pure cinema" in the former, in the latter they concocted a feast for the eyes in the film's imagery—and a feast for the ears in its dialogue.

To Catch a Thief is an unusual Hitchcock film in that it is something of a whodunit, yet it is typical of the director's work in that the denouement of the mystery is not his primary concern. The casual manner in which the mystery and suspense are handled do not detract from the romance plot or from the audience's enjoyment of its two stars. While the carefree design in itself might relegate *To Catch a Thief* to "lesser-Hitchcock" status—after all, even the director said of the film, "It was a lightweight story"—a careful study of the script reveals the development of several significant motifs, among them, hands, water, and games, some of which did not fully translate to the screen. Whereas *Rear Window* hit its target on all counts, *To Catch a Thief* misses on a few. Nonetheless, the finished film does exhibit Hitchcock's brilliance at building a story through the use of seamlessly integrated visual images and verbal clues.

The markers of a John Michael Hayes screenplay are much in evidence. The isolated protagonist who rejoins a larger community; the down-to-earth mother figure; and the literate descriptive passages, clever dialogue, and double entendres are all woven into the colorful fabric of *To Catch a Thief* and combined with the usual attention to detail found in a Hitchcock shooting script. Present are the director's characteristic concerns—fear of intimacy, betrayal of trust, and transfer of guilt—bolstered by a skillful display of recurring visual and verbal motifs. The central motifs are images of and references to hands and water, costumes and role-playing, and games and gambling.

Hitchcock frequently tied his films together with a linking image or idea. The use of triangles in *The Lodger*, food in *Frenzy*, drinking in *Notorious*, and doubles in *Shadow of a Doubt* and *Strangers on a Train* are only a few. In *To Catch a Thief*, there is an extraordinary number of close-ups of hands. It is appropriate, then, that the first scene in the script should end with a close-up on a pair of hands. After describing an open jewel case and its valuable contents bathed in a shaft of moonlight, the script notes:

```
a pair of black-gloved hands comes into
the picture—and with soundless and expert
dexterity, removes the jewelry from the
case.
```

The first scene is immediately followed by a shot of a black cat climbing a steep tiled roof. The cat is momentarily hidden by shadows, then reappears in the moonlight. The image of the black cat provides an aura of mystery and foreshadows the events that will follow. For later, on a similar rooftop, a cat burglar will emerge from the shadows, and its identity will be revealed.

The first time we see John Robie, the camera tilts up from his cat, asleep on a sofa, to him at work in his garden, creating a visual link between Robie and his cat. From an insert of Art Buchwald's column in the *Paris Herald Tribune*, we learn something of Robie's past career as a jewel thief. The insert serves a purpose similar to that of the cast, broken camera, and photographs in introducing L. B. Jefferies in *Rear Window*. Continuing the hand motif, Hitchcock and Hayes show that the cat has used its claws to tear through the newspaper article that questioned the innocence of its master.

Like a cat, both at the opening and through much of the film, Robie remains coolly detached. He is independent, having retreated to the isolation of his villa in the hills above the Grande Corniche. His arc as a character, although it fully develops late in the film, comes only when he readily admits and accepts his dependency on others, particularly Francie. That he only admits it casually—and not without her prompting—leads the reader and viewer to suspect he hasn't changed all that much, like Lisa at the end of *Rear Window*.

Early on, Robie toys with the police. From an upstairs bedroom he watches the police enter his driveway. He takes out a shotgun, loads it, and rests it on an armchair before returning to the living room to meet Commissaire Lepic and his assistant, Mercier. This is an example of Hitchcock's ability to manipulate his audience. The question—what does he intend to do with the shotgun?—draws the reader and viewer into the action.

The detectives want Robie to go to the police station so that they can question him about the recent jewel robberies. Robie agrees, but asks if he can change from his casual clothes into something more formal. Careful attention is paid in the script to the clothing of nearly every character, in almost every sequence—thus, the "costumes" represent the characters, or at least their intended role within a given scene. This role-playing motif culminates in a grand costume ball.

Robie's request to change his clothes is merely a ruse, though. He goes to his bedroom, and the sound of the door locking behind him causes Lepic and Mercier to follow. Suddenly the sounds of a shotgun blast and the thud of a falling body break the silence. Believing that Robie has committed suicide, all the detectives rush into the villa. John Robie, of course, has not committed suicide, and the camera reveals he has escaped to the roof. While Lepic and his men busy themselves breaking into Robie's bedroom, the sounds of an engine starting and a car speeding away cause the police to run back to their own car to make chase along the twisting mountain roads. The police eventually catch up to the speeding car, but it is Robie's housekeeper, Germaine, who is revealed to be the driver. She is a decoy, luring the police away from the villa so that Robie can escape. Filming the chase from the air shows off the beautiful topography, but it is also a cheat, because the audience, too, is led to believe Robie is the driver of the vehicle. Hitchcock generally did not film car chases objectively; note that the driving sequences in *Notorious*, *North by Northwest*, and *Family Plot* are all treated very subjectively, as is the sequence in *To Catch a Thief* in which Francie and Robie are being followed by the police.

Arriving at the restaurant of Augustus Bertani, an old Resistance friend who employs their former Maquis comrades, Robie's presence causes Foussard, the wine steward, to clumsily open a bottle of champagne, emphasized by a close-up of the wine spilling over his hands. Robie tells Bertani of the visit paid him by the police. Significantly, Bertani checks his appearance in a wall mirror, which Hitchcock frequently used to convey a difference between appearance and reality.

Although it was written as a master scene, Hitchcock shot this first meeting of Robie and Bertani as a separation. Throughout, Bertani is photographed in a position of superiority, from low angles. Robie, on the other hand, is suppressed in the frame, photographed from high angles. If Bertani and Robie were truly friends and allies, in the Hitchcock visual lexicon, they would be photographed together. Robie realizes he will have to catch the thief himself—a feat Bertani immediately discourages. Bertani is called to business, allowing Robie an opportunity to see former comrades who work in the kitchen. Robie's former friends believe he has returned to a life of crime and display their anger. A kitchen helper pours and offers Robie a saucer of milk. A vegetable chef uses his hands to remove the tops from a bunch of carrots, making a sound like a neck being broken. Finally, a dishwasher known as La Mule orders Robie out of the kitchen, backing up his threat by smashing a dinner plate and approaching Robie with the jagged end of one half. Robie again resorts to games to disarm the threat by tossing a wine bottle at the brute. In each instance—the milk poured into the saucer, the twisting of the carrots, the smashed dinner plate, and the tossed wine bottle—the action is conveyed through hands. There is no need for a clichéd dialogue scene in which Robie's former comrades denounce him; it is clear they believe him to be guilty and are therefore angry.

Bertani arranges for Robie to be taken to the beach club at Cannes by Foussard's daughter. In the script, the first clue that Danielle Foussard is the new cat burglar is her association with heights, for she is sitting atop a ladder. Further, the script indicates that while inexpensive, her light summer dress reveals a stylishness that shows she is not one of Bertani's regular employees. In fact, in the film her dress top is a female parallel to Robie's striped shirt. Danielle then baits Robie with continuous references to the cat burglar, and after he becomes annoyed, she asks, "Did I brush your fur the wrong way?"

Danielle, of course, is playing a game of cat and mouse with Robie, since she knows he is innocent. Thus the name painted on the side of the speedboat she drives—*Maquis Mouse*—is apt. When water sprays on Robie, Danielle continues baiting him, saying, "It must be true what they say. Cats don't like water." Danielle's game is deceptive. Although she knows Robie is innocent, she accuses him openly and offers to help him by inviting him to run away with her to South America. Danielle is much like Francie—excited by the danger and thrill of catching a thief. But whereas

Danielle knows Robie is innocent, Francie at first believes him to be guilty.

Following Robie's arrival at the beach club—where he is seen by Francie for the first time—he receives a telephone call from Bertani, who tells him that he has arranged a meeting at the flower market between Robie and a man who has made inquiries about the stolen jewels. The flower-market sequence opens with a high shot, then cuts to a close-up of a cart of colorful flowers moving away from the camera. A hand in the foreground appears in close-up—Robie's, tossing a coin. Several cutaways to the police detectives watching Robie remind us that he is on the run. H. H. Hughson, the insurance man from Lloyd's of London, is then introduced. Hughson is out of place in a business suit and homburg—attire more appropriate for his London office than for a summer afternoon on the Riviera. His first word upon recognizing Robie through the prearranged signal of tossing a coin is "Tails?" In this way, the theme of games is carried forward.

Hughson explains that his firm insured a good deal of the jewelry that has already been stolen during the recent crime wave. Robie, who likens insurance to gambling, offers Hughson a chance to recover his company's losses in exchange for information. Thus the stakes are now revealed. Robie risks eight years in prison, while Hughson faces the loss of his professional reputation and job by agreeing to provide Robie with a list of his wealthiest clients.

At the top of Hughson's list are Mrs. Stevens and her daughter, Francie, whom Robie sets out to meet at the casino. Standing on the opposite side of a roulette table, Robie tries to make a connection with Mrs. Stevens by means of shared humor. Mrs. Stevens is the type of woman who would find humor in an embarrassing situation, so Robie uses a casino chip and the cleavage of the woman in front of him as a ruse to meet Mrs. Stevens and Francie. While the crowd around the table moves to place their bets, Robie—his poised fingers in close-up—drops a 10,000-franc chip down the front of the woman's dress. Her scream causes all attention to be focused on Robie, whose mock confusion and embarrassment results in a moment of eye contact and shared laughter between him and Mrs. Stevens. It is an elaborate way of bringing about a meeting, but the sheer ridiculousness of the situation is so much fun.

In the scene following the casino sequence, we see Robie has successfully gained Mrs. Stevens's confidence, as the group is sitting over late-night cocktails. As filmed, the second shot of this sequence is a close-up of Francie, in profile, facing screen right, which recalls the second shot of the earlier dinner sequence, which was another close-up of Francie in profile, facing screen left. The director noted, "I deliberately photographed Grace Kelly ice-cold and I kept cutting to her profile, looking classical, beautiful, and very distant." This was Hitchcock's manner of building suspense with regard to sex. Sex on the screen, the director believed, is best when the tension is developed gradually throughout the course of a film.

When Robie accompanies the ladies to their suite, Hitchcock reveals the sex he has been building toward. In close-up, Francie turns in her open doorway to Robie and unexpectedly presses her lips to his. She then retreats into her suite and closes the door behind her. Her action reveals her true character and recalls Hayes's description of Lisa Fremont as "a lady in the drawing room and a minx in the bedroom." Of this scene Hitchcock told Peter Bogdanovich, "It's as if she's unzipped Cary's fly."

The following morning Hughson informs Robie and Mrs. Stevens that there's been another robbery. Hughson hopes he has not been betrayed by Robie and pleads with Mrs. Stevens to place her jewelry in the hotel safe. Mrs. Stevens reacts by extinguishing a cigarette in the yolk of a fried egg—emphasized by a close-up—and comparing insurance to gambling, she asks Hughson if he intends to welch if her jewels are stolen. Francie enters the room, no longer the cool and reserved woman of the previous evening. She is bright, gay, and quite coquettish. Has she already guessed Robie's identity?

Robie and Francie meet later in the hotel lobby on their way to the beach. Francie wears a very chic black and white sports outfit and sun hat which draws attention from the guests who pass her in the lobby. An idea in the script that only half made it into the fin-

ished film is that Robie believes *he* is the one being closely scruti-
nized.

At the beach Danielle resumes her cat-and-mouse game, signaling to Robie to swim out and meet her at the float. Again Danielle
takes a position of height over Robie, climbing onto the float while
he remains in the water. The sequence brings up several interesting
points. Robie asks Danielle if she knows who informed the police
that he would be at the flower market. Robie knows that Bertani
sent him there, but the idea is quickly dropped. Also never really
brought into question is whether the infatuation Danielle reveals
for Robie is genuine or merely part of her charade.

Francie then joins Robie and Danielle at the float, and the rivalry between the women becomes clear. Francie's presence is an
addition from the first draft and is her only screen time with
Danielle in the finished film. Trying to cover that he and Danielle
know each other, Robie says that he was asking about renting water
skis. But Francie doesn't bite:

                    FRANCIE
     Are you sure you were asking about
     water skis? From where I sat it
     looked as if you two were conjugating
     some irregular verbs.

Of course, Danielle is not about to let Francie get the better of her,
and all Robie can do is watch with a mixture of growing discomfort
and amusement. "She looks a lot older up close," quips Danielle.

                    FRANCIE
     To a mere child, anyone over twenty
     might seem old.

                    DANIELLE
     A child? Shall we stand in shallower
     water, and discuss that?

Danielle's challenge to Francie contained in the previous line has a double meaning. One is her desire to have Robie compare them; the other, a challenge to a real cat fight, recalling her earlier line to Robie about cats disliking water. But more about water later.

The next five movements of the film make up the crux of Francie's pursuit of Robie. But this, too, is just a game. At this point in the story, her amorous words are not backed by any true feeling other than a desire for adventure. "What do you get a thrill out of most?" Robie asks. "I'm still looking for that one," replies Francie. Still under the observation of a pair of detectives since their departure from the beach, Francie attempts to elude them by speeding along the dangerously narrow, curving roads during the final stretch of their drive. She also hopes to break through Robie's cool demeanor. Francie wants to see if he will give in first—she is playing a game of chicken. This sets up the only logical conclusion to the sequence—a chicken crossing the road—which allows Robie and Francie to get away from the police.

Here again the hand motif is used to convey the attitude of a character. The script indicates that Francie smiles at Robie with an "Enjoying the ride?" expression, to which he smiles in response. His hands, however, reveal the truth.

```
INT. CONVERTIBLE — (DAY) — CLOSEUP
Robie's hands on his knees. He wipes them
slightly.
```

Only after the police wreck their car to avoid the chicken crossing the road does Robie tell Francie to slow down. Having won this game of chicken, Francie chooses her moment to unmask Robie.

The picnic lunch at La Turbie begins with another high shot, overlooking the winding road and Monte Carlo. The meal, of course, is cold chicken. As Lisa Fremont did before her, Francie proudly displays her feminine intuition. "I hope you try to bluff me, Mr. Robie," she says, "then I can have the fun of telling you how clever I was." These are the same feelings Lisa Fremont experienced as she became more involved with the investigation of Thorwald. But soon Francie goes too far, offering herself as Robie's accomplice in a jewel robbery: "The cat has a new kitten. When do we start?" Robie takes hold of her wrist to stop her. The hand motif continues when she says, "You're leaving fingerprints on my arm." Finally, Robie pulls her close to him and leans her toward the picnic basket, where this time he kisses her.

The fireworks, or seduction, scene immediately follows. After dinner in her suite, Francie moves about the room turning off lamps, neatly reversing Lisa's action of turning on the lamps in Jeff's apartment in *Rear Window*.

FRANCIE
   If you really want to <u>see</u> fireworks,
   it's better with the lights out.

She snaps out the light. Then she crosses
and comes down behind the sofa. Robie
turns again, his eyes following her. As
she walks, she says:

FRANCIE
   I have a feeling that tonight you're
   going to see one of the Riviera's
   most fascinating sights.

She comes into the foreground, pauses
in front of a table lamp, bending over
it slightly: The jewels around her neck
catch the light and seem quite prominent.
She turns her head and looks across at
Robie.

FRANCIE
   I was talking about the fireworks.

The fetishism of *To Catch a Thief* is most explicitly expressed in this sequence. Francie, who had earlier spoken of her intense dislike for gambling, raises the ante by challenging Robie to resist her. Francie wants Robie precisely because she believes him to be guilty, and is willing to stake her virtue on it. She wants him to *take* it. This is about as close as one in 1950s Hollywood could get to portraying a rape fantasy, as Francie likens theft to lovemaking:

```
                 FRANCIE
     All right.
(She begins painting a mood picture)
     You've studied the—layout—drawn the
     plans, worked out the timetable—put on
     your dark clothes, with your crepe-
     soled shoes and your rope. Maybe your
     face blackened. You're over the roofs
     in the darkness, down the side of the
     wall to the right apartment—and then,
     the window is locked! All that elation
     turned into frustration. What would you
     do? The thrill is right in front of
     you, but you can't quite get it. The
     gems glistening on the other side of
     the window. Someone on the bed, asleep,
     breathing heavily.
```

Robie tells her, "I have about the same interest in jewelry that I have in horse-racing, politics, modern poetry, or women who need weird excitement. None."

Francie reintroduces the hand motif, challenging Robie to deny he's the cat burglar while holding her necklace in his hand. The motif continues as they move to the sofa, where Francie takes Robie's hand in hers and kisses his fingertips, finally placing the necklace in his hand, inviting, "Ever had a better offer in your whole life?" But Robie knows that Francie's feelings for him are no more genuine than the stones in her necklace: "You know, as well as I do, that necklace is imitation." The kiss is photographed from above, as Robie leans Francie back into the corner of the sofa.*

Now that the relationship has been consummated, the thrill Francie had been searching for is gone. And soon after, she angrily bursts into Robie's room. "Give them back to me," she demands, speaking of her mother's jewels. Francie likes to gamble, but she isn't prepared to accept the risks. While Francie searches Robie's room, he goes to her suite to study the crime scene. Hitchcock's minute attention to detail is illustrated by the inclusion in the script of a shot of Francie's bathing suit—worn earlier the same day—draped over the back of a chair. The script indicates: "It makes us almost feel she's in the room." The motif of clothing representing character is reinforced. When she returns to her suite, Francie exposes Robie, telling her mother that he's not the American lumber magnate he claimed to be but a famous jewel thief. As evidence, Francie announces that while searching his room, she found that all his clothes had French labels in them.

But Mrs. Stevens is not swayed by her daughter's histrionics and takes Robie's side. Francie calls for the police, sending Robie into hiding. In one sense, Francie feels betrayed, upset at the thought that after making love to her—stealing her virtue, essentially—Robie is able to steal not only another woman's jewels but her own mother's.

Disguised as a fisherman, Robie meets Hughson at the end of a pier. That Robie chooses a location near the sea as a hiding place is no casual occurrence, as it relates directly to the water imagery associated with the criminals in *To Catch a Thief*. The water imagery is first introduced by Bertani, who owns a seaside restaurant. It is also Bertani who orders Foussard to have Danielle bring Robie by

*The final kiss in the sequence is preceded by a sweeping circular camera move, opposed to the straight-on, static shots of Francie kissing Robie in the hotel corridor and Robie kissing Francie in the convertible. Hitchcock frequently photographed kisses in circular or semicircular movements to express fulfillment of a romance—*Suspicion, Notorious, Vertigo,* and *Torn Curtain* are a few examples of films demonstrating this perspective.

sea to the beach club at Cannes. The trio of criminals is immediately associated with water.

At the beach club, a fourth character associated with water is introduced. The appearance of the concession attendant, Claude, is meant to throw the audience off: because of his physique, the audience is supposed to suspect he is the new Cat. (With regard to the water motif, it should also be noted that in the carnival sequence cut from the first draft script there was an episode involving a float with King Neptune and a cast of fishermen and mermaids.)

Later Danielle beckons Robie into water for another rendezvous. At the hotel float she plays her cat-and-mouse game, again trying to get Robie to stop searching for the new thief. Following the scene at the hotel float, Robie discovers that someone has been searching through the clothes he locked in a cabana and found the insurance agency list. The giveaway clue is a wet thumbprint (the hand motif again). The only logical culprit is Claude, who would have been able to enter Robie's cabana while Danielle held his attention at the float.

It would seem that the criminals want to keep Robie in or near water, where he is vulnerable; recall Danielle's line about cats disliking water. However, when Robie goes into hiding, he returns to the sea. Robie tells Hughson of a threatening note he received, warning him to stay away from the Silvas' villa. Hughson warns, "This note is obviously the bait for a trap." But Robie intends to turn the tables with bait of his own.

The sequence at the Silvas' villa brings a conclusion to the water imagery. It is only fitting that the Silvas' villa is referred to in the script as the SEA VILLA. It is here that Foussard and an unidentified character—who logically must be Claude—attempt to murder Robie. In the struggle, Foussard is struck by his accomplice and plunges to a watery grave.

Yet again, the significance of hands is apparent in the script:

```
A man's arm is seen, as we SHOOT UP toward
the moonlit sky. The hand grips a long
```

> blackjack. It descends successively and
> heavily down on one of the struggling men.

Robie's attacker has been struck (by a monkey wrench instead of a blackjack, in the actual film) and plunges to his death. The dead man is Danielle's father, Foussard—Bertani's wine steward with the limp.

At Foussard's funeral Francie apologizes to Robie for believing he was guilty and offers to help clear his name once and for all. But he remains distant, saying they should return to their "mutual disregard" of each other. As Robie turns to go, Francie grabs his arm with her hand and holds him—shown in an unscripted close-up—finally admitting that she's in love with him. Francie no longer regards words as playthings, which she has done up to this point, so Robie asks for her help in getting into the Sanford gala.

The costume motif reaches its climax at the Sanford gala, where the characters arrive in eighteenth-century dress. The first close-up of the sequence in the script is of Bertani closely watching the arriving guests. As written, the camera reveals the mastermind behind the new Cat. In the film, however, Hitchcock uses this scene to set up another ruse. The scene begins in a medium shot, with Bertani's back to the camera. He stands beside Antoinette, who is dressed as a serving maid. He then turns and moves to Danielle, who is also dressed as a serving maid, unpacking bottles of champagne. Bertani makes a consoling gesture to lift Danielle's spirits, then moves toward the party, the camera panning him. Instead of the close-up of Bertani, which seems intended as a visual clue, Hitchcock reveals a different clue, which is quickly forgotten: Antoinette and Danielle are dressed in identical costumes.

Mrs. Stevens, Francie, and Robie make their entrance in costume. Robie is dressed as a blackamoor attendant to Francie, his face and hands concealed by a black mask and gloves. Within earshot of Lepic and Mercier, Mrs. Stevens feigns a need for heart pills in order to drink champagne and asks Robie to retrieve her purse. Lepic and Mercier turn their attention to the costumed fig-

ure of Robie as he enters the villa. Lepic and Mercier quickly inform the Sanfords and the other police officers of Robie's presence,
giving a description of his costume.

Unknown to the police and the audience, Robie secretly meets
with Hughson, who is wearing an identical costume. Robie's costume—and subsequent disappearance and replacement by Hughson at the party—recalls the black cat from the film's opening
scene: the one that disappears into the shadows and then reappears.
The police and a substantial part of the audience believe that Francie and Robie are dancing all evening. The crowd at the gala dwin-
dles until they are the last couple on the dance floor. The orchestra
finally stops playing, so Francie and Hughson (as Robie) retire to
her room in the villa, observed by Lepic and his men, who are satisfied that they have Robie under surveillance for the night.

Inside Francie's bedroom it is revealed that it is Hughson, not
Robie, who has been dancing all evening. Hughson says, "Frankly, I
didn't think this scheme of yours would work, Francie. But it has."
The line emphasizes that Robie did need Francie's help.

The next shot reveals Robie on the rooftop, looking down.
While waiting for something to happen, Robie sees Bertani climbing into his car, but he is puzzled by what appears to be Danielle
getting into the car before him. Robie is exasperated and seems on
the verge of giving up when he hears a sound elsewhere on the
rooftop. Just as Robie is fooled by the serving maid—Antoinette in
costume—getting into the car with Bertani, so, too, is the audience.
By now, most of the audience has come to suspect Danielle. But
Hitchcock prolongs the guessing, even if only briefly, as the final
chase reveals Danielle to be the new Cat.

In the final tag, Francie gets Robie to admit that he needed her
help. They shake hands and Francie moves to leave, but Robie
pulls her toward him and kisses her passionately. She is radiant, saying, "So this is where you live? Oh, Mother will love it up here." A
bell sounds, and Robie eyes Francie sideways. Francie's last line,
like Lisa Fremont's reading of her *Harper's Bazaar*, adds a final
ironic touch.

The Act of Confessing in The Trouble with Harry

For their third collaboration, Hitchcock and Hayes returned to the classic dilemma of what to do with an unwanted corpse. In *Rear Window* they had the murderer cut his wife into pieces and scatter them along Manhattan's East River, taking their cue from an actual murder case. In *The Trouble with Harry*, though, the main characters are so affable that through most of the film, none of them is able to dispose of Harry for more than a few hours. Lacking the complexity and suspense of the majority of the director's 1950s films, *The Trouble with Harry* stands out as an oddity to be studied further, yet, strangely, it has been ignored by all but a few commentators. While the basic material did not necessarily lend itself well to Hitchcock's cinematic treatment, relying more on dialogue than visuals to tell the story, its thematic concerns are ones the director focused on throughout his career: sex, death, and redemption.

Like his previous scripts for Hitchcock, which focused on the integration of an isolated protagonist with a larger community, Hayes's screenplay for *The Trouble with Harry* is also concerned with self-imposed isolation. In this case, it is not just an individual but a community of people, each of whom, for various reasons, lives alone. Until an outsider named Harry Worp invades their Edenic environment, the principal characters manage to remain strangers.

The Trouble with Harry is similar to *Rear Window* and *To Catch a Thief* in that a quartet of characters occupies its center and that, by the end of each film, a couple is united in love: L. B. Jefferies and Lisa Fremont, John Robie and Francie Stevens, Sam Marlow and Jennifer Rogers. A set of paternal figures occupies each film as well: a wise mother figure (Stella McCaffery, Mrs. Stevens, and Miss Gravely) is balanced by a father figure, who also holds some official status (Lieutenant Thomas J. Doyle, H. H. Hughson of Lloyd's, and Captain Albert Wiles). In the first two, the paternal figures are not coupled, but in *The Trouble with Harry* they are.

To appreciate *The Trouble with Harry* fully, one must see how the motif of the confession is alluded to in nearly all the director's films. In screenwriting, the term for a character's change or revelation is the "arc," or "spine," or "through-line." This is the character's pivotal moment, when he or she will take action that will lead to freedom or further enslavement and, on occasion, death. In Hitchcock's films, which tend to be romances, this pivotal moment usually occurs between the hero and heroine, often acknowledging something that we, the audience, have known all along. The act of confessing in Hitchcock's films, as in life, takes many forms. It is not merely in the literal (or legal) sense that Hitchcock's characters acknowledge their sins and shortcomings, and frequently the director's protagonists have more to confess than his villains.

Movie characters reveal themselves through a combination of dialogue and action. Often dialogue is used for exposition, while action serves to reveal the character's reactions to obstacles that prevent him from achieving his goal. In Hitchcock's best films, though, his protagonists not only overcome the plot's obstacles through their own actions but are provided with an opportunity to articulate their revelations, usually in the form of a confession.

For example, in *Rear Window*, while Lars Thorwald is offscreen telling the detectives the manner and location in which he disposed of his wife, Jefferies is busy confessing to Lisa that he'd been lying to himself all along, refusing to see that he loves her deeply. In *To Catch a Thief*, John Robie forces Danielle to confess to the police that she is the new cat burglar by dangling her over a courtyard. Moments later, Francie corners Robie on the terrace of his hillside villa and gets him to confess that he needed her help. In *Notorious*, Devlin—another Cary Grant role—is able to save a dying Alicia only by confessing his true feelings, saying, "I was a fat-headed guy full of pain." Devlin whisks Alicia out of harm's way, leaving Alex Sebastian to face his co-conspiritors. In *Vertigo*, Scottie—another James Stewart role—forces Judy to confess her role in the murder of Madeleine Elster and, in the process, overcomes his acrophobia. The list of confessions in Hitchcock is long; it culminates in *I Confess*, another personal, underappreciated film, one in which nearly every character has something to confess.

Just as Uncle Charlie arrived to shake up the Newton household in *Shadow of a Doubt*, it is an outsider, Harry Worp, who is the catalyst for both change and unification among the principals in *The Trouble with Harry*. In coming together, three of the four principal characters are liberated from a life of repression by each making a confession of sorts.

Miss Gravely's quiet reservedness, which allows her to remain silent when Captain Wiles accepts the responsibility for Harry's death, and which has ultimately resulted in her spinsterhood, is replaced by a newfound freedom and sexual reawakening. She begins to focus her attentions on the captain, but still remains somewhat coy in front of the others. Once Miss Gravely confesses to Captain Wiles, she is liberated and no longer fears community gossip.

After losing her husband and marrying again for the security of her child rather than love, Jennifer Rogers hides from the world. Even the script notes that the "circumstances of her life have forced her to run away from the thing she wants most," love. With Harry's death, Jennifer regains her freedom but not entirely her belief in love. However, Sam is able to revive Jennifer's faith in the power of a loving relationship.

Captain Albert Wiles plays the role expected of a retired sea captain as he spins tales of danger and adventure on the high seas. Through his tales Captain Wiles masks his fears and conceals his true self. He, too, confesses his faults—that he was not the adventurer he claims to be but merely a tugboat captain who never went more than a mile offshore. Only after facing up to his shortcomings and lies does he prove, to everyone's surprise, that he truly is a hero by stealing Harry's shoes out of the deputy sheriff's car; in so doing, Captain Wiles makes it possible for the group to return Harry's body to the woods, where it can be found again.

Sam Marlow is the character least in need of change. From beginning to end, he is open and frank, showing little concern for social convention. This attitude, however, does not take the form of a feeling of superiority—as it does with Brandon Shaw in *Rope*—but instead allows Sam to take pleasure in sharing and spreading his energy and freedom. He sings while walking through the countryside, assists Miss Gravely with her makeover, openly compliments Jennifer, inspires bravery in Captain Wiles, and is unconcerned with an art critic's opinion of his paintings when a millionaire wishes to buy them; even in the selling of his work, he profits not monetarily but by bartering his paintings to obtain gifts for his friends. Through these subtle changes of character and by emphasizing certain aspects of Jack Trevor Story's novel, Hitchcock and Hayes have taken ownership of Story's characters.

Given the relatively low number of scenes for a Hitchcock shooting script (321 by comparison to 481 for the *Rear Window* script), at 154 pages *The Trouble with Harry* is still close to the average length for one of the director's scripts. The length is more the result of Hayes's descriptive passages, for the writer drew upon his familiarity with the New England setting to layer the script with vivid details in an almost poetic style.

The screenplay for *The Trouble with Harry* begins with a close shot of a sugar maple branch, intended as a time-lapsed or stop-motion sequence to run beneath the main titles. The script describes in colorful detail the life cycle of a single bud on this branch—beginning as a tiny bud, then uncoiling itself into a small five-lobed leaf, and spreading out and growing to a deep green maturity. Then, as the leaf's stem turns brown and its tips turn red, the leaf changes from a pale red to orange and finally to yellow.

In the script it is clear that death will come to this leaf, but also that the branch will continue to grow and a new bud will form with the coming spring, thus illustrating the cycle of nature. This image—through its evocation of seasonal change embodied by the changing leaves—mirrors the process of life and the inevitability of death, and might have been the perfect way to begin the movie. The sequence depicting the cycle of nature never made it into the film, though, and the main titles appear over Saul Steinberg's rendering of autumn foliage, small-town New England structures, and a series of birds, all leading up to a line drawing of a man lying on his back, eyes closed, wearing an enormous pair of shoes.

While the film is set in autumn, Story's novel takes place during the summer, so that the symbolism surrounding nature's death and rebirth—the ongoing process—remained incomplete. This theme of rebirth, which recurs throughout the film, is also representative of the confession/redemption theme. Once absolved of sin and no longer burdened by the weight of a guilty conscience, one is, in effect, reborn. Although Captain Wiles says at one point that he possesses no conscience, he acts remarkably as if he does, and later proves that in fact he does through his confession to the others.

Following the main titles, the film opens with a series of shots of the Vermont landscape. Into this idyllic setting walks a small boy named Arnie Rogers, armed with his disintegrator ray gun. A series of aural details follow—three loud shotgun blasts, the sounds of a physical struggle, a man's voice exclaiming, "Okay—I know how to handle your type!" and then a crashing sound. These sounds cause Arnie to pause momentarily, with the wonderment and fear of a four-year-old boy, then resume his quest until he comes upon the body of a man lying on his back, with a small wound on his forehead—quite dead. The sight of the dead man sends Arnie running toward home.

The first of the main characters, Captain Wiles, is then introduced while he is hunting. He strides through the woods, hoping to bag at least two rabbits, but finds instead a freshly shot beer can, a NO SHOOTING sign, and, finally, the body of the man whose presence alarmed little Arnie Rogers a moment earlier. White and shaken, believing himself responsible, Captain Wiles says in a most Hitchcockian manner, "Mother always said I'd come to a bad end." Captain Wiles decides he'd better dispose of Harry's remains. But before Captain Wiles can complete his task, Miss Gravely comes upon him as he is dragging Harry by the ankles and greets him in a surprisingly calm manner, asking, "What seems to be the trouble, Captain?"

Captain Wiles explains that he mistook Harry for a rabbit, shot him, and now intends to bury him. Although the viewer is not yet aware of this, Miss Gravely believes she has killed Harry, and so she is touched by the captain's accepting responsibility for the death. This transfer-of-guilt theme is common in Hitchcock, from *Under Capricorn* to *Strangers on a Train* to *I Confess*. As a result, Miss Gravely invites Captain Wiles to her cottage for coffee, blueberry muffins, and elderberry wine. We learn that they have been neighbors for three years but have yet to exchange social calls.

Following Miss Gravely's departure, Captain Wiles is subjected to a series of passersby who come upon Harry in the woods, all of whom prevent the captain from completing his business of burying the body. This sequence is treated quite subjectively, in the Hitchcock manner. Captain Wiles watches from his hiding place as Arnie Rogers returns with his mother, Jennifer. "Thank Providence. The last of Harry!" she says breathlessly. Her indifference gives the reader a surprising introduction to one of the principal characters, but we are no more shocked by her reaction than by those of Captain Wiles and Miss Gravely.

Captain Wiles then watches as Dr. Greenbow, engrossed in a book of poetry, stumbles over the body, mutters an apology, and moves along. Soon a tramp passes through and, on seeing Harry, proceeds to steal his shoes. In his excellent essay on *The Trouble with Harry*, Ed Sikov notes that in the book of Deuteronomy (25:5–10) the punishment indicated for a man who refuses to marry (i.e., copulate with) the wife of a dead brother is that she will "come unto him in the presence of the elders, and loose his shoe from off his foot, and spit in his face . . . And his name shall be called in Israel, The house of him who hath his shoe loosed." Jack Trevor Story made good use of this idea in his novel, which Hitchcock, of course, expanded on with a vengeance, filling *The Trouble with Harry* with as many images of feet as *To Catch a Thief* has images of hands. Examples of this foot motif include the following: Harry's feet in red-tipped socks, close-ups of both Miss Gravely and the tramp kicking Harry to make certain he's dead, a close-up of Calvin's foot opening a sketchpad to see Sam's portrait of Harry, Arnie's observation that even with four rabbit's feet the rabbit still got killed, Dr. Greenbow stumbling over Harry's feet twice, Sam first noticing Harry when he sees his feet in a sketch of a landscape, Miss Gravely defending herself by striking Harry with her hiking shoe, the shadow of Harry's feet looming on the wall of Jennifer's living room, Captain Wiles stirring from a nap when he touches Harry's foot, Harry's bare feet sticking out of the bathtub, and, finally, the movie's last shot, which is of Harry's shoes.

Sam Marlow's introduction at once establishes his self-assured and carefree nature. His singing voice precedes him throughout the hillsides and down to the meadow, heard over various shots of both natural landscapes and the other characters in the story. In fact, nearly all the adult male characters in the film are heard before they appear on-screen. The dissonant shout of an unseen man, which startles Arnie Rogers, turns out to be a sex-crazed Harry attacking Miss Gravely, moments before dropping down dead. Captain Wiles is introduced through three shotgun blasts—a sign of virility. The noisy motor of Calvin Wiggs's antique car is heard before he is seen, representing his outdated, antiquated, even rusty ideals. And even Dr. Greenbow and the millionaire are announced at times through sound. But in Sam's song—and the emphasis it is given in the script and film by cutting to the various characters who hear it; even in a witty close shot of Harry's shoeless feet—Hitchcock calls our attention to Sam as a representative of harmony and sensitivity.

In the same way that *To Catch a Thief* is linked to its darker counterpart, *Marnie*, by its shared fetishism, *The Trouble with Harry* finds its parallel in *Rope*. Both films share a gallows humor, but where the humor of *Rope* tends to leave a bad taste, the humor in *The Trouble with Harry* is a little more innocent. While the two films could not be more different in tone, they are similar in that the director deviated from his usual cinematic style in approaching the material. In *Rope*, Hitchcock virtually rejected the use of montage, and in *The Trouble with Harry*, he severely limited the variety of shots he employed, using very little camera movement and only a handful of close-ups, so that together the films form a unique part of the Hitchcock canon. The films are further linked in their discussions of art, a central theme in both. Brandon Shaw in *Rope* expresses his desire for artistic talent as well as his desire to kill, saying, "The power to kill can be just as satisfying as the power to create." Sam Marlow, perhaps the most grounded character in Hitchcock's work, can find satisfaction only in the power to create.

After stopping to drop off his latest painting at Wigg's Emporium, where he also helps Miss Gravely with her new makeup and hairdo, Sam searches the countryside for inspiration and finds it near the place where Captain Wiles left Harry. As Sam sketches the landscape, he notices something out of place in his drawing. He looks and sees a man's shoeless foot, which is first shown in the film in an insert of the sketch, then in a shot of the landscape. Sam walks over to Harry and asks, "Would you mind moving out of my picture?" The choice of the word "picture" conveys a double meaning, taken in the context of Sam, the artist, being a surrogate for Hitchcock. It is as though Hitchcock were trying to create a landscape of a film with no reference to murder, or corpses, as he so often felt forced to do. We hear more of Sam's voice as Hitchcock's later, in the scene with the millionaire and the art critic.

When Sam notices the man is dead, he first reacts as Arnie did, turning to leave the woods quickly. On reflection, though, he returns to Harry and, inspired, decides to sketch Harry's portrait. Captain Wiles, who is sleeping nearby, awakens to find Sam at work over Harry. Rather than lie, the captain decides to plead his case and beg for mercy. Sam tries to ease Captain Wiles's conscience, telling him that if he did indeed kill Harry, he should feel honored that he was able to aid a man in the fulfillment of his destiny. But Captain Wiles, who is also something of a surrogate for Hitchcock, says it's not his conscience that bothers him but his fear of the police.

                          CAPTAIN
          It's me. It's me that's worrying me.
          Me and my future life. I know the po-
          lice and their suspicious ways.

> You're guilty until you're proved in-
> nocent, and I want nothing to do with
> them. Bury him, I say, and have done
> with him. He's no good to anyone now.
> Lay him to rest. Put him under the
> sod. Forget him. You never saw him
> and I never did it.

Fearing Captain Wiles may get himself into trouble, Sam offers to call on Mrs. Rogers and ask if she intends to inform the authorities about Harry's death. Sam wants to help Captain Wiles, but also is glad of the opportunity to speak with Jennifer Rogers. On meeting Jennifer, Sam is so open and confident that he is able to pull on her skirt and ask to paint her nude figure. Sam says and does as he feels. Harry, as we learn later, was bound by conventions for which Sam has no use. Harry would just as soon have *not* made love to his wife, because a magazine horoscope told him not to. However, Jennifer only smiles at Sam's offer, saying, "Some other time, Mr. Marlow," before going into the house to bring him a glass of lemonade.

As Sam waits, Arnie comes out of the house carrying a dead rabbit and getting into a discussion with Sam about time. Arnie's understanding of time—that tomorrow is yesterday and today is tomorrow—is something only hinted at in the novel's opening passages. Here Hayes turns it into the charming characterization of a small boy, as well as a bit that pays off at the end of the film.

While Arnie's timing might be off, he does possess a wisdom about death beyond his years, saying, "You never know when a dead rabbit might come in handy." Arnie makes trades for the dead rabbit, obtaining a frog from Sam and, later, two blueberry muffins from Miss Gravely. The grownups profit from death, too: Harry's death grants Jennifer her freedom to remarry, provides a tramp with a pair of shoes, inspires Sam, and emotionally resurrects Miss Gravely, as if from the grave, as suggested by her name. She later says, "Thank you for burying my body." The rabbit is also suggestive of birth, since dead rabbits also bring to mind newly conceived babies.

In the first of the film's confessions of sorts, Jennifer explains the truth about Harry. Jennifer describes to Sam the circumstances of her living alone—the death of her husband Robert, whom she loved, her discovery that she was pregnant with Arnie, and her subsequent loveless marriage to Harry, whom she left the morning after their wedding night. Jennifer is frank and tells Sam that Harry did not show up to perform his husbandly duties. "Some things I don't like to do by myself," Jennifer says innocently. The script is loaded with similar double entendres.

Jennifer's deadpan reaction to Sam's offer to paint her nude, her willingness to speak of her wedding night, and the warning she gives Sam when he kisses her are illustrations of her reawakened sexual desire. But Jennifer is not alone in this rebirth of feminine sexual identity, for even Miss Gravely welcomes the attentions of Captain Wiles. Wiggy, on the other hand, is something of a sexless creature—the script describes her as "a neutral woman"—so that when Sam sells his paintings to the millionaire, Wiggy says without hesitation that she'd like a chromium-plated cash register that rings a bell.

After Sam's visit to Jennifer, he and Captain Wiles bury, dig up, and bury Harry all over again when the captain accounts for all his bullets and realizes that he didn't shoot Harry. At this point comes the film's second confession, when Miss Gravely tells Captain Wiles that she struck Harry on the head with the heel of her hiking boot, which has a metal cleat on the end. Miss Gravely explains that when she met Captain Wiles on the path dragging Harry by the ankles, she couldn't help feeling that it was convenient that Captain Wiles thought he had shot Harry. "You must forgive me for thinking that," she says.

Once seated, Miss Gravely remains so throughout her confession, while Captain Wiles moves about the room nervously at every mention of Harry. After explaining the circumstances which caused her to strike Harry—that he pulled her into the bushes, believing that she was his wife—Miss Gravely insists that they dig up Harry, inform the authorities, and return to her cottage for hot chocolate.

The story resumes with Sam and Jennifer at her cottage, having moved from the front porch to the living room, where they are having coffee. Jennifer admits to Sam that she feels awfully comfortable with him, and he confesses the same. In spite of their ease with each other—or perhaps because of it—Jennifer reveals her concern over Harry. Sam is trying to reassure her when Captain Wiles and Miss Gravely arrive, carrying a shovel. Miss Gravely quickly announces, "I killed Harry Worp with the leather heel of my hiking boot." The group tries to dissuade her from going to Calvin Wiggs until it is revealed that Harry has been dug up yet again. After discussing the matter further, it is decided that Harry should be buried again, quickly, so that the details of Jennifer's marriage do not become public knowledge.

Night has fallen as the next sequence begins. On their way back from the burial spot, the group hears the sudden trumpetlike sound of an automobile horn blown three times—like the three gunshots of the film's opening—followed by a shout and running feet. Mrs. Wiggs arrives with the news that a millionaire has come and that he wants to buy all of Sam's paintings: "He says you're a genius, Mr. Marlow."

If *The Trouble with Harry* resembles a fairy tale, the millionaire is rather like a fairy godfather. He bestows a set of wishes upon Sam, who in turn shares them with his friends. This sequence, which has no parallel in Story's novel, is Sam's key moment. When the millionaire starts to offer the art critic's opinion, Sam rejects it, saying, "Don't think I'm rude, but it doesn't matter to me what an art critic says." Sam is representing Hitchcock here. His next line in the script reads, "You see, I know my pictures are good. And he doesn't want them—you do." Significantly, the script uses the word "pictures," although in the film the word "paintings" is substituted.

After some encouragement from the others, Sam asks Jennifer what he should do. "It's your genius, Sam. It's up to you," she advises, and with that he asks her what she likes more than anything else in the world. "Strawberries, I guess," she answers. Sam then proceeds to ask the millionaire for modest gifts, not only for Jennifer, but for the others as well: two boxes of fresh strawberries every month for Jennifer, a smelly chemical set for Arnie, a chromium-plated cash register for Wiggy, a hope chest for Miss Gravely, and a shotgun, ammunition, and a hunting outfit for Captain Wiles. The millionaire tells Sam to ask for something for himself. He thinks it over for a moment, then discusses his request in private with the millionaire. But Hitchcock and Hayes reserve the punch line—Sam's answer—for the film's ending.

Sam seeks Jennifer's approval and then proposes marriage. Scene 177 begins as a close shot of Jennifer's profile, facing screen left. Sam moves into the frame and faces her. Then the camera pulls back slightly to a medium-close shot:

                    SAM
          Did I do the right thing?

                  JENNIFER
          You did <u>just</u> the right thing, Sam.

                    SAM
          That's good. I mean it's important
          that you think so.

                  JENNIFER
          Why?

                    SAM
          Because I love you. I want to marry
          you.

                  JENNIFER
          But . . . but I've only just got my
          freedom. Just today.

```
Sam shrugs.

             SAM
    Easy come, easy go. Besides, if you
    married me, you would keep your free-
    dom.


          JENNIFER
          (Smiles)
    You must be practically unique then!


             SAM
    I respect freedom. More: I love free-
    dom. We would probably be the only
    free married couple in the world.
```

Before Jennifer can answer, though, Calvin Wiggs arrives, carrying Harry's shoes, which he got from the tramp. Although he doesn't believe the tramp's story about getting the shoes from a corpse, Calvin decides to call in a report to the state police. Back at her cottage, Jennifer accepts Sam's proposal; in a reversal of the earlier scene, there is a close shot of their profiles, with Jennifer now facing right and the camera moving in. Miss Gravely and Captain Wiles congratulate the couple, before Sam realizes that in order for Jennifer to be free to marry, they'll need to prove that Harry is dead.

The group returns to the burial site to dig up Harry yet again, and finally reaches the conclusion that it would be best if they just told the truth about the day's events. When Dr. Greenbow reappears suddenly, this time reciting Shakespeare, he notices Harry for the first time and asks what happened. Thinking quickly, Sam asks the doctor if he could render an opinion as to what caused Harry's death. The doctor agrees to meet everyone back at Jennifer's cottage and says of Harry, "He's going home for the last time."

Actually, a theme of returning home—specifically to one's mother—pervades the script and film, more so than in the novel.

Arnie twice runs toward his mother's house when he comes upon
Harry at the beginning and the end of the film. When Sam gives
Arnie a frog, Jennifer says, "It's hungry. It needs a mother." Jennifer
tells Sam that she left Harry after their wedding night and went
home to her mother. Although the dialogue was cut from the film,
the script indicates that Calvin Wiggs has been divorced and also returned to live with his mother. Sam sings of "flaggin' the train that's
homeward bound" and of getting "back to the gal I left behind."
And in a sense, Harry too has returned home to Mother Earth.

While waiting for Dr. Greenbow to arrive, Jennifer, Sam, and
Miss Gravely work at making Harry presentable, but they are interrupted by the arrival of Calvin Wiggs, who questions Sam about his
portrait of Harry. Before long, Captain Wiles panics and leaves in a
hurry, much to Miss Gravely's disappointment. As Calvin continues
to insist the drawing matches the tramp's description of the corpse,
Sam takes the portrait and bluffs an explanation of his art, while
seizing an opportunity to alter the sketch. "A raised eyelid—a line of
fullness to the cheek—a lip that bends with expression—and
there!" Sam thus revives Harry.

```
INSERT
The drawing of Harry Worp, the dead man,
has now been transformed into the face of
a happy human being, eyes open, mouth
smiling broadly, with no hint of death,
injury, or decay.
```

"You destroyed legal evidence!" exclaims Calvin. Hitchcock illustrates Calvin's closed-mindedness and ineptitude through his inability to comprehend a work of art. There are similar occurrences
in both *Suspicion* and *Rear Window*, when a police detective appears to become puzzled by a painting. Calvin remains suspicious
and doesn't leave until he hears someone honking his car horn.
Captain Wiles gets Calvin to leave, then himself returns to the cottage. Miss Gravely asks if he's gotten over his fright. Captain Wiles
begins to talk of his adventures, when he stops himself:

                    CAPTAIN
    Frightened?
                    (he chuckles)
    That's not why I left. I'm not easily
    frightened, you know. Why after all
    those years sailing the four corners
    of the globe—strange ports—a rough
    lot of men—

    He stops, rubs his chin thoughtfully.
    Something seems to be bothering him. Then
    he faces Miss Gravely.

                    CAPTAIN
    Miss Gravely, what would you say if I
    told you I was only the captain of a
    tugboat—in the East River—and I never
    got more than a mile, or so, off
    shore?

Miss Gravely is touched by Captain Wiles's sincerity in front of the
group, and after his confession, Captain Wiles reveals that he lifted
Harry's shoes from Calvin's car. They're all impressed by his bravery
and cunning.

    Not long after he arrives, Dr. Greenbow announces that Harry
died of a heart seizure. Jennifer explains why Harry is in the condition he's in, but the explanation is too much for the doctor, who
leaves in a rage, believing this all must be a nightmare. The group
decides that they will return Harry to the place where he died so
that Arnie can find him all over again and explain to Calvin Wiggs
that he found him "tomorrow."

    The final tag or sequence begins the following morning as the
quartet waits for Arnie to come across Harry once again. He does,
and then runs home to tell Jennifer. Miss Gravely and Captain
Wiles exchange first names—Ivy and Albert—and Sam reveals that

he asked the millionaire for a double bed. The two couples are happily united, and Harry's feet point toward the heavens. The end title comes up—THE TROUBLE WITH HARRY IS OVER.

The Structure of the Unexpected in The Man Who Knew Too Much

Alfred Hitchcock and John Michael Hayes's fourth and final collaboration is one that has sparked a debate over the difference between the director's British period and his career in Hollywood. By remaking *The Man Who Knew Too Much*, Hitchcock might even have encouraged the controversy by creating two versions of the same story for comparison—but such was not his intention. Production values and technological advances notwithstanding, the conflict between the principal characters and the meticulous structure of the 1956 Paramount release—heightened over what was in the earlier version—resulted in a richly textured and enduring masterwork.

Given the social climate of 1950s America, Hitchcock's reworking of *The Man Who Knew Too Much* was very much ahead of its time. While American popular culture was spewing out entertainment that suggested a woman's place was in the home or that a mother's position in the family should be subservient—a view effectively promulgated through such television series as *I Love Lucy* and *Father Knows Best*—Hitchcock and Hayes developed a story that said quite the reverse.

As in their previous collaborations, *The Man Who Knew Too Much* explored a male's insistence on self-reliance. The story is a social drama in the pleasant disguise of a Hitchcock thriller. However, *The Man Who Knew Too Much* relies more on its dramatic elements than on the kinds of comic elements present in Hayes's previous scripts for the director, although the script and film are not without their comic diversions. Still, the double entendres of *To Catch a Thief* or *The Trouble with Harry* would be out of place here. This is a story about a family, about a long-standing marriage in some difficulty, and so is unlike Hitchcock's romantic films.

The Man Who Knew Too Much marked a return to Hitchcock's characteristic cinematic style, following a brief venture into the distinctly understated treatment of The Trouble with Harry. Like Hayes's screenplays for Rear Window and To Catch a Thief, the shooting script of The Man Who Knew Too Much bears the cinematic identity of the director: the subjective camera technique, long sequences without dialogue, suspenseful set pieces, and the ironic use of framing and transition. Nearly every sequence in the storyline is designed so that an unexpected event propels the plot and characters forward. It is this theme of chance, accident, and inevitability that is reinforced by three of the four musical selections in the film: "Whatever Will Be (Que Sera, Sera)," "The Portents Hymn," and the "Storm Cloud Cantata." Not until the husband and wife successfully work together—in the final sequence at the embassy—does a single sequence come off as they had planned.

The mechanics that propel the plot and characters of The Man Who Knew Too Much are 1. conflict, 2. action, and 3. progression. This is a very simple design, and not unlike a film such as Rear Window, which was constructed on a triad of subjective treatment. In the case of The Man Who Knew Too Much, however, the catalyst that propels the plot is something outside the protagonists' control. Hitchcock mastered this form of storytelling in his 1930s thrillers for Gaumont-British, and used it effectively in such Hollywood productions as Foreign Correspondent, Saboteur, Strangers on a Train, and North by Northwest, in which the protagonists are thrust into extraordinary circumstances over which they have no control.

The film's main titles appear over a shot of an orchestra, while slowly moving into a close-up of a musician who picks up a pair of cymbals, strikes them, and holds them up to the camera. A title reads "A single crash of Cymbals, and how it rocked the lives of an American family." Following the main titles, The Man Who Knew Too Much opens with a medium-close shot of Ben, Jo, and

Hank McKenna sitting at the back of a bus en route to Marrakesh. The image of the McKenna family together—father, mother, and child in between—is an ironic one. For as unified as the family seems in this shot, the sequences that follow reveal a need for this family to pause and do a little stock-taking. These sentiments will be echoed by the villain in his bogus sermon late in the picture.

The first line of dialogue is a question to Ben—"Daddy—you *sure* I never been to Africa before? It looks familiar"—revealing the irony of the film's title. Ben is a father, husband, and doctor—three roles revered by American society in the 1950s. In typical Hitchcock fashion, it is not Ben's knowledge of the assassination that is our concern; in fact, Ben knows very little about it—as does the audience, who is never told why the ambassador of an unnamed foreign power wishes to have his own country's prime minister assassinated. Our real concern is the challenge to Ben's position within his family, for it is Ben's supposition of knowledge that is at odds with his family's needs, particularly those of his wife.

Jo comments that the landscape looks no different than it did during their drive to Las Vegas the previous summer, and tells Hank that it is not really Africa but French Morocco. Early on we get indications of tension between Ben and Jo. Throughout the film, Ben corrects Jo. "*Northern* Africa," he tells her.

Bored with the scenery passing outside the window, Hank decides to explore the bus and moves down the aisle. As the camera retreats with the boy, we see a familiar image in the background— Jo has taken up a magazine and Ben has put his head back so that he can sleep, recalling the final tag of *Rear Window*. The conflict over the professions of Jefferies and Lisa that was never resolved in *Rear Window* is in effect going to surface here. The bus jolts, and Hank accidentally removes an Arab woman's veil, causing a great commotion as the woman's husband shouts out sharply at the boy. A charming Arabic-speaking Frenchman, Louis Bernard, intervenes and calms the Arab down. "There are moments in life when we all need a little help," he says to the grateful Ben. Significantly, this is what Ben needs to learn, as did Jefferies in *Rear Window* and Robie in *To Catch a Thief*, as well as, to a degree, the main characters in *The Trouble with Harry*.

Ben introduces himself and his family to Louis, who is confused over Jo's name until Ben explains it is short for Josephine, and that he's called her Jo for so long that no one knows her by any other name. However, Ben has a short memory if he is taking the credit for the abbreviation, for, as we learn, Jo is her professional name; moreover, she is known internationally by another full name—not Jo McKenna but Jo *Conway*. Ben's dismissal of his wife's professional identity introduces a motif of patriarchal dominance. This motif occurs not only between Ben and Jo, but also in the relationship of the Draytons, the minister husband and his subservient wife—another couple in which the female's needs are suppressed. Further illustrating this point is the fact that in the native culture where the McKennas have chosen to vacation, an Arab woman never removes her veil except in the presence of her husband.

Each of the key sequences in the film will follow a pattern set by the first. Each begins with the introduction of the principal characters and the establishing of their circumstances (although the conflict between Ben and Jo is only just hinted at). An incident beyond their control occurs (for example, Hank's removal of the woman's veil) and results in an event that moves the plot and principal characters in an unexpected direction (as when the McKennas meet Louis Bernard, who begins asking questions about Ben's background and arranges to meet them for cocktails in their suite and, later, dinner that evening).

When Hank sings the lyric asking his mother what he will be when he grows up, Ben turns to Jo, smiling, and says that Hank will follow in his footsteps and become a doctor. The line is another clue to the conflict between the couple. Jo smiles in return and joins Hank in the song. Of course, the lyrics of the Jay Livingston / Ray Evans song "Whatever Will Be" are in keeping with the previously mentioned theme of chance. Here also Hitchcock and Hayes set the audience up for the payoff later by including a whistling accompaniment by Hank.

After a waiter arrives with Hank's dinner, Jo joins Ben and Louis for cocktails, when a man comes to the McKennas' suite by mistake. It is later revealed that this man is the assassin, whose name in the script is Rien, which is apt since *"rien"* is the French word for "nothing" and the whole business of the assassination is merely the film's MacGuffin. So this scene serves several purposes. First, it forces Louis to break his dinner date with the McKennas, since he apparently recognizes Rien, and second, it sets up the payoff later when Rien and Jo recognize each other in the Albert Hall. But why would Rien have made the mistake of going to the McKennas' room? This is a question left unanswered by the script— and one meant to be quickly forgotten. Hitchcock regarded such moments as "icebox talk," a point that the audience doesn't give a second thought to until *after* the movie, when they've arrived home and opened the icebox for something to eat. Again, this sequence is patterned on the first, as the mistaken visitor has disrupted the McKennas' dinner plans. Louis is called away to deal with an important matter, and the McKennas will have to dine alone.

At the restaurant Jo notices a couple from the hotel that stared at her earlier and tells Ben they are staring again. He complains that she is just imagining things. Then, surprisingly, the man and woman turn and introduce themselves as Lucy and Edward Drayton, fans of Jo's. Ben interjects that they are Dr. and Mrs. McKenna. Questioned about her singing career, Jo reveals her conflict with Ben over giving up the stage in favor of supporting him in his medical practice.

Before long the two couples join each other, and Drayton explains the local custom of eating with only the first two fingers and thumb of the right hand. When Louis Bernard appears in the restaurant in the company of a woman, Jo becomes upset to the point that she and Ben have another argument. Mrs. Drayton attempts to quell the McKennas' bickering by inviting them to go shopping in the marketplace tomorrow and by changing the subject to the weather:

                        MRS. DRAYTON
    Of course, I know our English weather
    is awful, but I sometimes think we
    don't know when we're lucky. All this
    sunshine, day after day. It seems un-
    natural, somehow.

It is ironic that twice in the script the most meaningful words are
spoken by the Draytons. The implication is that the McKennas
should be grateful for each other.

The restaurant sequence is punctuated by a brief exchange between Louis Bernard and his female companion that adds to the air
of mystery surrounding Louis and draws the reader and viewer in.
Louis's unnamed companion glances in the direction of the
McKennas and Draytons and asks in French, *"C'est les deux que
vous cherchez?"* (Is that the couple you are looking for?) To which
Louis replies, *"Oui."* (Yes.) More "icebox talk," as Louis's companion never reappears. She is obviously another spy, and very likely
the person Louis telephoned from the McKennas' suite after recognizing Rien. But at this point in the story it is not clear whether they
are speaking of the McKennas or the Draytons.

The sequence in the marketplace opens on an array of tourists,
natives, vendors, carts, donkeys, and acrobats, all gathered in the
square. The setting is established as a crowded, happy place—the
perfect place for Hitchcock to set a murder. Two sets of dialogue
were written for Ben and Jo in the marketplace. As in Hayes's first
draft, Version A is an argument about Jo's career. When Jo finally
seems to be enjoying herself, Ben reminds her of what she said to
the Draytons at dinner the previous evening and asks if she'd rather
be in New York rehearsing. Jo replies:

                        JO
    Oh, all that talk last night was just
    social chit chat. Every woman who
    ever gave up the stage for marriage

is supposed to want to go back. I was
just playing a part expected of me.

Ben is surprised by Jo's attitude. He had expected an argument.

                    BEN
Then, if that's the way you feel
about the stage—do me a favor, huh?

                    JO
Anything you say.

                    BEN
               (Kindly)
Stop trying to make a chorus boy out
of Hank.

Her eyes widen a little in surprise, and
somewhat hurt, at his statement.

                BEN (CONT'D)
Oh, I know it's just a song and a
dance here and there . . . but it's
all he thinks about. Show business.

                    JO
Ben, you're setting a trap for me.

                    BEN
He has a good mind. Give him a chance
to develop it.

                    JO
You mean give him a chance to be a
doctor?

BEN

I didn't say that.

As a compromise, Jo promises that for every matinee performance Hank attends, he will have to learn two chapters of *Gray's
Anatomy*. Beneath the humor, though, is still an undertone of resentment.

Version B, the one used in the film, provides a fresh comic
look at the McKennas, a contrast to the arguments we have seen
so far. Jo says it's funny that their trip is being paid for by Mrs.
Campbell's gallstones and Bill Edwards's tonsils and so on.
Ben joins in the laughter and remarks that his patients' ailments
have also paid for his new suit, and if business keeps up, they'll
be able to redecorate their house completely. Although the conversation is humorous, the implication is that the McKennas
have attained pleasure from other people's suffering while taking
their own good lives for granted. Just as the spoiled Melanie
Daniels will learn "what it's like to be on the other end of a gag"
in *The Birds*, the McKennas will have to weather a storm of their
own.

Jo decides this is a good time and place to ask Ben when they're
going to have another baby. "You're the doctor, you've got all the
answers," she teases. Of course, another child is not the solution to
the McKennas' marital problems. They will have to lose their son,
temporarily, to be reminded of what they have—bringing to the
viewer's mind Mrs. Drayton's speech about taking our fair-weather
days for granted. That metaphor is carried further by the "Storm
Cloud Cantata" played in the Albert Hall. At the same time, Hitchcock is lulling his audience into a false sense of security, to illustrate
that at any moment disorder can erupt into the lives of innocent
people, even while they are on a holiday.

As had happened on the bus journey to Marrakesh, chaos
suddenly erupts in the marketplace when the police chase two
white-robed Arabs. While everyone's attention is drawn to the commotion, Hank dashes over to get a better view of the action:

```
EXT. MARKET PLACE — (DAY) — MEDIUM CLOSE SHOT
Jo and Ben miss Hank. Then see him moving
through the crowd.

                    BEN
    Hank! Hank—come back here!


                    JO
    Hank!


She starts forward after him, but Mrs.
Drayton moves faster than anyone. She
passes both of the McKennas and overtakes
Hank.
```

This is an important moment for Mrs. Drayton, revealing her maternal instinct, which develops even more later. But there is the possibility of a second motive to her actions. Mrs. Drayton is, as we later discover, *aware* that a man is going to be killed in the marketplace—she could be protecting the boy and also making sure he does not get in the way of their plans. She tells Hank, "It looks as though the police are chasing somebody." This is exactly what it *looks* like, but appearances can be deceiving: the truth is that this is to be a murder attempt on a French spy.

One of the Arab figures is stabbed in the back and, dying, approaches Ben. Ben sees that the stabbed man is actually Louis Bernard in dark makeup; Louis tells him, "A man . . . a statesman . . . is to be killed . . . assassinated . . . in London . . . soon . . . very soon . . . tell them . . . in London . . . to try Ambrose Chappell . . ." Louis dies, and Ben writes down the message. The French police quickly arrive on the scene and ask the McKennas to come to the police station to make a statement.

The sudden turn of events locks this family into a world of uncertainty. Drayton offers to accompany the McKennas to the police station, since he speaks French, and Mrs. Drayton offers to bring

Hank back to the hotel. The script leaves certain details ambiguous. Has Drayton had a chance at this point to tell his wife to kidnap Hank? Or since Drayton remains with Ben and Jo, accompanying them to the police station, could Hank's abduction have been entirely Mrs. Drayton's idea and, if so, could she have had an ulterior motive—perhaps wanting Hank for her own?

The McKennas are interrogated by a police inspector who reveals that Louis Bernard was an intelligence agent. The inspector also points out that the McKennas arrived on the same bus as Louis, shared drinks with him in their hotel room, and dined in the same restaurant later that evening. But Jo points out that they were seated at separate tables. The inspector's reaction to Jo's rebuttal reveals more about the attitude of male dominance in the film. The script notes: "The Inspector's eyes study her briefly, as if her comment was an unnecessary interruption. Then his eyes return to Ben." (A similar exchange occurs in the ambassador's study, when Mrs. Drayton interrupts him.) Angered by the inspector's harsh treatment, Ben stands—taking a position of superiority in the frame—and refuses to be further subjected to a police grilling. However, each time the McKennas try to take control of the situation, some outside force prevents them from doing so. In this case, the cause is a telephone call for Ben from a man with a foreign accent who threatens that if Ben reveals Louis Bernard's message to the police, Hank will be in danger. Once again the course of events has been altered.

Back at the hotel, Ben tells Jo that Hank has been kidnapped. Here the filmmakers portray one of the key conflicts in the story: Ben's use of logic versus Jo's emotionalism. To prevent Jo from becoming too emotional, Ben resorts to sedating her, which makes her collapse on the bed. Yet—later at the Albert Hall and also at the embassy—it is the emotional responses of Jo and Mrs. Drayton that save the lives of the prime minister and of Hank. Ben, on the other hand, displays his emotions at the most inopportune times—first in the restaurant, then in the police station and in the taxidermist's shop. Finally, when he is alone with Drayton in the chapel, he shouts out to Hank, when what he really needs to do is stall Drayton until Jo returns with the police.

Arriving in London, the McKennas are greeted at the airport by Jo's screaming fans—the result of Ben sending a wire to Jo's friends, Val and Helen Parnell, asking them to arrange their hotel accommodations. The McKennas are then led to an office where they meet Mr. Buchanan of the Foreign Office, who surprises them with the news that the British authorities are already aware that Hank was taken from them in Marrakesh. Ben remains cautious, revealing little and trying to learn what he can from Buchanan. In the film, Buchanan continually moves about the room, sitting at first on a desk and then on a chair somewhat small for his frame. The McKennas remain still, Ben standing at Jo's side. Jo stays seated, as she did both on the bus and in the inspector's office in Marrakesh.

Determined to find Hank on their own, the McKennas refuse to cooperate with the authorities. Buchanan, who is more sympathetic than Gibson—his counterpart in the 1934 version—remarks that as a parent, he, too, wouldn't know what to do. Just then Buchanan's assistant, Woburn, enters with a telephone call for Jo. The caller is Mrs. Drayton, who puts Hank on the line. Hank says, "I'm all right—I guess." Jo is overcome by tears, and Ben tries to get Hank to reveal some clue to his whereabouts before the call is cut off. Realizing that the McKennas have been through enough of an ordeal, Buchanan presses them no further, but he gives them a telephone number at which he can be reached should they decide to cooperate.

Since their arrival in London, a shift in authority has begun to take place between the McKennas. Ben will slowly yield his position as head of the family and share the role with Jo. The reversal is made clear when Jo's friends arrive at the McKennas' hotel suite and one of them addresses Ben as "Mr. Conway." But Jo's friends represent another obstacle in the McKennas' effort to recover Hank. Intent on meeting Ambrose Chappell (the name spoken by Louis Bernard while dying), Ben makes an awkward, if not rude, exit, to the bewilderment of Jo's friends.

The Ambrose Chappell whom Ben locates in Camden Town is an innocent taxidermist. When Ben enters the shop, several workmen are stuffing exotic animals. After some initial confusion between the elder Ambrose and his son, Ambrose Jr., Ben proceeds to question the latter. The sequence is shot as a separation, with both Ambrose Jr. and Ben shown in separate medium-close shots. Hitchcock frames both angles so that a stuffed tiger is poised menacingly toward Ben. In the confusion of his questioning, Ben gives the taxidermist the impression that he wants to have a dead Frenchman stuffed. Horrified by what he believes Ben is suggesting, young Ambrose tells his father to telephone the police. Ben's desperation turns to anger, and the taxidermist calls on his workers to restrain Ben. A mini-riot ensues, after which Ben realizes he has made a terrible mistake and barely manages to escape.

Back in the hotel room, Jo remains detached from the gossip and shoptalk of her theater friends. When Val asks about the man that Ben went to see, he substitutes the name Church for Chappell and Jo is struck by the revelation. Rising slowly, she says, "It's not a *man*, it's a *place!*" Jo's rise from her seated position, emphasized by a close-up, is significant. Previously, Jo has remained seated in moments of crisis, deferring to her husband on the bus, at the inspector's office in Marrakesh, and at the airport when interviewed by Buchanan. Away from Ben, she is able to take action, and here rises to the occasion. After she and Val look up the chapel's address, she runs out, instructing her friends to explain everything to Ben. They're left to ponder: "Explain what?"

After Jo goes to the chapel and telephones Ben about her discovery, the point of view shifts away from the McKennas for the first extended period. Inside the chapel, a figure places numbers on a hymn board and turns to the camera. It is Mrs. Drayton. It is significant that Mrs. Drayton should pick up the narrative at this point, since she has become a surrogate mother to Hank. Mrs. Drayton is protective of the boy, and when it is suggested that Hank be given another sleeping pill, she refuses and orders instead that he be brought milk and biscuits.

In another back room, Drayton and Rien—whom the audience will remember as the man who mistakenly came to the McKennas' suite in Marrakesh—are dressing for the evening. Both wear white dress shirts and black trousers. As Drayton puts on a minister's surplice, Rien straps on a shoulder holster; it is clear their actions are linked. Drayton then goes over the plans of the assassination plot in the Albert Hall with Rien, while playing a recording of the cantata to indicate the precise moment when his gunshot will be concealed by the crashing cymbals.

When the McKennas reunite in front of Ambrose Chapel, Jo wants to call the police right away, but Ben insists that they continue trying on their own. Inside the chapel is a congregation of about thirty people singing a hymn. Although the lyrics of the hymn can only be faintly understood, Hitchcock's selection is, of course, not an instance of sheer chance. According to production correspondence, the lyrics of what was referred to as "The Portents Hymn" appear to date back to 1791 from a volume entitled *Psalms and Hymns of Magdalene Church*. The lyrics read:

> *From whence these dire portents around*
> *That Earth and Heaven amaze?*
> *Wherefore do earthquakes cleave the ground?*
> *Why hides the sun in shame?*
>
> *Let sin no more my soul enslave*
> *Break now the tyrant's chain.*
> *Who save me when thou cans't to save,*
> *Nor bleed nor die in vain.*

The hymn warns of the greater stakes in the two musical sequences to follow at the Albert Hall and at the embassy. The first verse, growing darker with earthquakes and the sun hiding in shame, is a foreshadowing of the Albert Hall sequence and its thunderous musical selection, the "Storm Cloud Cantata." The second verse foretells Mrs. Drayton's rebellion against her husband at the embassy—"Let sin no more my soul enslave/Break now the tyrant's chain"—when she decides to help Ben escape with Hank and stands up to Drayton, saying, "You've got to let the boy go!"

The McKennas join in the hymn, soon recognizing Mrs. Drayton as she walks down the aisle with a collection plate. The Ambrose Chapel sequence is great visual storytelling. On seeing the McKennas, Mrs. Drayton backs away in fear, but she is unable to warn her husband in front of the whole congregation. Confident Hank is near, Ben tells Jo to leave the chapel and telephone Buchanan. Having been told he is the one with all the answers, Ben now admits, "I don't know how else to do it, honey." Ironically, it is Drayton's sermon that provides the lesson the McKennas need to learn:

> DRAYTON
> Few of us pause to think how life's
> adversities work in our behalf, to
> make better men and women of us. But
> I believe we should pause now to do a
> little stock-taking—to look into our
> own hearts and see what we find there.
> Therefore, instead of continuing the
> service, I think we should all return
> to our homes for private meditation,
> remembering how little we have to
> complain of and how much to be grate-
> ful for.

The sentiments of Drayton's sermon are echoed in the lyrics of "Whatever Will Be." With the chapel cleared, Drayton confronts Ben. Ben need only stall to allow Jo enough time to return with the police, but he becomes impatient and begins shouting for Hank, forcing Drayton's henchmen to subdue him.

When Jo returns with the police, she is shocked to find that the chapel has been abandoned. Since Woburn told her that Mr.

Buchanan is attending a diplomatic affair at the Albert Hall, Jo decides to go to the hall to see him. Thus it is by pure chance that Jo (and later Ben) arrives at the site of the assassination attempt. But when she arrives at the Albert Hall, Jo is unable to get close enough to Buchanan to ask for his help. However, she is recognized by Rien, who approaches her in the lobby with a warning (and in another sense, a prediction) that Hank's well-being will depend upon her tonight.

The Albert Hall sequence is one of the great set pieces in the Hitchcock canon, one in which the director ransacks his bag of cinematic tricks. Drayton's playing of the record and Rien's warning to Jo in the lobby of the hall prepare the audience for high-powered suspense, and so words are not necessary. Even when Ben arrives at the Albert Hall and Jo has to let him know what is happening, the script indicates that this is all conveyed wordlessly:

```
We do not hear what they are saying but by
their pantomime we see that Jo is telling
Ben all about the impending shooting.
```

In the finished film the Albert Hall sequence is a wordless twelve minutes in which Hitchcock employs cross-cutting to build suspense and uses subjective treatment to provide an emotional connection to the characters. From the musician's raised cymbals to the assassin's poised gun to Ben searching the theater boxes to the dignitary's pleased and smiling face, back to the poised gun, the crashing cymbals, and, finally, to Jo leaping forward with a scream, the cross-cutting increases with the music's tempo. Of course, Jo's scream foils the assassination attempt and Ben comes face-to-face with the assassin, who plunges to his death while trying to flee to another box. The sequence ends with a shot of a section of soprano singers, who scream in unison, hitting a single high note.

Amid the confusion, Ben and Jo meet in the lobby of the hall and are introduced to the grateful prime minister, who wishes to express his gratitude. He departs with his entourage while Buchanan waits for the McKennas at the top of the stairs. They go to him this time completely unified in purpose.

At the embassy, the Draytons meet with the ambassador in his study, where it is clear that he was the mastermind behind the assassination plot. The ambassador has betrayed his own prime minister, whose large portrait hangs on the wall behind him. The ambassador informs Drayton of the failed assassination and berates him for taking the McKennas' child. "Don't you realize Americans dislike having their children stolen?"

The ambassador orders Drayton to have Hank killed, and Mrs. Drayton cries, "Oh, no!" Recalling the inspector's gaze at Jo in the Marrakesh police station, the script reads: "The Ambassador pauses and looks up at her in such a manner that she almost shrinks." Again, the filmmakers set the clock ticking by raising the stakes about Hank.

Back at the Albert Hall, Ben and Jo are conferring with Buchanan and Woburn when they are informed that the Draytons are at the embassy, very likely with Hank. Buchanan explains that the complications of extraterritoriality leave them powerless. But Ben comes up with an idea that will allow him as well as Jo to get into the embassy to visit the prime minister. His plan hinges on the belief that the prime minister and his guests will not be able to resist asking the famous Jo Conway to sing for them. So while Jo holds their attention, Ben will be able to search the embassy for Hank. The implication is clear: Ben has learned that Jo is equally important to Hank's life and his, and he has now devised a plan by which they can both save their son.

The climax at the embassy virtually duplicates the structure of the Albert Hall sequence. The elegant setting, the musical background to be provided by Jo, Hank as the intended victim, Drayton as the assassin, Ben making his way through the corridors and stairways in search of the right room, and Mrs. Drayton as the mother figure who lets out a scream to save the child—nearly every aspect mirrors the action of the previous sequence.

Arriving at the embassy, Ben and Jo are greeted by the prime minister. Before the prime minister can even ask, Ben volunteers a song by Jo, and the guests are led into the music room. At a piano Jo begins another rendition of "Whatever Will Be." Her purpose is not to entertain but to make certain she is heard by Hank: "As she sings, her voice seems to be rather overpowering." Hitchcock shows the shocked reactions of the distinguished guests, insulted by what appears to be Jo's inability to modulate her voice to a performance appropriate for the intimate room rather than a concert hall.

In *The Art of Alfred Hitchcock*, Donald Spoto suggests that the theme of manners in *The Man Who Knew Too Much* emphasizes the false sense of security that is created by so-called civilized living. Throughout the script and film the McKennas are often the cause of or at the center of some offense: Hank removes an Arab woman's veil, Ben and Jo bicker in the restaurant, Ben grabs the chicken with all ten fingers, the McKennas repeatedly leave Jo's friends behind without explanation, Ben and Jo disrupt the hymn in the chapel, Jo screams during the concert at the Albert Hall, and Ben interrupts the prime minister, eagerly offering Jo to sing. But they have discovered that manners neither preserve nor protect life, and increasingly, the McKennas have had to set manners aside.

Jo's voice travels through the stairways and corridors of the embassy to a locked room where Hank and Mrs. Drayton are waiting. Hank instantly recognizes his mother's voice, telling Mrs. Drayton, "That's her! I know it!" Until this moment Hank's recurring phrase had been "I guess so." Mrs. Drayton tells Hank to whistle the song as loud as he can. Jo hears Hank's faint whistle and looks at Ben, who understands. Again, no words are necessary. The family—all three—were never more united than at this very moment. Ben finally makes his exit and moves up the stairs in search of Hank.

As earlier, Hitchcock cross-cuts, showing Drayton with two henchmen in the service stairs, preparing to strangle Hank. He tells them to wait and moves up the stairs. Back in the locked room, Mrs. Drayton consoles a teary-eyed Hank. In the background Jo can be heard singing "We'll Love Again." The uncertainty of the lyrics "Whatever Will Be" has now become a statement of the family's union—or, more precisely, their *re*union. Mrs. Drayton hears footsteps outside the door and believes her husband is coming for the boy. Hitchcock treats the moment subjectively, from Mrs. Drayton's point of view. She watches as the doorknob begins to turn slowly—and we, too, are unsure if it is Ben or Drayton on the other side. Mrs. Drayton screams, just as Jo did when she saved the prime minister.

Ben breaks through the door, and Hank rushes to his father. Ben is puzzled at Mrs. Drayton's actions when she tells him to take Hank, saying, "You must be quick!" Suddenly a gun appears at Hank's head. Drayton tells Ben that the three of them will go together to the nearest taxi rank. For the first time, Ben is able to control himself in a crisis and calmly leads Hank toward the stairway, while Jo's voice is still heard in the background. As the three move down the main stairway, Ben quickly grabs Hank and pushes Drayton, who stumbles and accidentally shoots himself.

The gunshot brings the guests out into the main hallway. Mrs. Drayton stands on the stairway, looking down at her dead husband. Ben brings Hank into the music room, and he runs into his mother's waiting arms. The family has finally been able to work together, and so in the final tag, as they enter their hotel suite and find Jo's friends asleep, the script notes that Ben, Jo, and Hank are a "smiling trio." The irony of the film's opening image is replaced by one of genuine affection. The Hitchcock-Hayes films of redemptive love and of the integration of the individual with a larger community, which began with a fear of intimacy and marriage in *Rear Window*, end with a most happy union.

Appendix I
Credits for the Hitchcock-Hayes Films

Note: Credits appear in the same order as they appear on-screen in each film. Following those are additional cast and crew who do not appear on-screen.

REAR WINDOW
A Paramount Release, Patron Inc.—1954

L. B. Jefferies	James Stewart
Lisa Fremont	Grace Kelly
Thomas J. Doyle	Wendell Corey
Stella McCaffery	Thelma Ritter
Lars Thorwald	Raymond Burr
Miss Lonely Hearts	Judith Evelyn
Songwriter	Ross Bagdasarian
Miss Torso	Georgine Darcy
Woman on Fire Escape	Sara Berner
Fire Escape Man	Frank Cady
Miss Hearing Aid	Jesslyn Fax
Honeymooner	Rand Harper
Mrs. Thorwald	Irene Winston
Newly Wed	Havis Davenport
Screenplay	John Michael Hayes
From the Short Story by	Cornell Woolrich
Director of Photography	Robert Burks

Technicolor Consultant	Richard Mueller
Art Direction	Hal Pereira and Joseph MacMillan Johnson
Special Photographic Effects	John P. Fulton
Set Decoration	Sam Comer and Ray Moyer
Assistant Director	Herbert Coleman
Editor	George Tomasini
Costumes	Edith Head
Technical Advisor	Bob Landry
Makeup Supervision	Wally Westmore
Sound	Harry Lindgren and John Cope
Music	Franz Waxman
Director	Alfred Hitchcock

Uncredited Cast

Dancer	Jerry Antes
Choreographer	Barbara Bailey
Miss Torso's Friend	Benny Bartlett
Bird Woman	Iphigenie Castiglioni
Party Girl	Marla English
Woman with Poodle	Bess Flowers
Stunt Detectives	Fred Graham
	Edwin Parker
Party Girl	Kathryn Grandstaff
Policeman	Len Hendry
Young Man	Harry Landers
Landlord	Alan Lee
Policeman	Mike Mahoney
Bit Part	Dick Simmons
Carl, the Waiter	Ralph Smiley
Detective	Anthony Warde

Uncredited Crew

Unit Production Manager	C. O. Erickson
Camera Operator	Bill Schurr
Assistant Camera	Leonard South

Special Visual Effects	Irmin Roberts
Song:	"Lisa"
	Lyrics by Harold Rome
	Music by Franz Waxman
Producer	Alfred Hitchcock

TO CATCH A THIEF
A Paramount Picture—1955

John Robie	Cary Grant
Francie Stevens	Grace Kelly
Jesse Stevens	Jessie Royce Landis
H. H. Hughson	John Williams
Augustus Bertani	Charles Vanel
Danielle Foussard	Brigitte Auber
Foussard	Jean Martinelli
Germaine	Georgette Anys
Screenplay	John Michael Hayes
From the Novel by	David Dodge
Director of Photography	Robert Burks
Technicolor Consultant	Richard Mueller
Art Direction	Hal Pereira and Joseph MacMillan Johnson
Second Unit Photography	Wallace Kelley
Special Effects	John P. Fulton
Special Photographic Effects	Farciot Edouart
Set Decoration	Sam Comer and Arthur Krams
Editor	George Tomasini
Assistant Director	Daniel McCauley
Makeup Supervision	Wally Westmore
Sound	Harold Lewis and John Cope
Music	Lyn Murray
Second Unit Director	Herbert Coleman
Costumes	Edith Head

Dialogue Coach   Elsie Foulstone
Director   Alfred Hitchcock

Uncredited Cast
Chef   John Alderson
Bit Part   Martha Bamattre
Commissioner Lepic   René Blancard
Cold Cream Woman   Margaret Brewster
Man with Milk in Kitchen   Lewis Charles
La Mule   Wee Willie Davis
Antoinette   Dominique Davray
Detective   Guy De Vestel
Bertani's Voice
(English dialogue)   Jean Duval
Mr. Sanford   Russell Gaige
Desk Clerk   Steven Geray
Monaco Policeman   Michael Hadlow
Elegant French Woman   Gladys Holland
Mercier   John Hébey
Detectives   Bela Kovacs
                            Don Megowan
Claude   Roland Lessafre
Kitchen Worker   Edward Manouk
Croupier   Louis Mercier
Vegetable Chef   Paul Newlan
Monaco Policeman   Leonard Penn
Chef   Otto F. Schulze
Woman on Bus with Bird Cage Adele St. Maur
Mrs. Sanford   Marie Stoddard
Woman in Kitchen   Aimee Torriani
Jewelry Salesman   Philip Van Zandt

Uncredited Crew
Unit Production Manager   C. O. Erickson
Script Supervisor   Sylvette Baudrot
Producer   Alfred Hitchcock

THE TROUBLE WITH HARRY
A Paramount Release, Alfred J. Hitchcock Productions— 1955

Captain Albert Wiles	Edmund Gwenn
Sam Marlow	John Forsythe
Miss Gravely	Mildred Natwick
Mrs. Wiggs	Mildred Dunnock
Arnie Rogers	Jerry Mathers
Calvin Wiggs	Royal Dano
Millionaire	Parker Fennelly
Tramp	Barry Macollum
Dr. Greenbow	Dwight Marfield
Jennifer Rogers	Shirley MacLaine
Screenplay	John Michael Hayes
From the Novel by	Jack Trevor Story
Director of Photography	Robert Burks
Technicolor Consultant	Richard Mueller
Art Direction	Hal Pereira and John Goodman
Editor	Alma Macrorie
Special Effects	John P. Fulton
Set Decoration	Sam Comer and Emile Kuri
Assistant Director	Howard Joslin
Costumes	Edith Head
Makeup Supervision	Wally Westmore
Sound	Winston Leverett and Harold Lewis
Music	Bernard Herrmann
Song	"Flaggin' the Train to Tuscaloosa"
	Lyrics by Mack David
	Music by Raymond Scott
Associate Producer	Herbert Coleman
Director	Alfred Hitchcock

Uncredited Cast

Chauffeur	Ernest Curt Bach
Harry Worp	Philip Truex
Art Critic	Leslie Woolf

Uncredited Crew

Unit Production Manager	C. O. Erickson
Producer	Alfred Hitchcock

THE MAN WHO KNEW TOO MUCH
A Paramount Release, Filwite Inc.—1956

Ben McKenna	James Stewart
Jo McKenna	Doris Day
Mrs. Drayton	Brenda De Banzie
Mr. Drayton	Bernard Miles
Buchanan	Ralph Truman
Louis Bernard	Daniel Gelin
Ambassador	Mogens Wieth
Val Parnell	Alan Mowbray
Jan Petersen	Hillary Brooke
Hank McKenna	Christopher Olsen
Rien, the Assassin	Reggie Nalder
Assistant Manager	Richard Wattis
Woburn	Noel Willman
Helen Parnell	Alix Talton
Police Inspector	Yves Brainville
Cindy Fontaine	Carolyn Jones

Screenplay	John Michael Hayes
Based on a Story by	Charles Bennett and
	D. B. Wyndham-Lewis
Director of Photography	Robert Burks
Technicolor Consultant	Richard Mueller

Art Direction	Hal Pereira and Henry Bumstead
Special Photographic Effects	John P. Fulton
Process Photography	Farciot Edouart
Set Decoration	Sam Comer and Arthur Krams
Technical Advisors	Constance Willis
	Abdelhaq Chraibi
Editor	George Tomasini
Costumes	Edith Head
Assistant Director	Howard Joslin
Makeup Supervision	Wally Westmore
Sound	Paul Franz and Gene Garvin
"Storm Cloud Cantata"	Arthur Benjamin and
	D. B. Wyndham-Lewis
	Performed by London
	Symphony Orchestra
	Conducted by Bernard
	Herrmann
	Covent Garden Chorus
	and Barbara Howitt, soloist
Music	Bernard Herrmann
Songs:	
"We'll Love Again"	
"Whatever Will Be"	Jay Livingston and Ray Evans
Associate Producer	Herbert Coleman
Director	Alfred Hitchcock

Uncredited Cast	
Arab	Abdelhaq Chraibi
Edna	Betty Baskomb
Chauffeur	Leo Gordon
English Handyman	Patrick Aherne
French Police	Louis Mercier
	Anthony Warde
Detective	Lewis Martin
Bernard's Girl Friend	Gladys Holland

Uniformed Attendant	John O'Malley
Headwaiter	Peter Camlin
French Policeman	Albert Carrier
Henchman	Ralph Neff
Butler	John Marshall
Special Branch Officer	Eric Snowden
Arab	Lou Krugman
French Waiter	Edward Manouk
Desk Clerk	Donald Lawton
Special Branch Officer	Patrick Whyte
Arab Woman	Mahin S. Shahrivar
Man	Alex Frazer
Assistant Manager	Allen Zeidman
Guard	Milton Frome

Players Hired and Used in England Only

Workmen in Taxidermist's Shop	Frank Atkinson
	John Barrard
	Mayne Lynton
	Liddell Peddieson
Foreign Prime Minister	Alexi Bobrinskoy
Box Office Women	Janet Bruce
	Alma Taylor
Ladies in the Audience	Naida Buckingham
	Janet Macfarlane
Sir Kenneth Clarke	Clifford Buckton
Girl Friend of the Assassin	Barbara Burke
Ambassador's Wife	Pauline Farr
Edington	Harry Fine
Aide to Foreign Prime Minister	Wolf Press
Guard	Walter Gotell
Ambrose Chappell, Sr.	George Howe
Butler	Harold Kasket
Patterson	Barry Keegan
General Manager Albert Hall	Lloyd Lamble

Lady Clarke	Enid Lindsey
Aide to the Ambassador	Richard Marner
Inspector at Albert Hall	Leslie Newport
Woman Cook	Elsa Palmer
Ticket Collector	Arthur Ridley
Footman	Guy Verney
Police Sergeant	Peter Williams
Ambrose Chappell, Jr.	Richard Wordsworth

Uncredited Crew

Unit Production Manager	C. O. Erickson
Assistant Director (London)	Basil Keys
Contributor to Screenplay Construction	Angus MacPhail
Producer	Alfred Hitchcock

Appendix II

Rules and Rigors of a Book-Fed Scenarist

by John Michael Hayes

The following is an essay written by John Michael Hayes in 1957, which originally appeared in *The New York Times*.

RULES AND RIGORS OF A BOOK-FED SCENARIST
Seasoned Adapter Analyzes the Art of Transforming Novels into Films
by John Michael Hayes

A recent *New York Times Book Review* cartoon showed a clergyman thumbing through a Bible while sitting in a theatre watching a certain current Biblical spectacle movie. The caption underneath was:

"I wonder if it has the same ending as the book."

This, in rather ultimate terms, touches on everyone's attitude when he goes to see a film based on a classic or best-selling book.

Since I am one of those engaged in the nefarious business of adapting novels to the screen, it apparently falls on my shoulders to offer some word of defense, or at least, explanation, in this matter of cinematic transformation of books.

To begin with, all novels are difficult to adapt to the screen. Some are more difficult than others. A good share of them are so difficult they are virtually impossible. It has been my experience that the novels I draw for assignment are generally in this last category.

Obstacles

In many novels the action takes place over a span of generations so that it is impossible to get the proper actors for them because they do not "age" well. Having Marilyn Monroe play the young Grandma Moses is fine, she possessing certain attributes of the American primitive. But those later years! You can gray her hair and crack her voice—but that pinafore is still going to bulge, and you can't write it off.

Even the least of screen writers learns quickly that he must not talk about action, but show it. However, not only do novel writers rarely show action—they don't even talk about it. They only think about action. Everything happens in the minds of their characters. Thought certainly has its uses—but not in a screenplay. What men think and what men do are often quite different things. On the screen we must have them "do." Result: loud complaints that the picture cheapened all the characters.

The average novel today visits seventeen cities, half a dozen states, Las Vegas, Paris, Greenwich Village, 10 Downing Street and an isolated honeymoon cottage in the Canadian Rockies. In pictures there is a thing called "budget." Just to put the number "10" on a studio-built Downing Street door costs $65 when you add up art direction, property department, set designing, set building, secretarial and producer-writer conferences.

Many novelists have an unfortunate tendency toward sloppiness in their writing. They seem to know little if anything about construction of a story. Sometimes they know this little, deliberately construing art to be something that has nothing like a middle, beginning and end.

Consequence

When the screen writer finally translates, interpolates and straightens out the storyline it fails to make sense—so he has to rewrite it. Result: the critics kill him for having touched sacred words, and the original author is heard saying around Eastern bistros: "What can you expect? Hollywood! They wouldn't recognize culture if it fell on them out of a DC-7. I just took their money and ran."

Despite the rich, expressive possibilities of the motion picture cameras, it is likely that many novels should not be made into pictures. They are too often chosen simply to capitalize on the name of the author, or title of the book, or the fact that a few thousand people (enough to put it on a best-seller list) have purchased it, or because competitive bidding makes a studio afraid that it might lose out on something.

Once the choice of a novel is made, and its anticipated production announced, the screen writer and producer are usually in for a barrage of criticism. People are liable to be horrified, angered or disgusted at your choice. The Negro press will demand to know how you're going to handle the race problem, or become angry because they've heard a rumor that you're going to make the Negroes into Italians in the film version.

Then the Catholics have probably banned the book in toto, the Bostonians in part, and the Legion of Decency gunners are already gleefully tracking you with radar. Certain state review boards and censorship czars have categorically announced that the book is unfit to be placed in the American home, pointing out that it makes a mockery of motherhood and the sacred institution of the family, and they are sharpening their scissors for the eventual kill when the picture arrives in their States. Even the script writers' friends have their say.

To top all this off, when the picture finally does emerge through this barrage of criticism and pressure, there is widespread disappointment because it isn't as daring as the book.

I used to argue with these people, but no more. We're all hypocrites, and these same back-fence critics and censors have made us so.

My current assignment is Grace Metalious' best-selling novel, *Peyton Place.* A book that's controversial and one that virtually everyone has an opinion about. Such a book could not avoid being made into a movie. And the public will be watching the results more closely than usual. I know already that I will never satisfy anyone completely—including myself. The author won't like me for bringing order to her disorder. The public will miss the pornography, the censors will read it into the picture anyway. The critics will have new grist for their mills. The studio might make a bundle, in which case they will be encouraged to snap up more novels to give screen writers more nightmares.

As for myself, I might even be offered another job by Jerry Wald Productions. But next time I think I'll turn it down. I'm going to take a year off to write a novel. Then I'll sit back on a mountain of money and watch some script mechanic grow gray wondering why I didn't write a better book.

Adapt it myself? Don't be ridiculous!

Notes

In addition to Steven DeRosa's many interviews with John Michael Hayes, the main sources for *Writing with Hitchcock* were the Paramount Production and Budget Records Collection, the Alfred Hitchcock Collection, and the Production Code Administration Collection, all of which are in the Margaret Herrick Library of the Academy of Motion Picture Arts and Sciences.

The primary sources for script drafts, treatments, story outlines, and story notes were John Michael Hayes's personal collection, the Paramount Script Collection, and the Alfred Hitchcock Collection. Larry McCallister and Robert McCracken of the Paramount Pictures Corporation also made certain script materials available.

Key to Abbreviations:

AMPAS	Margaret Herrick Library of the Academy of Motion Picture Arts and Sciences, Beverly Hills, CA
AHC	Alfred Hitchcock Collection at the AMPAS
JMH	John Michael Hayes (The Hayes papers will eventually be housed in the Special Collections Department of the Dartmouth College Library, Hanover, NH)
PAR	Paramount Pictures Collection at the AMPAS
PCA	Production Code Administration Collection at the AMPAS
SLD	Steven L. DeRosa
WB	Warner Bros. Collection at University of Southern California, Los Angeles, CA
WGF	The Writers Guild Foundation, Los Angeles, CA

Introduction

ix "The most enjoyable": Budge Crawley, Fletcher Markle, and Gerald Pratley, "Hitch: I wish I didn't have to shoot the picture," *Take One* 1, no. 1:14–17.

x–xi "A lot of people": Digby Diehl, "Q&A Alfred Hitchcock," *Los Angeles Herald Examiner*, June 25, 1972, p. 21.

xi "radio writer": François Truffaut, *Hitchcock* (New York: Simon & Schuster, 1967), p. 163.

xi "very best screenplay": Ibid.

xii In his book: Thomas M. Leitch, *Find the Director: And Other Hitchcock Games* (University of Georgia Press, 1991), p. 165.

xiii "John Michael Hayes looks": Peter Evans, *London Variety*, August 7, 1957, p. 30.

xiii "You've obviously 'fripperied' your lid": John Michael Hayes, unproduced screenplay for *Un Carnet de Bal* (December 15, 1959). (JMH)

xiii–xiv "Sure. A series": John Michael Hayes, screenplay for *But Not for Me* (January 1959). (JMH)

xiv "conjugating some": John Michael Hayes, screenplay for *To Catch a Thief* (May 28, 1954). (JMH)

xiv "One of the hardest things": Hayes to SLD, March 26, 1994.

xiv "schmucks with Underwoods": Tom Stemple, *Framework: A History of Screenwriting in the American Film* (New York: Continuum, 1988), p. 85.

xiv "BY CHANGING SCENES": Telegram from Hayes to Howard Koch, September 23, 1964. (JMH)

Prologue

3–4 "I was heading": John Michael Hayes to Steven DeRosa (SLD), March 26, 1994.

1 / A Perfect Treatment

5 At Hitchcock's request: In a memo from Peggy Robertson to Hitchcock, dated September 9, 1965, Robertson offered the following names as candidates to doctor the screenplay for *Torn Curtain*: Al Morgan, Arnold Schulman, Terrence Rattigan, John Michael Hayes, Arthur Ross, Randall MacDougal. Hayes's name appears again in the General Writers File kept by Robertson. In a memo dated November 8, 1967, Hayes appears on a list that includes the writers John Osborne, Nunnally Johnson, Robert Shaw, Terrence Rattigan, and Frederick Knott. (AHC)

6 In March: *The New York Times*, April 9, 1953.

6 "Do you know": Hayes to SLD, March 26, 1994.

7 "Hitchcock had his agents": Ibid.

11 "Mr. Hitchcock": Ibid.

12 In his biography: Francis M. Nevins, Jr., *Cornell Woolrich: First You Dream, Then You Die* (New York: The Mysterious Press, 1988), p. 24.

14 That autumn: An evaluation by Sanford John Dody was made on November 17, 1944. (PAR)

14 the following May: Tom Bierbaum, "MCA Loses Legal Ground in '*Rear Window*' Dispute," *Variety*, December 12, 1988, p. 2. (Although other sources indicate that DeSylva paid $9,250 for the film rights to *After Dinner Story*, a handwritten letter from Cornell Woolrich to George Stevens of the J. B. Lippincott Co., dated March 15, 1945, indicates the author's "approval of the picture sale of *After Dinner Story* for $7,250, with the understanding that the radio and dramatic rights are not included." A copy of this letter exists in the records of U.S. District Court, Central District of California, Case No. 84-2489 AAH [JRX]. I have not seen documentation to support the transaction at the price of $5,000, as suggested in Nevins's book, p. 475.)

14 In 1950: Copyright Office records for the motion picture *Rear Window* and the card indices of the Library of Congress. On December 26, 1945, B. G. DeSylva Productions assigned an undivided 9/10 interest in *After Dinner Story* to George DeSylva and an undivided 1/10 interest to George W. Cohen. On January 13, 1950, George DeSylva and George W. Cohen assigned all their interest to the individual story "Rear Window" to Orange Productions, Inc.

14 Hayward first: Attached to the correspondence between Hitchcock and Samuel J. Briskin, the Hollywood chairman for the "Movietime U.S.A." campaign is an agenda for Hitchcock, which lists his meetings with Sidney Bernstein and Leland Hayward and the properties which they were to discuss. (AHC)

15 Logan's thirteen-page treatment: Joshua Logan's thirteen-page outline exists in *The Alfred Hitchcock Collection*.

16 In his autobiography: Joshua Logan, *Movie stars, real people, and me* (New York: Delacorte Press, 1978), p. 241. (Logan didn't even get to direct *Mister Roberts*. The film was directed by John Ford and Mervyn LeRoy.)

16 Hitchcock paid: (PAR)

17 "It started with": Hayes to SLD, March 26, 1994.

18 According to Kelly biographer: Robert Lacey, *Grace* (New York: G. P. Putnam's Sons, 1994), pp. 138–39.

18 "She even": Ibid.

18–19 "Hitchcock said": Hayes to SLD, March 26, 1994.

19 Capa even visited: Richard Whelan, *Robert Capa: A Biography* (New York: Alfred A. Knopf, 1985), pp. 243–45, and Donald Spoto, *Notorious: The Life of Ingrid Bergman* (New York: HarperCollins, 1997), p. 210.

19 "not the marrying kind": Ingrid Bergman, with Alan Burgess, *My Story* (New York: Delacorte Press, 1980), p. 181.

19 A good case: Steve Cohen, "*Rear Window*: The Untold Story," *Columbia Film View* 8.1 (Winter/Spring 1990), pp. 2–7.

20 However, on one occasion: Hayes to SLD, March 26, 1994. (In 1974 literary agent Sheldon Abend, who acquired the rights to "It Had to Be Murder," initiated a copyright infringement suit against Hitchcock, James Stewart, MCA Inc., and the American Broadcasting Company when *Rear Window* was televised without his permission. The suit was settled out of court. In his deposition Hitchcock stated that the character of Lisa Fremont was modeled on Anita Colby.)

20 Anita Colby: " 'The Face' has a brain to match," *Time*, January 8, 1945, pp. 39–44.

20 No doubt: Gary Fishgall, *Pieces of Time: The Life of James Stewart* (New York: Scribner, 1997), p. 179. (Anita Colby made this claim in *The New York Times*, August 11, 1970; she also claimed to have turned down a marriage proposal from Clark Gable.)

21 "In the case": Hayes to SLD, March 26, 1994.

22 "a blunt": Passages are cited from John Michael Hayes's treatment for *Rear Window* dated September 12, 1953. (JMH)

23 "I like a character": Hayes to SLD, March 26, 1994.

25 The treatment follows: Woolrich's story makes something of the postmark, in which the time and month are legible but the year and date have been blurred by water. Hayes dropped that device, and Jeff holds his ground, telling Boyne to find the trunk: "Open it—and inside will be Anna Thorwald!"

26 The shorter zinnias: Cornell Woolrich, "Rear Window," a.k.a. "It Had to Be Murder," in *After Dinner Story*, reprinted in *The Best of William Irish* (New York: J. B. Lippincott, 1960), p. 289.

29 Hayes turned in: Daily production reports for *Dial M for Murder* indicate that on Friday, September 11, 1953, and Saturday, September 12, 1953, Hitchcock was at Warner Bros. shooting Scenes 289 through 292 on Friday and Scenes 293 through 301 on Saturday. (WB)

29 The treatment: A list of the story materials submitted to the Production Department indicates that Hayes's "typed" draft of the *Rear Window* treatment was delivered from MCA Artists to Marge Wonder on September 11, 1953, for retyping. (PAR)

30 "Hitch was still working": Hayes to SLD, March 26, 1994.

30 "I always insist": Hitchcock quoted in *Oui*, February 1973, p. 119.

31 "Jeff is afraid": Hayes to SLD, March 26, 1994.

31 Hitchcock often stated: Truffaut, *Hitchcock*, p. 141.

31–32 "When we were casting": Hayes to SLD, March 26, 1994.

32 By the time: "Rear Window Orange-Patron Consideration Agreement," dated October 14, 1953, and signed by Arthur Park and Leland Hayward. Copies of the signed agreements between Orange Productions and Patron, Inc. are in the records of U.S. District Court, Central District of California, Case No. 84-2489 AAH. (JRX)

33 "We sat down": Hayes to SLD, March 26, 1994.

33 The first twenty-one pages: *Rear Window* first draft script by John Michael Hayes, October 20, 1953. (PAR) (Unless noted, all quotes from the *Rear Window* first draft script are from the draft cited here.)

34 Hitchcock described the Patrick Mahon case on *Monitor 137*, recorded on July 8, 1964.

34 Filson Young, *The Trial of H. H. Crippen* (Edinburgh and London: William Hodge & Company, Ltd., 1920).

37 Seeing him look: In this draft Thorwald attacks Jeff with a heavy metal tripod—which he uses in detailed description—". . . smashes the tripod at Jeff's arms and hands. Sudden blood shows on the back of Jeff's hands."

38 "Herbie was there": C. O. "Doc" Erickson to SLD, telephone interview, October 18, 1994.

39 "Hitchcock told me": Edith Head and Paddy Calistro, *Edith Head's Hollywood* (New York: E. P. Dutton, Inc., 1983), p. 109.

40 The storyboards: John M. Woodcock, "The Name Dropper: Alfred Hitchcock," *American Cinemeditor* 40.2 (Summer 1990), p. 36. (Woodcock was the assistant editor assigned to *Rear Window* under George Tomasini.)

40 Although *Rear Window*: C. O. "Doc" Erickson to SLD, telephone interview, October 18, 1994.

40 In the film: Donald Spoto was first to point out the exact location in *The Art of Alfred Hitchcock*, 2nd ed. (New York: Anchor Books, 1992), p. 217.

40–41 Hitchcock insisted: Hitchcock in interoffice communication dated November 5, 1953. The request is also referred to in a memo by Erickson dated November 9, 1953. (PAR)

41 Additionally, two days later: Memo from Gordon Cole to the Production Department dated November 7, 1953. (PAR)

41 The first photography tests: Production reports for Production #10331, *Rear Window*. (PAR)

41–42 "I went": David Atkinson, "Hitchcock's Techniques Tell *Rear Window* Story," *American Cinematographer* (January 1990), p. 37.

42 "It is apparent": Letter from Joseph I. Breen to Luigi Luraschi, November 20, 1953. (PCA)

43 "the physical setup": Memo dated November 27, 1953, to the PCA file on *Rear Window*, indicating that Mr. Murphy and Mr. Dougherty conferred on the set at Paramount with Alfred Hitchcock and Luigi Luraschi.

43 Principal photography: Production reports for *Rear Window*. (PAR)

44 Hitchcock and his crew: Ibid.

44 "We had one shot": Arthur E. Gavin, *"Rear Window," American Cinematographer* (February 1954), pp. 77–78, 97.

44 Many of the film's special effects: Ibid.

45 *Rear Window* was also: Although *Rear Window* was photographed with the intention of being exhibited in the aspect ratio of 1.66:1, exhibitors had the option of screening *Dial M for Murder* in either 1.33:1 or 1.66:1. (WB)

45 Hitchcock shot the scene: Production reports for *Rear Window*. (PAR) (Although Frank Cady played Gunnison in the unused footage, it is not his voice in the film, when Jeff has a telephone conversation with his editor. No indication in the credits identifies the actor whose voice was used. A bit player and character actor, Frank Cady made a brief but memorable appearance in Billy Wilder's *Ace in the Hole* and was best known for his role as Mr. Drucker, the grocer in the television series *Green Acres*.)

46 With the exception: Personal injury reports for *Rear Window*. (PAR) (Besides Raymond Burr, stuntman Len Henchy was treated for a cut on his scalp he got from the badge on his policeman's hat while catching Stewart's double as he fell from the window. Henchy later sprained his right ankle jumping a wall in the courtyard set. Ted Mapes, Stewart's double, was cut on his right thigh sliding out of the window, and dancer Gretchen Husser scratched her right leg being fitted for a costume.)

47 "to be underwear": Memo dated February 15, 1954, to the PCA file on *Rear Window*. (PCA)

47 "It was a common practice": Hayes to SLD, March 27, 1994.

47 In a telephone conversation: Memo dated February 16, 1954, to the PCA file on *Rear Window*. (PCA)

48 "He should sound like": *Rear Window* Dubbing Notes (February 18, 1954). (JMH) (All quotes from Hitchcock's dubbing notes for *Rear Window* are from those in Hayes's collection.)

50 "I was a little disappointed": Alfred Hitchcock, "Rear Window," *Take One* 2, no. 2 (November–December 1968), p. 18.

50 "This was one of the most": Summary of *Rear Window* 1st Preview

(April 1, 1954). (JMH) (All quotes from the audience comment cards are from the Summary of *Rear Window* 1st Preview in Hayes's collection.)

50–51 *"Rear Window* is": *The Hollywood Reporter,* July 13, 1954.

51 *Rear Window* premiered: *The New York Times,* August 5, 1954.

2 / A Match Made in Hollywood

56 "I must have been": Richard Schickel, director, *The Men Who Made the Movies,* 1972.

56 "evening confessions": Quoted in Donald Spoto, *The Dark Side of Genius: The Life of Alfred Hitchcock* (New York: Little, Brown and Company, 1983), p. 18.

57 A student: Richard Schickel, "We're living in a Hitchcock world, all right," *The New York Times Magazine,* October 29, 1972.

57 "The Hayes boy": *Worcester Telegram,* 1935.

58 "I didn't get": Hayes to SLD, March 26, 1994.

59 "My mother was": Patricia Hitchcock O'Connell in BBC's *Omnibus,* 1986.

60 Filmed in Munich: Alfred Hitchcock's second film, *The Mountain Eagle,* is believed to be lost. In the August 1995 issue of *The MacGuffin,* a newsletter devoted to the study of the work of Hitchcock, a piece entitled "Missing, Believed Lost: Hitchcock's *The Mountain Eagle*" by Jenny Hammerton traces the release history of the film and details how and why it may have become lost.

60 *"The Lodger"*: Quoted in Truffaut, *Hitchcock* (New York: Simon & Schuster, 1967), p. 30.

60–61 Ivor Montagu: Roy Armes, *A Critical History of British Cinema* (New York: Oxford University Press, 1978), p. 71.

61 "I beg permission": Hitchcock on the *AFI Salute to Alfred Hitchcock,* recorded April 29, 1979.

63 "I entered": Hayes to SLD, March 26, 1994.

65 The writing and production: No doubt Hitchcock enjoyed borrowing the title from G. K. Chesterton's 1922 collection of short stories.

65 "In the morning": Charles Bennett in BBC's *Omnibus,* 1986.

66 Although popularized: Ivor Montagu, "Working with Hitchcock," *Sight and Sound* 49 (Summer 1980), pp. 189–93, and Hitchcock in Peter Bogdanovich, *Who the Devil Made It* (New York: Knopf, 1997), p. 502.

66 "It's called": Richard Schickel, director, *The Men Who Made the Movies,* 1972.

67 "What do they have": Quoted in Truffaut, *Hitchcock*, p. 74.

68 "Well, it's not": Ibid., p. 91.

70 This was followed: Ibid., p. 102. (There are contradictory accounts about the intended ending of *Suspicion*, which initially went into production under the title of the Francis Iles novel on which it is based, *Before the Fact*. Hitchcock told François Truffaut that his original intention was to have Johnnie guilty of the crimes for which he is suspected, and that Lina, aware of her husband's guilt, writes a letter to her mother indicating she knows Johnnie is planning to kill her and that she intends to allow her own murder to take place. Later, Johnnie brings a glass of poisoned milk to Lina, and she gives him the letter to mail. The last scene would have been Johnnie mailing the incriminating letter.

(It is interesting to note how this intended ending would complete a theme of the finished production. In the opening sequence it is a postage stamp that Johnnie borrows from Lina that ultimately brings them together. Using the stamp to pay his fare, Johnnie remarks to the annoyance of the conductor, "Write to your mother," thus foreshadowing the ending of Lina's incriminating letter to her mother. At crucial moments in the film, letters are sent and received. When Lina elopes with Johnnie, her excuse to her parents when she goes out is that she is going to the post office. The theme of "letters" is carried forward in the game of anagrams that Lina plays with Beaky. At the moment when Lina decides she will leave Johnnie, she writes a letter to him, ultimately tearing it up. He then enters with a telegram containing news of her father's death. Finally, Hitchcock makes his cameo appearance dropping a letter into a mailbox. Very early in pre-production the following titles were listed as alternates to *Before the Fact*: *Letter from a Dead Lady*, *Posthumously Yours*, and *A Letter to Mail*. These titles are listed in a December 10, 1940, interdepartmental communication from Harry E. Edington to Peter Lieber.

(This ending, of course, was never actually filmed, nor is there evidence that it was ever scripted that way. The first ending shot by Hitchcock, and seen by preview audiences, has Lina drink the milk that she believes contains poison. Believing she is about to die, she embraces Johnnie and forgives him. When Johnnie realizes the implications, that Lina believes him to be a murderer, he leaves. War has broken out and Lina searches for Johnnie. In a scene mirroring the opening sequence on the train, Lina sees an *Illustrated London News* photograph with Johnnie in an RAF pilot's uniform. She is next seen at the base where an Air Force commodore explains that James Allen [Johnnie] is one of their best pilots—a real hero. Johnnie has changed his ways, and their future seems bright. Lina watches as Johnnie flies off on a dangerous mission over Berlin and sees that he has named his fighter after her, *Monkeyface*.

(It is possible, then, that the ending Hitchcock always claimed he wanted for the picture was foiled because RKO did not wish to have Cary Grant portray a murderer. It is more plausible, however, that the Production Code would not permit Lina to allow herself to be murdered. Criminals could commit suicide within the code, but a heroine could not, in spite of the fact that her actions would help convict a murderer.)

70 "I would say": Quoted in Truffaut, *Hitchcock*, p. 109.

71 Still eager: The script of *Lifeboat* was ultimately written by Jo Swerling. On seeing the finished draft, Steinbeck complained to studio chief Darryl Zanuck that Hitchcock had distorted the story and characterizations, and requested that his name be taken off the picture. His request was denied, though, as his name was clearly a selling point of the film.

72 "I wrote": Hayes quoted in *Worcester Telegram*, May 4, 1952.

73 "I went down the block": John R. Wiggins, "John Hayes Commutes to Hollywood," *The Ellsworth American*, May 31, 1967, p. 3.

74 "The first time": E. Jack Neuman to SLD, telephone interview, December 13, 1994.

75 "the fastest writer": *Worcester Telegram*, May 4, 1952.

76 "The Song of the Dragon": The story had been serialized in *The Saturday Evening Post* in 1921 and was the source of a 1927 silent movie called *Convoy*, starring Dorothy Mackaill.

76 "He was": Translation by Valerie Masset of a French interview with Hitchcock dated 1972. From the clipping files at the Academy of Motion Picture Arts and Sciences Library.

78 Recently, Arthur Laurents: Arthur Laurents at "Working with Hitch: A Screenwriter's Forum," chaired by Walter Srebnick, Hitchcock: A Centennial Celebration, New York, October 14, 1999.

78–79 "I went over": Hayes to SLD, January 14, 1995.

79 "What in the world": Hayes to SLD, March 26, 1994.

81 "There were two other": Ibid.

82 "It is my hope": Hitchcock to Philip K. Scheuer, *Los Angeles Times*, March 9, 1950.

82 "*Stage Fright*": Bosley Crowther, *The New York Times*, February 24, 1950.

83–84 "He relied": Hayes in BBC's *Omnibus*, 1986.

84 "He was the master": Samuel Taylor in BBC's *Omnibus*, 1986.

84 "My agent said": Hayes to SLD, March 26, 1994.

3 / You've Never Been to the Riviera?

87–88 Although it had been submitted: Story department records indicate David Dodge's novel was submitted to Paramount Pictures by Curtis Brown, and evaluated by Helene Hanff on July 17, 1951. (PAR) Budget records for *To Catch a Thief* indicate the cost for story rights was $105,000. (PAR)

89–90 Although David Dodge: David Dodge, *The Rich Man's Guide to the Riviera* (Boston: Little, Brown and Company, 1962), pp. 1–15. (David Dodge wrote his account of how he came to write *To Catch a Thief* in the first chapter of this book. He also told how his real-life housekeeper, Germaine, enjoyed the film so much that she saw it twenty-seven times.)

90 In Hornung's: E. W. Hornung, *Raffles: Further Adventures of the Amateur Cracksman* (New York: Charles Scribner's Sons, 1901), pp. 120–158. (Hornung's *Raffles: The Amateur Cracksman* was filmed twice—in 1930, with Ronald Colman in the title role, and again in 1939, with David Niven. Hornung's gentleman thief seems also to have been the inspiration for William Dieterle's film *Jewel Robbery* [1932], which starred William Powell and Kay Francis. *Jewel Robbery* influenced two Hitchcock films— *To Catch a Thief* and the director's final film, *Family Plot*, which borrows its ending from the Dieterle film. In the final moments of *Jewel Robbery*, Kay Francis looks directly into the camera and puts a finger to her lips, inviting the audience to keep her secret—that she's turned the tables on jewel thief Powell. In *Family Plot*, Barbara Harris feigns a trance in front of Bruce Dern that leads them to discover a diamond hidden in a chandelier. When she's out of Dern's sight, she looks at the camera and gives a final wink to the audience.)

90 Hitchcock's first mention: *Los Angeles Times*, February 15, 1953.

91 "Well, let me": Hayes to SLD, March 26, 1994.

91–92 "So we went over": Ibid.

92 The result: The nine-page story outline exists in the PAR.

92 "Plotting was not": Hayes to SLD, March 26, 1994.

92 "All that survived": Dodge, *The Rich Man's Guide to the Riviera*, p. 10.

93 "I learned": Hayes to SLD, March 26, 1994.

93–94 "I would say": Hayes to SLD, March 26, 1994.

94 "Hitch was": Ibid.

95 "I had an actress": Hitchcock to Tom Snyder on *Tomorrow*, NBC (November 1973).

95 "Hitch could be": Hayes to SLD, January 14, 1995.

96 The first draft: The 212-page first draft script, dated March 23, 1954, exists

in the PAR. (Unless otherwise noted, all quotes from the March 23 draft are from this script.)

98 "I would like": Memo from Hitchcock to Hugh Brown, dated March 16, 1954. (PAR)

98–99 "An English girl": François Truffaut, *Hitchcock* (New York: Simon & Schuster, 1967), p. 167.

101 The research file: The gala depicted in the research photographs was given by Marquis de Cuevas on September 1, 1953. (AHC)

101 With the first draft: In a memo from Doc Erickson to Hugh Brown, dated February 12, 1954, Erickson indicates: "Scripts must be submitted in French and English for approval by the National Centre of the Cinema, which grants permission to shoot in France. It must also be submitted to the Ministry of Work and the Union of Cinema Technicians in order to obtain work permits for the American personnel going to France. I do not know how far in advance of shooting the script must be submitted or whether a treatment is acceptable." (PAR)

101–2 "Hitchcock had me": Hayes to SLD, March 26, 1994.

102 Under this agreement: There is a document in Paramount's production and budget records, dated March 30, 1954, "Notes pertaining to the Hitchcock Contract," which includes the details of agreements between Alfred Hitchcock and Paramount, and Cary Grant and Paramount, for *To Catch a Thief*. (PAR)

102 He completely eliminated: In an April 15, 1954, letter to Frank Caffey, Doc Erickson indicated, "According to Mr. Hitchcock the entire Nice carnival sequence is being eliminated from the story. However, we still have the chase and capture in the flower market. We should pass the information along to de Segonzac so he can release the carnival floats." (PAR) (It has been incorrectly reported elsewhere that the carnival sequence was dropped from the film due to weather delays caused at the start of principal photography. In fact, Hitchcock decided to drop the sequence more than a month before arriving in the South of France.)

104 "unacceptable elements": Letter from Joseph I. Breen to Luigi Luraschi, dated May 6, 1954. (PCA)

105 "a remarkably fine job": Hitchcock to A. H. Weiler, *The New York Times*, May 9, 1954.

105–6 "The condition": Letter from Doc Erickson to Hugh Brown, dated May 25, 1954. (PAR)

106 "I heard it was a loan": Passages are cited from the May 28, 1954, draft of *To Catch a Thief*. (JMH)

107 "It would have made": Catherine DeLa Roche, "Conversation with Hitchcock," *Sight and Sound* 25, no. 3 (Winter), pp. 157–58.

109 Principal photography: Production reports for Production #11511, *To Catch a Thief*. (PAR)

109 "John, this": Hayes to SLD, June 5, 1994.

109–10 "We managed": C. O. "Doc" Erickson to SLD, telephone interview, October 18, 1994.

110 "We would often": Oleg Cassini, *In My Own Fashion* (New York: Simon & Schuster, 1987), pp. 252–53.

111 "So far": Letter from Erickson to Caffey, dated June 1, 1954. (PAR)

111 "We have discussed": Letter from Erickson to Caffey, dated June 6, 1954. (PAR)

111 Although Hayes: John Mock issued a closing notice for Hayes on *To Catch a Thief* effective June 12 and a starting notice for *The Trouble with Harry* for June 14, 1954. (AHC)

111 "total story cost": There is a document in the Paramount production and budget department files, dated March 30, 1954: "Notes pertaining to the Hitchcock Contract," which includes the details of agreements between Alfred Hitchcock and Paramount for *To Catch a Thief*. (PAR)

112 "NEW CHANGE": Telegram from Doc Erickson to Edith Head, dated June 20, 1954. (PAR)

112–13 "When people ask me": Edith Head and Paddy Calistro, *Edith Head's Hollywood* (New York: E. P. Dutton, Inc., 1983), p. 109.

113 "Cary is marvelous": Laurent Bouzereau, *The Alfred Hitchcock Quote Book* (New York: Citadel Press, 1993), p. 167.

113 "Edith dressed the women": Head and Calistro, *Edith Head's Hollywood*, pp. 112–13.

113–14 "Hitch, I have an idea": Hayes to Joe Pinder, *Worcester Telegram*, December 7, 1986.

114 "Grace said": Hayes to SLD, June 5, 1994.

115–16 "Dear Herbie": Cable from Hitchcock to Herbert Coleman, dated July 8, 1954. (PAR)

116 "poised fingers": Letter from Breen to Luraschi dated July 9, 1954. (PCA)

116 "She had": Hayes to SLD, June 5, 1994.

117 "They tried": Ibid.

117–18 On this set: Paramount Pictures production notes on *To Catch a Thief*.

118 "Hitchcock had Edith Head": Grace Kelly, quoted in "Salute to Hitchcock Genius," *Los Angeles Times*, May 4, 1974.

118 "Could I have": Cassini, *In My Own Fashion*, p. 253.

118–19 "John Michael Hayes": Hayes to SLD, June 5, 1994.

119 "Proper casting": Hitchcock to Howard McClay, *Los Angeles Daily News*, July 20, 1954.

119 "Originally": *Variety*, August 16, 1954.

119–20 "We had a fight": Hayes to SLD, June 5, 1994.

120–21 "I didn't want": Hitchcock to Truffaut, *Hitchcock*, 168.

121 Before then: Production reports on *To Catch a Thief*. (PAR)

121 Hartman asked: Letter from Herbert Coleman to Frank Caffey, undated, listing Hartman's request for changes. (PAR)

121 Grant received: Final cost breakdown for *To Catch a Thief*. (PAR)

121 Coppel received: Ibid. (Hitchcock would later engage Alec Coppel to write the screenplay for *Vertigo*. Although Samuel Taylor would write the final screenplay, Coppel received co-screenplay credit on *Vertigo*.)

122 The retakes: Production reports for *To Catch a Thief*. (PAR)

122 John Williams: Memo from Herbert Coleman to William Cowitt, dated January 31, 1955, requesting payment be made for the dubbing session. (PAR)

122 "with the understanding": Letter from Geoffrey Schurlock to Luigi Luraschi, dated February 24, 1955. (PCA)

122 "very sensuous manner": Lyn Murray in "Flashback: Chords and Discords," *American Film* 11, no. 8 (June 1986), pp. 17–20.

123 "when one experiments": *The Hollywood Reporter*, July 14, 1955.

123 "In his accustomed manner": Bosley Crowther, *The New York Times*, August 5, 1955.

4 / An Expensive Self-Indulgence

125 Ernest Lehman: Donald Spoto, *The Dark Side of Genius: The Life of Alfred Hitchcock* (New York: Little, Brown and Company, 1983), p. 388.

125–26 "When we were": Hayes to SLD, June 4, 1994.

126 "Hitch would": Hayes to SLD, March 27, 1994.

126 "He's . . . not exactly": Letter from David Selznick to his future wife Irene, August 9, 1939. Rudy Behlmer, editor, *Memo from David O. Selznick* (New York: Samuel French, 1989), p. 269.

128 "This is": Paramount reader's report by Francis Millington, dated October 18, 1950. (PAR)

128 "To my taste": Hitchcock to François Truffaut, *Hitchcock* (New York: Simon & Schuster, 1967), p. 169.

128 Unaware of: Letter from Jack Trevor Story to Alfred Hitchcock, November 3, 1954 (AHC), and *London Sunday Telegraph*, October 7, 1977. (Ac-

cording to Hitchcock biographer Donald Spoto [*Dark Side of Genius*, p. 353], Story received $11,000 for selling the rights to Hitchcock in 1954. I could find no corrobation for this. In any case, $11,000 was hardly a modest fee in 1954. Hitchcock purchased the rights to Robert Bloch's *Psycho* for $9,000 in 1959 and, in 1951, paid $15,000 for the rights to David Dodge's *To Catch a Thief*.)

129 "It's the story": Hitchcock to A. H. Weiler, *The New York Times*, May 9, 1954.

129 Although Paramount: The production was budgeted at $1,035,000 on August 26, and prepared from the 134-page "green" script dated July 27, 1954. (PAR)

129 "Hitch said": Hayes to Steve Cohen, "Setting the Record Straight," *Columbia Film View* (Winter/Spring 1990), p. 10.

129 "It was a relief": Hayes to SLD, March 26, 1994.

130 John Michael Hayes: John Mock had issued a starting notice to Sidney Justin for Hayes on *The Trouble with Harry*, effective June 14, 1954. (AHC)

130 "It was rather faithful": Hayes to SLD, March 26, 1994.

130 "the autumn foliage": The 157-page first draft script dated July 12, 1954, exists in the PAR. (Unless noted, all quotes from the July 12 draft are from this script.)

131 Both in the novel: Since the Douglases and D'Arcys appear only in Hayes's first draft script, I exclusively use the spelling of D'Arcy and Cassy from Jack Trevor Story's novel within the text to avoid confusion. In the first draft, however, D'Arcy is spelled Darcy and Cassy is spelled Cassie.

134 "mumbling something": Jack Trevor Story, *The Trouble with Harry* (London: T. V. Boardman and Company, Ltd., 1949), pp. 118–19.

134 "He never went": Hayes to SLD, March 26, 1994.

135 Joe Breen: Letter from Joseph I. Breen to Luigi Luraschi, dated August 5, 1954. (PCA)

136 "We were on our way": C. O. "Doc" Erickson to SLD, telephone interview, October 18, 1994. (While filling in for the injured Carol Haney, Shirley MacLaine had been seen by Hal Wallis, who, after shooting a screen test, signed her to a five-year contract to do two pictures a year.)

137 "His first name": Lesley Brill, *The Hitchcock Romance: Love and Irony in Hitchcock's Films* (New Jersey: Princeton University Press, 1988), p. 284.

138 "right to the end": Jack Trevor Story, *The Trouble with Harry*, p. 35.

138 On Saturday: Travel records for *The Trouble with Harry*. (PAR)

138 "I shall have": Hitchcock quoted in MCA/Universal Classics press materials for the 1984 reissue of *The Trouble with Harry*.

138 The following Wednesday: Travel records for *The Trouble with Harry*. (PAR)

140 "It's my favorite sonnet": Hayes to SLD, March 27, 1994.

140 "It rocked": Hayes to SLD, March 26, 1994.

140–41 Scott, a conductor: *Variety*, April 13, 1955.

141 The company: Production reports for Production #10332, *The Trouble with Harry*. (PAR)

141 "We stayed in the Lodge": Hayes to SLD, June 5, 1994.

141 "Only the elite": C. O. "Doc" Erickson to SLD, telephone interview, October 18, 1994.

142 The main exteriors: *Morrisville News & Citizen*, September 30, 1954.

142–43 "Would you like": Hayes to SLD, June 5, 1994.

143 During the first: Production reports for *The Trouble with Harry*. (PAR)

143 Then, as if: Production reports and personal injury reports for *The Trouble with Harry*. (PAR) (Personal injury reports for the entire production indicate Shirley MacLaine had to be treated for burning eyes and a headache by studio location doctors, Dr. Pease and Dr. Rogers, and was later sent to a specialist, a Dr. Morrow of Burlington, Vermont. Jerry Mathers was also treated by Dr. Pease after he stumbled over a piece of wood and burned his left hand when he fell against a salamander heater.)

143 "Hollywood's experiment": *Morrisville News & Citizen*, October 14, 1954.

144 Production resumed: Production reports for *The Trouble with Harry*. (PAR)

144 "When she came down": Hayes to SLD, June 5, 1994.

144 "I remember": Shirley MacLaine to Richard Brown on *Reflections on the Silver Screen*, American Movie Classics.

145 "In every spare moment": Hayes to John McDonough, *Chicago Tribune*, June 3, 1984.

145–46 "I once": Hitchcock to Brian Forbes, *Hitchcock at the National*, BBC, 1969.

146 Shortly after completing production: Letter from Jack Trevor Story to Hitchcock, November 3, 1954. (AHC)

146 A few weeks later: Letter from Alfred Hitchcock to Jack Trevor Story, November 30, 1954. (AHC)

147 "I have no intention": Jack Trevor Story in the *London Sunday Telegraph*, July 10, 1977. (Perhaps the $11,000 figure mentioned in Spoto's biography was paid to Story at this time for the renewal rights, since the author had refused to sign the rights over for no fee.)

147 In late November: Lyn Murray, "Flashback: Chords and Discords," *American Film* 11, no. 8 (June 1986), pp. 17–20.

147 Herrmann's score: Steven C. Smith, *A Heart at Fire's Center: The Life and Music of Bernard Herrmann* (University of California Press, 1991), pp. 191–94. (In his biography of Herrmann, *A Heart at Fire's Center*, Steven

C. Smith points out that several of the film's cues were originally written by the composer for the CBS radio series *Crime Classics*.)

148 Production reopened: Production reports for *The Trouble with Harry*. (PAR)

148 For the film's opening: Interoffice communication from Herbert Coleman to Paramount attorney Sidney Justin, dated July 22, 1955, regarding contract and payment for Saul Steinberg's drawings for use in the film. (PAR)

148 In attendance: Spoto, *Dark Side of Genius*, pp. 374–75.

148 "It is not": Bosley Crowther, *The New York Times*, October 18, 1955.

148–49 "Assimilating": Penelope Houston, *Sight and Sound* 26, no. 1 (Summer 1956), pp. 30–31.

149 "I'm afraid": Hitchcock on *Monitor 137*, BBC (recorded on July 8, 1964).

149 "Yes, I made one": Ibid.

5 / Into Thin Air

151 The visit to Morocco: Expense memo dated August 16, 1955, detailing expenses incurred during Mr. and Mrs. Alfred Hitchcock's trip to Europe, and charged to Production #10366, *The Man Who Knew Too Much*. The total charged to the production was $7,617.52. (AHC)

151–52 "Hitch would say": Hayes to SLD, March 26, 1994.

152 "British International": Bennett quoted in Lee Server, *Screenwriter: Words Become Pictures* (New Jersey: The Main Street Press, 1987), p. 18.

152 Hitchcock did: François Truffaut, *Hitchcock* (New York: Simon & Schuster, 1967), p. 59.

152–53 The story: Donald Spoto, *The Dark Side of Genius: The Life of Alfred Hitchcock* (New York: Little, Brown and Company, 1983), p. 141.

153 Abbott, the anarchist leader: In his book *Hitchcock's British Films* (Connecticut: Archon Books, 1977), Maurice Yacowar indicates that the name Levine from the script was changed to Ramon in the film to avoid offending Jewish people, p. 297.

154 "Hitchcock Plans": A. H. Weiler, *The New York Times*, January 23, 1955.

154 The Scottish writer: Ivor Montagu, "Working with Hitchcock," *Sight and Sound* 49 (Summer), pp. 189–93.

154–55 Nearly two years prior: A series of letters and cables to Hitchcock from MacPhail during January, February, and March 1953. (AHC)

155 Later in 1953: Undated letter from Sidney Cole, Monja Danischewsky, Basil Dearden, Frank Launder, and Michael Pertwee. (AHC) (I was unable to locate any information as to whether or not Hitchcock contributed to this fund.)

155 "to work on": Memo from John Mock to Sidney Justin, dated January 24, 1955. (PAR)

156 "A routine setup": All quotes from Angus MacPhail's notes on *The Man Who Knew Too Much* come from those contained in the AHC.

156–57 This device was inspired: I am grateful to Bob Dell for pointing this out to me.

160 "The idea": Truffaut, *Hitchcock*, p. 171. (The idea almost seems inspired by the pursuit of the white-robed Malay sailor in H. G. Wells's short story "Through a Window." Wells's story is described in detail in the first chapter, as it also seems to have been an inspiration for the basic situation in *Rear Window*.)

164–65 In a letter: Letter from Herbert Coleman to Richard Meland of Paramount London, dated January 31, 1955. (AHC)

165 That same day: Letter from Hitchcock to Edward de Segonzac of Paramount Paris, dated January 31, 1955. (AHC)

165 On February 5: Wire from Russell Holeman to Jack Karp, dated February 5, 1955, on behalf of Edward de Segonzac. (AHC)

165 Selznick then: Spoto, *Dark Side of Genius*, p. 359.

166 Acting on Hitchcock's behalf: Cable from Sidney Bernstein to Hitchcock, dated February 10, 1955. (AHC)

166 "They were all": *Worcester Telegram*, February 14, 1955.

166–67 "I was going": Hayes to SLD, March 27, 1994.

167 "Will you kindly": Memo from John Mock to Sidney Justin, dated February 23, 1955. (PAR) (By "third commitment" Mock was referring to the existing multipicture contract Hayes had with the studio. *Rear Window* and *To Catch a Thief* had each been single-picture deals. *The Trouble with Harry* and *The Captain's Table* were Hayes's first two assignments under his new contract.)

167 "Hayes on Hitchcock Pic": *The Hollywood Reporter*, February 1955.

167 "I never saw": Hayes to SLD, March 26, 1994.

168 "I'd never heard": Gino Falzarano, *Jo Stafford: The Portrait Edition* (New York: Sony Music Entertainment, Inc., 1994), p. 12.

169 "The wife of the minister": Hayes to SLD, March 27, 1994.

169 In a matter of days: Letter from Herbert Coleman to Hitchcock, dated March 12, 1955. (AHC)

170–71 "It went like this": Letter from Herbert Coleman to Hitchcock, dated March 17, 1955. (AHC)

171 "Hitch had to have": Hayes to SLD, March 27, 1994.

171 which both Hayes and Herbert Coleman: Spoto, *Dark Side of Genius*, p. 366. (Plagued by illnesses, Angus MacPhail died at the age of fifty-nine,

seven years after *The Man Who Knew Too Much* was in production. In the obituary that appeared in *The London Times*, producer Monja Danischewsky wrote: "In recent years [Angus MacPhail] led a very solitary life. But while he discouraged visitors, including his close friends, he kept up a prodigious correspondence in which self-pity never intruded and in which his delightful sense of humour always predominated. Many breakfasts in his friends' homes must have been enlivened by these always amusing and sometimes outrageous letters" [April 28, 1962]).

172 "Angus wasn't": Brian McFarlane (editor), *An Autobiography of British Cinema* (London: Routledge, Chapman and Hall, Inc., 1998), p. 419. (Diana Morgan is credited as co-writer with MacPhail on *The Halfway House*, *Fiddlers Three*, and *Went the Day Well?* and is mentioned several times by MacPhail in his correspondence to Hitchcock during the 1950s.)

172 Notes from: The authorship of this set of notes is questionable. While the inventory listing in *The Alfred Hitchcock Collection* states that these notes were "dictated by Mr. Hitchcock," the final page bears the typed initials "A MacP:JW." This would indicate that these are MacPhail's notes, which would have been typed by Hitchcock's secretary Julie Wyman. (AHC)

174 "The first time": Doris Day quoted in A. E. Hotchner, *Doris Day: Her Own Story* (New York: William Morrow and Company, 1976), p. 146.

174 A studio memorandum: Interoffice communication from Frank Caffey, dated March 22, 1955. (PAR)

174 "Hitch asked Bob Burks": Henry Bumstead to SLD, telephone interview, May 22, 1996.

175 "a carnival spieler": Martin Gottfried, *Nobody's Fool: The Lives of Danny Kaye* (New York: Simon & Schuster, 1994), p. 134.

177 "I didn't think": Steven C. Smith, *A Heart at Fire's Center: The Life and Music of Bernard Herrmann* (University of California Press, 1991), pp. 194–98.

177 Hitchcock selected: Letter from Roy Fjastar to Frank Caffey, dated June 7, 1955. The letter indicates the existence of an Eddie Wolpin song titled "Che Sera, Sera" on Mercury Records. (PAR)

177 The lyrics: Letter from Geoffrey Shurlock to Luigi Luraschi, dated April 18, 1955. (PCA)

178 "Asked what it's like": *The Third Degree*, Newsletter of the Mystery Writers of America, Inc., Volume II, no. 4 (April 1955), p. 3.

178 "John Michael Hayes": Ibid., p. 6.

178 "You know": Hayes quoted in Spoto, *Dark Side of Genius*, pp. 360–61.

178 "Young man": Ibid.

179 "highest level possible": Letter from Hitchcock to Richard Meland, dated April 14, 1955. (AHC)

180 "too much on the nose": Unless otherwise noted, all of Hitchcock's notes are from April 27, 1955, his notes on Hayes's first draft script. (JMH) (AHC)

181 "a whistling obbligato": Ibid.

185 "I'm afraid": Angus MacPhail's notes, April 25, 1955. (AHC)

185 Without time: Travel records for *The Man Who Knew Too Much*. (PAR)

185 Before departing: Letter from Geoffrey Shurlock to Luigi Luraschi, dated May 5, 1955. (PCA)

185 The director also: Wire to Russell Holeman, dated April 28, 1955. (AHC)

185 Character names: Memo from Hitchcock to Hayes, MacPhail, and Coleman, dated April 28, 1955. (AHC)

186 "We feel the danger": Letter from Geoffrey Shurlock to Luigi Luraschi, dated April 29, 1955. (PCA)

187 Although Angus MacPhail: Wire to John Mock, dated May 5, 1955. (AHC)

187 "Hitch went off": Hayes to SLD, March 26, 1994.

187 That same day: Memo from Herbert Coleman to John Mock, May 10, 1955. (AHC)

188 "There were two sets": Hayes to SLD, March 27, 1994.

188 Both marketplace scenes: Letter from Geoffrey Shurlock to Luigi Luraschi, dated May 13, 1955. (PCA)

188 A day earlier: Hayes's itinerary had been laid out by Herbert Coleman in a memo dated April 23, indicating his departure from Los Angeles on May 15, departure from New York on May 16, and arrival in London on May 17, where he was scheduled to remain at the Savoy Hotel through June 6. (PAR)

188 Principal photography: Production reports for *The Man Who Knew Too Much*. (PAR)

188 "On *The Man Who Knew Too Much*": C. O. "Doc" Erickson to SLD, telephone interview, October 18, 1994.

189 "Saturday, May 21": Letter from Erickson to Hugh Brown, dated May 21, 1955. (PAR)

190 Furthermore, Hayes: In a letter from Alfred Hitchcock to Jack Warner, dated February 7, 1952, Hitchcock promised to direct an additional picture for the studio during the original contract period and to take no additional salary for his services. (WB)

190 "I felt that": C. O. "Doc" Erickson to SLD, telephone interview, October 18, 1994.

190 "We were all": Ibid.

190–91 Production resumed: Production reports for *The Man Who Knew Too Much*. (PAR)

191 A reply: Night wire to Jacob Karp from Richard Meland, dated June 9, 1955. (AHC)

191 Hitchcock still wanted: When Hitchcock agreed to direct an additional, or fifth, picture for Warner Bros. in 1952, he stipulated that this would be within the time of the existing contract, which was to expire on May 22, 1955. As Hitchcock and the studio did not select a property during that time, the studio requested an extension until December 31, 1955, in a letter dated December 6, 1954. When it became clear that Hitchcock would still be tied up with *The Man Who Knew Too Much*, he and Warner Bros. agreed that he would commence his services to the studio as producer-director of *The Wrong Man* on completion of *The Man Who Knew Too Much*. Agreement between Hitchcock and Warner Bros., dated April 13, 1955. (WB)

191 Work on *Flamingo Feather*: In a letter to Hitchcock dated July 1, 1955, from Angus MacPhail's London agent, Roger Burford of Christopher Mann Ltd., Burford requested information regarding when Hitchcock would want MacPhail to begin work on *Flamingo Feather*. He also indicated that MacPhail suggested Geoffrey Gorer as a collaborator. In response, Hitchcock wrote in a letter to Burford, dated July 8, 1955: "Cannot name any date on *Flamingo Feather* as yet, but will do so as soon as I can. Why does Angus want a collaborator called Geoffrey Gorer? Is this an indication that Angus doesn't feel capable of doing a job on his own? I am mystified." (AHC)

191 "Bumstead plans": Letter from Erickson to Caffey, dated June 7, 1955. (PAR)

192 Production continued: Production reports for *The Man Who Knew Too Much*. (PAR)

192 "You will recall": Letter from Geoffrey Shurlock to Luigi Luraschi, dated June 16, 1955. (PCA)

192 The company completed: Production reports for *The Man Who Knew Too Much*. (PAR)

192–93 "Hitch never spoke": Doris Day quoted in Hotchner, *Doris Day*, pp. 152–54.

193 "I knew Hitch": James Stewart quoted in ibid., p. 156.

194 "It is something": Memo from David O. Selznick to R. H. Dann and Alfred Hitchcock, June 22, 1945. (AHC)

194 Hitchcock continued shooting: Production reports for *The Man Who Knew Too Much*. (PAR)

194 On the afternoon: Memo from Hitchcock to John Mock, dated August 4, 1955. (AHC)

195 But scenes: Production reports for *The Man Who Knew Too Much*. (PAR)

195 Years later: Doris Day quoted in Hotchner, *Doris Day*, pp. 154–55. (Doris Day exaggerated considerably when she stated that she and James Stewart managed to complete the scene in one take.)

195 Principal photography: Production reports for *The Man Who Knew Too Much*. (PAR)

195 The following day: The letter from Reece Halsey to Mrs. Barbara Paul of the Screen Writers' Guild, dated August 25, 1955, is referred to in an October 21, 1955, letter from John Mock to Ned Brown, Hayes's agent, requesting that Brown inform Hayes of the counter-protest on MacPhail's behalf. (PAR)

195–96 "Hitch loved": Henry Bumstead to SLD, telephone interview, May 22, 1996.

196 During September: Production reports for *The Man Who Knew Too Much*. (PAR) (Herbert Coleman also directed retakes on October 17.)

196 Allardice, whose services: Memo from John Mock to Sidney Justin, dated September 23, 1955, and interoffice communication from Herbert Coleman to John Mock, dated September 28, 1955, indicating that six forewords had been delivered to Hitchcock. (AHC)

196 *Alfred Hitchcock Presents*: Hitchcock directed two episodes of *Alfred Hitchcock Presents* during this period. "Breakdown," starring Joseph Cotten, was directed before the premiere episode for the series, "Revenge," which starred Vera Miles.

196 On November 1: Letter from Mary Dorfman, Credit Arbitration Secretary, Writers' Guild of America West, to John Mock. Copied are Sidney Justin, Jack Karp, Alfred Hitchcock, and Herbert Coleman. (AHC)

197 *The Man Who Knew Too Much*: Letter from Geoffrey Shurlock to Luigi Luraschi, dated February 27, 1956. (PCA)

197 On the morning: Production reports for *The Man Who Knew Too Much*. (PAR)

197 A preview: *Variety*, May 1, 1956.

197 "projects for brotherhood": *Los Angeles Examiner*, May 23, 1956.

199 Article 8: *Motion Picture Basic Agreement*, Writers' Guild of America, West, Inc. (November 1955), p. 10. (WGF)

199 "I was told": Hayes to SLD, March 26, 1994.

199 Stefano made extensive notes: Joseph Stefano at "Working with Hitch: A Screenwriter's Forum," chaired by Walter Srebnick. Hitchcock: A Centennial Celebration, New York, October 14, 1999.

200 Hunter recently confirmed: Evan Hunter at ibid.

200 Coincidentally: Jay Presson Allen to Richard Allen at ibid., October 17, 1999.

200–1 "I miss the things": Arthur Knight, "Conversation with Alfred Hitchcock," *Oui*, February 1973, p. 120.

201 Had MacPhail written: According to the WGA rules, the "Adaptation by" credit is appropriate in certain unusual cases where a writer shapes the direction of screenplay construction without qualifying for "Screenplay by" credit. In those special cases, and only as a result of arbitration, the "Adaptation by" credit may be used. The WGA also states that it is possible to consider the writer of a story or treatment as eligible for screenplay credit, but only in those cases where the story or treatment is written in great detail, to an extent far beyond the customary requirements for a story or treatment. (WGF)

6 / Un-Hitched

205 "The collaboration": Hayes to SLD, June 4, 1994.

206 "I asked my agent": Hayes to SLD, March 27, 1994.

207 "I have always believed": *The Hollywood Reporter*, April 5, 1956, p. 5. (A copy of the ad signed by Don Hartman hangs on the wall of John Michael Hayes's study.)

208 "Trying to please": Hayes to SLD, June 5, 1994.

208 Ultimately: In Gary Fishgall's biography of Burt Lancaster, *Against Type*, Delbert Mann, the director of *Separate Tables*, attributes, disdainfully, an early draft script to John Michael Hayes in which the Lancaster character, John Malcolm, is a retired baseball player. Hayes's work on the screenplay of *Separate Tables* is unfairly dismissed by Mann, who is quoted as saying, "That script didn't last very long." The finished film follows Hayes's draft (dated September 16, 1957, with changes through September 30) very closely, and in that draft John Malcolm is a journalist. Mann is quoted in Gary Fishgall's *Against Type* (New York: Scribner, 1995), p. 171.

209 "You know, John": Hayes to SLD, January 14, 1995.

209 When hired to write: Joseph Stefano to SLD, March 2000.

210 Ernest Lehman: Donald Spoto, *The Dark Side of Genius* (New York: Little, Brown and Company, 1989), p. 409.

210 Evan Hunter was dismissed: Evan Hunter at "Working with Hitch: A Screenwriter's Forum," October 14, 1999.

210 "Perhaps I am too old": George Tabori to Hitchcock, December 6, 1952. (AHC)

211 "The script was written": Hayes to SLD, March 26, 1994.

212 "John Michael Hayes": Warren G. Harris, *Audrey Hepburn: A Biography* (New York: Simon & Schuster, 1994), p. 182.

212 "But after the shoot": Shirley MacLaine, *My Lucky Stars* (New York: Bantam, 1995), pp. 350–54.

212–13 "It was an unhappy picture": Hayes to SLD, June 5, 1994.

213 "cultural antique": Bosley Crowther, *The New York Times*, March 15, 1962.

213 "He had a big office": Hayes to SLD, June 4, 1994.

213–14 "I READ THE SCRIPT": Telegram from Joe Levine to Hayes, Paramount Pictures Corp., January 28, 1963. (JMH)

214 "the producer": Quoted in Carroll Baker, *Baby Doll* (New York: Arbor House, 1983), p. 255.

215 "I wrote": Hayes to SLD, June 4, 1994.

216 "The director": Ibid.

216–17 "I got called in": Hayes to SLD, June 5, 1994.

217–18 "I said": Hayes to SLD, March 27, 1994.

220 "*Rear Window*": John Michael Hayes's notes for a sequel to *Rear Window*. (JMH)

222 Hayes declined: The television movie *Rear Window* premiered on Sunday, November 22, 1998, on ABC. The teleplay was by Eric Overmeyer, playwright and writer/producer for *Homicide: Life on the Street*.

7 / The Screenplays—An Analysis

223–24 "There was a book": Hayes to SLD, March 26, 1994.

224 "Subjective treatment": Hitchcock quoted in "On Style," *Cinema* 1, no. 5 (August/September 1963).

224 "At all times": Alfred Hitchcock, "Film Production," Sidney Gottlieb, editor, *Hitchcock on Hitchcock* (University of California Press, 1995), p. 218. (This was originally published in the *Encyclopaedia Britannica*, Vol. 15, 1965 ed., as a section of the eight-part entry "Motion Pictures.")

226 "Can you see me": Passages cited are from the shooting script of *Rear Window* dated December 1, 1953, with changes to January 5, 1954. (JMH)

233–34 "It's what I call": Hayes to SLD, March 27, 1994.

235 "It was a lightweight story": Hitchcock to François Truffaut, *Hitchcock* (New York: Simon & Schuster, 1962), p. 166.

236 It is appropriate: In the finished film, the close-up of the thief's black-gloved hands does not appear until the sixth shot, following the main titles.

236 "a pair of black-gloved hands": Passages are cited from the shooting script of *To Catch a Thief* dated May 28, 1954, with changes through August 30. (JMH)

239 Thus, the name: The irony of Danielle driving a boat called *Maquis Mouse*, when, in fact, she is the new "cat" burglar, recalls Philip's line near the end of *Rope*: "Cat and mouse, cat and mouse. Only which is the cat and which is the mouse?" As Brandon and Rupert go at it, Philip observes that each of them believes himself to be the "cat."

241 "I deliberately": Hitchcock to Truffaut, *Hitchcock*, p. 168.

241 "a lady in the drawing room": John Michael Hayes, *Rear Window* treatment, September 12, 1953, p. 15. (JMH)

241 Of this scene: Peter Bogdanovich told this story while presenting an evening of rare materials from the Hitchcock Collection at the Museum of Modern Art, June 6, 1999.

252 "circumstances of her": Passages are cited from the shooting script of *The Trouble with Harry*, dated September 20, 1954, with changes through October 13, 1954. (JMH)

255 In his excellent: Ed Sikov, *Laughing Hysterically* (New York: Columbia University Press, 1990), p. 161.

256–57 The films are further linked: Dave Kehr, "Hitch's Riddle," *Film Comment* 20, no. 3 (May–June), pp. 9–18. Kehr's fine essay makes a case for each of the five Hitchcock films reissued in 1983–84 by MCA/Universal Classics as having a particular art as its central theme. Literature in *Rope*, photography in *Rear Window*, painting in *The Trouble with Harry*, music in *The Man Who Knew Too Much*, and the cinema in *Vertigo*.

267 "Daddy—you *sure*": Passages are cited from the shooting script of *The Man Who Knew Too Much* dated May 7, 1955, with changed pages through August 26. (JMH)

268 Of course, the lyrics: Music plays a vital role in the sound films of Alfred Hitchcock as early as the sound version of *Blackmail* in 1929. There are musical sequences, songs, or melodies used for dramatic purposes, or as plot devices, in such films as *The 39 Steps*, *Young and Innocent*, *The Lady Vanishes*, *Shadow of a Doubt*, *Stage Fright*, *Rear Window*, and the 1934 version of *The Man Who Knew Too Much*.

281 In *The Art of Alfred Hitchcock*: Donald Spoto, *The Art of Alfred Hitchcock* (New York: Hopkinson and Blake, 1976), pp. 272–73. (In *The Art of Alfred Hitchcock*, Spoto relates this theme of appearance versus reality as a major concern in the Hitchcock canon and suggests that in *The Man Who Knew Too Much* manners offer a false sense of security.)

Selected Bibliography

Baker, Carroll. *Baby Doll* (New York: Arbor House, 1983).

Behlmer, Rudy, editor. *Memo from David O. Selznick* (New York: Samuel French, 1989).

Bergman, Ingrid, with Burgess, Alan. *My Story* (New York: Delacorte Press, 1980).

Brill, Lesley. *The Hitchcock Romance: Love and Irony in Hitchcock's Films* (New Jersey: Princeton University Press, 1988).

Cassini, Oleg. *In My Own Fashion* (New York: Simon & Schuster, 1987).

Dodge, David. *The Rich Man's Guide to the Riviera* (Boston: Little, Brown and Company, 1962).

———. *To Catch a Thief* (London: Michael Joseph, 1953).

Fishgall, Gary. *Pieces of Time: The Life of James Stewart* (New York: Scribner, 1997).

Gottlieb, Sidney. *Hitchcock on Hitchcock* (University of California Press, 1995).

Head, Edith, and Calistro, Paddy. *Edith Head's Hollywood* (New York: E. P. Dutton, Inc., 1983).

Hotchner, A. E. *Doris Day: Her Own Story* (New York: William Morrow and Company, 1976).

Lacey, Robert. *Grace* (New York: G. P. Putnam's Sons, 1994).

Leitch, Thomas M. *Find the Director: And Other Hitchcock Games* (University of Georgia Press, 1991).

Nevins, Francis M., Jr. *Cornell Woolrich: First You Dream, Then You Die* (New York: The Mysterious Press, 1988).

Sikov, Ed. *Laughing Hysterically* (New York: Columbia University Press, 1990).

Smith, Steven C. *A Heart at Fire's Center: The Life and Music of Bernard Herrmann* (University of California Press, 1991).

Spoto, Donald. *The Art of Alfred Hitchcock* (New York: Hopkinson and Blake, 1976).

———. *The Dark Side of Genius: The Life of Alfred Hitchcock* (New York: Little, Brown and Company, 1983).

———. *Notorious: The Life of Ingrid Bergman* (New York: HarperCollins, 1997).

Story, Jack Trevor. *The Trouble with Harry* (London: T. V. Boardman and Company, Ltd., 1949).

Truffaut, François. *Hitchcock* (New York: Simon & Schuster, 1967).

Whelan, Richard. *Robert Capa: A Biography* (New York: Alfred A. Knopf, 1985).

Woolrich, Cornell. *Rear Window and Other Stories* (New York: Penguin, 1994).

Young, Filson. *The Trial of H. H. Crippen* (Edinburgh and London: William Hodge & Company, Ltd., 1920).

Acknowledgments

There are many people I wish to thank for their assistance in this project. First and foremost, this book could not have been written without the generous cooperation and encouragement of John Michael Hayes. Mr. Hayes first telephoned me on December 30, 1993, in response to my written request for an interview. It was a cold, snowy day in New York and his call took me completely by surprise. We spoke for a good half hour and I hardly got a word in. I knew instantly that he was eager to tell his story. Mr. Hayes invited me to his home in New Hampshire, for what would be the first of many visits. There was excitement in his voice as he told me that in two weeks his new film, Disney's *Iron Will*, would be having a special premiere in his hometown, that he was featured in the current issue of *Premiere* magazine, and that rumors of a *Rear Window* sequel and his possible involvement were circulating, despite the likelihood that it would never be made.

Several professional associates of Alfred Hitchcock and John Michael Hayes were kind enough to grant interviews: Henry Bumstead, Herbert Coleman, Clarence Oscar "Doc" Erickson, and Daniel McCauley. The late E. Jack Neuman, Hayes's radio writing partner and a prolific television writer/producer, was very helpful. Doris Halsey, wife of the late Reece Halsey, Angus MacPhail's Hollywood agent in the 1950s, shared memories of her husband's association with MacPhail. John Strauss, James Stewart's longtime publicist, spoke with me on several occasions when the actor was in declining health. Molly Mock Caputo, daughter of the late John Mock, also spoke with me about her father and his years at Paramount.

I—and others who value the work of one of the twentieth century's great artists—owe a tremendous debt of gratitude to Patricia Hitchcock O'Connell, the only child of Alfred and Alma Hitchcock. Through her donation of her father's production files to the Academy of Motion Picture Arts and Sciences, Mrs. O'Connell made it possible for many to study in depth the life and work of Alfred Hitchcock.

The staff at the Margaret Herrick Library in Beverly Hills, California, made every research visit a joy. I wish to thank especially Sam Gill, Faye Thompson, and Kristine Krueger. Stuart Ng and Bill Whittingham at the USC/Warner Bros. Archive were also very helpful. At Paramount Pictures, Larry McCallister and, later, Robert McCracken made certain script materials available to me. Charles Silver at the Museum of Modern Art arranged a screening of *Downhill*. At the Writers' Guild of America, West, Karen Pedersen obtained for me a copy of the 1955 Motion Picture Basic Agreement. At the Mystery Writers of America, Priscilla Ridgeway provided information on the MWA's 1955 awards ceremony. Lynn Pittell-Minn and I were once comrades in the trenches of the archival footage business. Lynn was always eager to share valuable contacts and obtain obscure and valuable interview materials. Tom Toth made it possible for me to see many of Hitchcock and Hayes's films in original Technicolor prints, which has spoiled me completely. Robert Thixton believed in this book very early on, and without his encouragement and advice I might have taken a safer but less rewarding course. I am also grateful for the encouragement I received from several film and Hitchcock scholars, most especially to Sidney Gottlieb and Leonard Leff.

I first met Donald Spoto in 1987, when I was an undergraduate taking his class on Hitchcock entitled "The Masks of Love." It was the last time Dr. Spoto's class was being offered for credit at the New School. Had I not received an "A" from him then, I might not have undertaken this book several years later. Dr. Spoto read an early draft of the manuscript and, as always, was generous and helpful in many ways.

One of my oldest friends, Frank John Hughes, himself a gifted actor, introduced me to the cinema bookshop in Manhattan where I obtained my first copy of a Hitchcock shooting script. It was John Michael Hayes's script for *Rear Window*, which probably makes Frank responsible for planting the seed from which this book has grown. I am very fortunate to have Franco D'Alessandro as a friend. Franco never seemed to tire of hearing the most minute revelation I uncovered. Both as a wonderful playwright and an occasional writing partner, Franco is a constant source of inspiration.

John Arco and Matt Crisfield sat through dozens of movies and even more hours listening to me talk about movies, finally encouraging me to give their ears a rest and put it all down on paper. Jeffrey Kearney also was instrumental in my decision to begin the project, and I am grateful. Other friends whose patience and support continue to mean a lot to me are Anthony DiLeo, Karin and Dave Kulsar, Michele Naumann, Toné Vazquez, and Jay Wander. I am also grateful for the recently acquired friendship of Corey Ellis Hayes, John Michael Hayes's youngest son, and his wife, Rhonda.

Two dear friends passed away while I was writing, Rob Cates and Robert M. Dell. Rob Cates made my last year in the stock footage business thoroughly enjoyable. He was a true and great friend who is sorely missed. I first became a student of Robert Dell's during my sophomore year at Pace University. He encouraged my interest in cinema and, not long after, allowed me to adopt him as my academic advisor. Years later, when I began research for this book, I was even more privileged to be able to call Bob my friend. He was enthusiastic about my work from the start and was a generous host during many of my research trips to New England. I am deeply saddened that he passed away this past spring, but grateful for the guidance he provided over the years.

At Faber and Faber, I am very fortunate that this book ended up in the astute hands of my editor, Linda Rosenberg. Linda pushed me in areas where it was easy to be lazy, and reined me in when less said was better. Her dedication to this book is apparent on every page, and it is so much the better for it.

Edward Hibbert is a writer's dream agent. As an agent, Edward is fiercely loyal, dedicated to his client's best interests, unfailingly good-humored, often brutally honest, and always there for you. As a friend, Edward is all those things and so much more. And I am blessed that I can call him both. Edward and his colleagues at Donadio and Olson—Peter Steinberg and Neil Olson—made all this worthwhile, and not just because they made it possible for me to get paid.

Lastly, to my family:

To Mom and Dad; my sister, Donna; and my brother-in-law, Andrew—thanks for keeping me motivated.

To Sam, who was always nearby, thanks for helping me keep things in perspective.

To Elizabeth, who more than anyone else read and reread every chapter, paragraph, line, and word of the manuscript, in its many drafts, words cannot begin to express the depth of my gratitude. She lived with this book for more than three years, allowed me to turn our living room into a screening room, and remained my greatest champion, ally, confidante, and partner.

The love and support you provide, each in your own way, sustains me.

And to my grandparents, Frances and Louis Gagliano, who both passed away shortly after I started research for this book. I am blessed to have been able to spend so much time with them during their last years, many hours of which were spent watching movies. This book is for them; my love and gratitude to them all.

Steven DeRosa

August 2000

Index

Evans, Edith, 214
Evans, Ray, 177, 268
Evelyn, Judith, 41

Family Plot, 39, 125, 144, 174, 205, 238,
    306n
Famous Players–Lasky, 40, 59
Farmer's Wife, The, 61
Farrington, George, 54
Ferren, John, 141
Fiddlers Three, 314n
Filwite, Inc., 166
Finch, Jon, 205
Fishgall, Gary, 318n
Flamingo Feather (van der Post), 172n,
    191, 316n
Flanagan, Bud, 175
Fleming, Ian, 152
Fleming, Peter, 152
Fontaine, Joan, 20, 68
Foote, John Taintor, 76
Ford, John, x
Ford, Paul, 207
Foreign Correspondent, 69, 75, 137,
    266
Forsythe, John, 136–37, 140, 141
Foulstone, Elsie, 117
Francis, Kay, 306n
Franklin, Sidney, Jr., 80
Frenzy, 35, 205, 236
Fulton, John P., 39

Gable, Clark, xi, xiii, 209
Gainsborough Pictures, 59–60
Gardner, Ava, 75
Garland, Judy, 175
Garner, James, 213
Gaumont-British, 11, 37n, 64, 66, 144,
    152, 154, 200, 266
Gay, John, 208
Gelin, Daniel, 186–87
Gerrard, Edward, 191
Glaoui, Thami al-, 189, 190
Golden Globe Awards, 214
Gone With the Wind, 68, 77
Gordon, Richard, 146
Gorer, Geoffrey, 316n
Graham, Winston, 199
Granger, Farley, 83
Grant, Cary, xv, 110, 129, 205, 206; in
    North by Northwest, 99–100, 103; in
    Notorious, 251; in *Suspicion*, 67, 70,
    305n; in *To Catch a Thief*, xiv, 90, 92,

98–100, 102, 109, 112–14, 116, 117,
    120, 121, 241, 307n
Greenwood, Edwin, 152
Guys and Dolls, 182
Gwenn, Edmund, 82, 137, 148

Halfway House, The, 314n
Hall, Willis, 5
Halsey, Reece, 195
Hamilton, Patrick, 77
Hammerton, Jenny, 303n
Haney, Carol, 136, 310n
Hanff, Helene, 306n
Hannah, Daryl, 222
Harlow, 79, 215–16
Harlow, Jean, 215
Harris, Barbara, 306n
Harrison, Joan, 65
Hartman, 219
Hartman, Don, 91, 121, 207, 214
Hayes, Corey (son), 210
Hayes, Dorothea (sister), 54
Hayes, Ellen (sister), 54
Hayes, Ellen Mable (mother), 53, 151
Hayes, Garrett (son), 210
Hayes, John Michael: benefits of collabo-
    ration with Hitchcock for, 84–85, 205;
    birth of, 53; childhood and adolescence
    of, 54–56; as contract screenwriter,
    78–82; disenchantment with Holly-
    wood of, 210; family background of,
    53–54; first meeting of Hitchcock and,
    6–10; Hitchcock's break with, 5,
    193–201, 206; marriage of, 74; nature
    of relationship of Hitchcock and,
    125–26; newspaper writing by, 57–58,
    62; radio career of, 62–63, 69, 72–75;
    screenplays by, *see titles of specific
    films*; in World War II, 3–4, 69
Hayes, John Michael, Sr. (father), 53–54,
    151, 166
Hayes, Mel (wife), 10, 19–21, 74, 91,
    151, 166, 174, 210, 222
Hayes, Meredith (daughter), 210
Hayes, Rochelle (daughter), 151, 210
Hayward, Leland, 14–16, 30, 299n, 301n
Hayworth, Rita, 208
Head, Edith, 39, 112, 113, 118, 174
Hecht, Ben, 6, 71, 75, 76, 144, 154, 194
Hecht, Harold, 207, 208
Hedren, Tippi, 96
Hellman, Lillian, 211
Hello, Dolly, 207

STEVEN DeROSA

WRITING WITH HITCHCOCK

Steven DeRosa is a screenwriter and has also worked as an editor of movie theater previews. He received a B.S. in Art from Pace University and an M.A. in Media Studies from the New School for Social Research. He lives in Westchester County, New York.